PRAISE FOR

THE CHILD I LEFT BEHIND

"*The Child I Left Behind* is an empowering narrative about the trauma that shapes us, the resilience that allows us to survive, and the healing possible when we reconnect with our roots and our strength. Anjalia crafts a heartbreaking and hopeful story, reminding us that while the past cannot be undone, the future can still be shaped with love, wisdom, and care."

Jennifer L. Barnes, BS, RDH, entrepreneur

"Anjalia's journey of breaking generational patterns and healing her inner child are so beautifully portrayed in this book. Her courage and determination to meet herself with acceptance, compassion, tenderness, determination, and forgiveness is inspiring. Healing ourselves is a sacred calling and requires patient devotion, which is clearly portrayed in this book. I highly recommend this book to anyone who has left their inner child behind and wants to find peace and wholeness."

Lori Drell, RNC, neonatal intensive care, retired psychospiritual integration coach

"This book is a raw and emotionally charged account of a woman's journey through abusive relationships and the devastating decision to leave her child behind. The author's honest and vulnerable portrayal of her experiences will resonate with anyone who has faced adversity and struggled to find hope in the darkest of times. This book definitely pulls at the heartstrings and ultimately offers a message of resilience and the power of the human spirit to overcome even the most insurmountable obstacles."

Penny A. Kring, certified integration life coach

"A deeply vulnerable and harrowing examination of one's life and journey from childhood through motherhood in which the author confronts her guilt, pain, and trauma. Through this introspective and healing work we, the audience, are given a front-row seat to witness how one can transcend guilt and shame in order to achieve acceptance and self-love. A must-read for anyone who has struggled with events from their upbringing, who has struggled to feel as though they were enough as a parent, or who has struggled with codependency in their relationships."

Sherri Caudill, FNP-C nurse practitioner

"This book is a story of hope, one that we don't hear enough of in our world today. The author uses her lived experience to highlight what's necessary to find forgiveness, peace, and love. Anjalia's honesty about how healing isn't perfect and that it's a continuous effort, illustrates that we are all capable of moving on. The author demonstrates that we are to transform our hurt and pain to be of service to others, to lead them out of the darkness. Her incredible story will inspire and heal millions who share the same experience."

Henry Lucas, LCSW, LCADC, best-selling author, *Maximize*

"Anjalia has such an incredible talent describing her journey you feel as if you are right there with her on her path toward healing. Her ability to show compassion and understanding even for those who didn't or couldn't give her what she needed provides the reader with an authentic connection to her that is often missing in similar stories. This book shows the indomitable spirit, exceptional ability, unrivaled inner strength, and uncommon sense of commitment the author demonstrates by bringing healing and light, not only to herself, but also to those making their own journey through life's struggles."

Barbara L. Seals, LPC, LMFT retired

"*The Child I Left Behind* is not just a memoir; it's a masterclass in courage, resilience, and the power of grit and transformation. Anjalia's willingness to delve deep into her shadows and share her journey is a profound gift to anyone seeking to reclaim their story and find healing. In a world where this story has become all too common, it's one that must be told. Witnessing Anjalia's journey is both an honor and an inspiration, as her story invites others to embark on their own path toward forgiveness and self-love."

Steven Twohig, founder of Mastering Change, author of *Turning Within*

A Memoir

THE
CHILD
I LEFT BEHIND

A Mother's Journey Toward Healing & Forgiveness

Anjalia McGoldrick

ISBN: 979-8-9920320-0-0 (Paperback)
ISBN: 979-8-9920320-2-4 (Hardcover)
ISBN: 979-8-9920320-1-7 (eBook)

Library of Congress Control Number: 2024927335

This book is a memoir. It reflects the memories and recollection of experiences and events over time from the author's perspective. Some names and characteristics have been changed to protect the identity of those involved. Some events have been compressed and some dialogue has been recreated. The material in this book is intended for education. The healing journey within these pages is a personal journey the author has taken. It is not meant to take the place of diagnosis and treatment by a qualified medical practitioner or therapist and does not represent advocacy for illegal activities. Any application of the material set forth in the following pages is at the reader's sole discretion and risk, and the author and publisher assume no responsibility for any action taken now or in the future. No expressed or implied guarantee of effects of the use of the recommendations can be given or liability taken. Please note this book has content of domestic violence, sexual abuse, strong verbal language, and descriptions that may be triggering to some.

Front cover designer: Rajendra Kumar Mourya,
RKM Designs of 99designs, LLC
Book interior designer: Ines Monnet
Logo designer: Artlogo.com
Copyeditor: Joe Pierson
Developmental editor: Brianna McCabe
Marketing strategist: Rodney Hatfield
Author photographer: Jason Lester

First printing edition 2025.

Anjalia Productions, LLC
PO Box 98
Christiansburg, VA 24068

Contact information: anjalia@anjaliamcgoldrick.com
www.anjaliamcgoldrick.com

To my wounded inner child, I am glad I can finally see you!
And to my beautiful daughter,
the child I left behind.
I love you with all of my heart!

TABLE OF CONTENTS

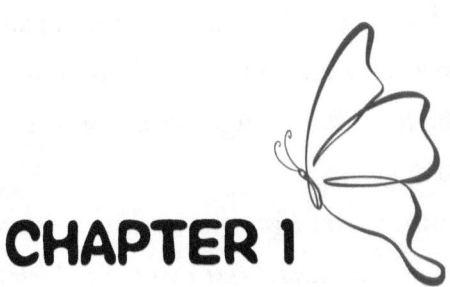

CHAPTER 1

Charlie grabbed my purse and slung it out of my hands. Then he hit me so hard it knocked me onto the hardwood floor in the dining room, which was vacant except for a small toybox that sat in the corner. He smacked me in the face then grabbed me by my hair and slammed my head against the floor, banging it into the hard surface again and again. I was afraid he was going to break my skull. He was so enraged I was afraid he had lost all control. I was swinging my arms and pushing him back trying to get him off me so I could get away from him.

"Please stop, Charlie, please!" I cried, but he wouldn't listen. "Charlie! Charlie, stop!" It was as if he was in a trance or out of his mind. He didn't drink or use drugs. He just needed power and control over me, and when he felt he was losing it, he came undone and would go crazy to get control back over me. It made him feel powerful.

I could taste the blood running from my nose and lip. My head was pounding, and I could feel my face beginning to swell.

He was on top of me, yelling, "You bitch, what are you going to do now?"

The coolness of the hardwood floor where my head rested brought comfort. I wondered what he was thinking, but I could never figure out what was going on inside of his head. I had always wanted so badly for us to be happy and for him to love me without hurting me. As he yelled and called me names, I lay there thinking about how I could ever get out of this mess and be free. The thought of being stuck here in his prison brought panic and anger.

I can't do this anymore. Am I going to be able to escape this time? I have lived in his prison for years, and I just want out. I left and survived once. Why in the hell did I ever come back? Why did I believe his lies that things would be different this time? I wanted to believe him. I wanted things to be better. I wanted the fairy tale I had dreamed about, but this is a nightmare that is never going to change. Because I had left him, he punishes me every chance he can. He will never let me forget the pain I caused him.

I knew if I didn't figure it out soon one of us would end up hurt or maybe even dead. And it scared the shit out of me.

He continued to shout at me and was knocking me around and slapping me across my face, to make sure he had my attention.

I shouted, "Please, Charlie, stop this!"

I could hear the door to Lea's room squeak as she opened it and ran from her bedroom, awakening from her nap by the rumble of his voice and screech of the scream that came reactively from my lips. Her blankie was wrapped in her arms and snuggled up to her body for comfort. Her blonde hair lay in curls and bounced as she approached me and began to plead, "Please, Daddy, don't hit Mommy! Why are you hurting Mommy?" She ran and lay down beside me and gently rubbed her tiny hand across my face to wipe the tears that fell down my cheek. It broke my heart for her to see this. I wanted so badly to jump up and take Lea and run out the door and leave and never look back.

I stopped fighting him as I pulled Lea into my chest. He looked at her and stopped hitting me. He got up and started pacing, rummaging through the house, throwing my stuff everywhere, kicking it across the floor, shouting and calling me names. I didn't get up to try and stop him this time. I didn't care anymore. I was so sick of this. None of these things meant anything to me. I was just empty, numb, and tired of fighting. I just wanted out.

I cringed as he walked closer to my body curled up in a fetal position, lying still on the floor, holding Lea and thinking of how I could get out of here. I could see a spider crawling across the floor, making its way to its well-spun web, oblivious to the fear I felt or the pain I was in. I wanted to flinch, but I kept still. I didn't dare move, in fear of him hitting me again, but just as the thought left me, he kicked me in the back with his boot, and instantly my body coiled up in reaction to the pain. I couldn't control the movement that naturally occurred as my body tried to protect itself.

"Get the fuck up, Angel, and get this fucking house cleaned up."

I screeched out in pain and pulled Lea closer to my chest.

I have to get out of here. If I don't go now, I may never get out.

I gained enough strength to pull myself up from the floor. I knew if I didn't leave now, he was going to kill me; if not today, someday, someday soon. I began picking my things up and straightening the house back up from his tirade as he demanded. I noticed my purse and keys were lying on the floor near the door where he knocked them out of my hand. Just as he went into the kitchen, and I was several feet away from him, I grabbed Lea and my purse and ran for the door, stumbling down the stairs of our two-story flat, running with Lea in my arms as fast as I could. Immediately he came running after me, grabbing my arm the final few steps at the bottom of the stairs. I pushed him backward as I went out the door and got a few steps ahead of him. I ran and got in the car.

My hands were trembling as I fumbled with the key, rushing, trying to get it into the ignition before he got to me. Lea was crying. "It's okay, baby. We are going to go for a ride." Just as I got the car started, he ran to the passenger side and found the door unlocked and jumped inside. My heart sank. He began trying to grab for the key, and I put the car in drive and drove off with him in it. *If I can just get somewhere in public, he won't hurt me in front of other people, or at least they can help me.* I didn't know where I was going. I thought quickly, *I can take him to his mom's. She only lives a few miles away, and I can drop him off. She can calm him down, and I can leave. She will tell him to stop acting this way.*

He slammed his fist into the dashboard and was shoving me while I was driving, trying to get me to pull over. I feared he was going to crash the car, but I was more afraid of stopping.

"Charlie, please stop! You are going to wreck us!"

"You need to pull over! Right now, Angel!" he shouted.

My foot was shaking so bad, I could barely keep it on the gas pedal. I drove as fast as I could to get to his mother, even hoping I would get pulled over by the police. I finally got to his mother's house. I jumped out of the car, leaving Lea behind. Blood, snot, and tears were running down my face. I was hysterical. I banged on the door as hard as I could.

Dottie ran out. "What in the hell is going on?"

"Charlie has gone crazy, and he won't calm down. Please help me!"

She shook her head. "Now, I am sick and tired of this fighting going on. You all need to get it together! I don't know about the two of you. Why can't you stop all this foolishness and figure this out for this baby?" Charlie was her baby, and she always sided with him.

Charlie ran upon the porch with Lea in his arms blaming me. "It's her, Mom. She's trying to leave and take my baby. I am not going to let her do it again."

He began screaming in my face. Lea was crying and reaching for me. I tried to get her out of his arms. She was scared, and I wanted to comfort her, but he kept pushing and shoving me away. I just wanted to get her out of his arms and leave. I was done with all this. I just wanted out. At some point while we were arguing, Dottie went back into the house.

Then suddenly, Mitch rushed out on the porch with a double-barrel shotgun, the same gun that, weeks before, Charlie had pulled on me. He pointed the gun at me. "Get the hell off of my porch!" he shouted.

I was in shock, and my mind raced. I wanted so bad to grab Lea from Charlie's arms, but I knew if I did, he would shoot me. I ran off the porch, screaming for my life. Mitch continued to chase me with the gun. I ran as fast as I could and got into my car, trembling. I knew any second, he was going to pull the trigger, and I would be dead. I managed somehow to get the key into the ignition and got the car started as he was staring me down. I pulled away, leaving my baby girl crying for me in Charlie's arms.

I felt like I was in a nightmare I couldn't wake up from. *This can't be happening.* I thought as I drove as fast as I could to get off their street. I didn't know where to go or what to do. I was a nervous wreck and in shock over everything that had happened this morning. I knew going to the police was a waste of time. I drove in a trance, trying to get my thoughts together and figure out what to do. *I don't have anywhere to go.*

I sobbed as devastation rose up within me. *My poor baby girl. Oh, I should have stayed quiet. I shouldn't have run out of the house. None of this would have happened.* I blamed myself, just like Charlie did, adding insult to my injuries. *What am I going to do? I have nothing. I don't even have my uniform for work. I have no money, no friends, and nowhere to turn. I burned all my bridges.*

My mind raced as I drove aimlessly, farther away from Dottie and Mitch's house, trying to calm myself down, but I just couldn't. I remembered school. *Yes! I can go to the Teen Parent Program. They will help me! They will help me for sure!* An ounce of hope came through my tears as I drove onto I-75 South toward the school.

CHAPTER 2

As a child, our small three-bedroom yellow bungalow house sat on a dead-end street backed up to a brickyard with a railroad track just on the other side. Many times at night, I lay awake, listening to the train shake the glass panes in our windows as it passed. Honeysuckle vines entangled the fence between the brickyard and the twelve small houses on our little street. All the houses were similar but unique in their own way. They each had a different color brick and shingles and were landscaped to match the personality of the homeowner. Tall evergreen trees stood in some yards, while a hedge of bushes lined another. You could smell the seasons, especially spring and summer, when nature came back to life after a long winter's rest. The air was so fresh with the fragrance of flowers and recently cut grass, and sometimes you could smell butterscotch from a nearby factory that made food flavoring.

We often awoke to the songs of birds chirping in the early morning sun and saw the lightning bugs by the hundreds that lit up the night sky that we chased and caught to put in mason jars to illuminate our rooms while we slept. Playing baseball or swimming in the public pool around the corner at Caldwell Park was an event that took place nearly every day in the summer in the small village of Carthage, on the outskirts of Cincinnati, where I spent most of my childhood. We often walked or rode our bikes a few blocks to the corner pharmacy on Vine Street and Seymore Avenue to buy penny candy by the bagful. There was never a time in those days when you didn't see kids outside riding their bikes, playing ball, or roller skating. We never considered staying in the house. Even during the coldest months of winter, we were outside making snowmen or snow mountains to sled down. We used our imagination every day to create a magnificent adventure.

My parents grew up in Appalachia, in the coal fields of Harlan, Kentucky, and were called hillbillies. Their difficult circumstances shaped their lives. It was a place where poverty reigned and hope of a better life was drained if you stayed around too long. Education wasn't as important as surviving. Daddy only had a third-grade education, and Mom only finished the eighth grade. They both went to work to help their families survive. Both of my parents lived in a dirt-floor home with an outhouse for a bathroom. They had to get up before daylight to bring water in from the well to wash for school. Clothes were washed on a washboard and hung out in the sun to dry. They never owned a television or a telephone. The first time Mom ever saw either of these was when she was nine years old, ironing for the rich folks in town. Mom was the baby of fourteen children, and her dad died when she was only three years old, leaving the family in poverty. She rarely had any toys. That was a luxury her family couldn't afford.

She used sticks for dolls and played with rocks. She would at least get one new pair of shoes a year, but if she wore them out, she'd have to go barefoot. For Christmas, she felt blessed if she got an orange and some nuts and a piece of candy in her sock that hung on a nail near the coal stove that was worn with holes and stitched together to hold the contents. Food was another scarce commodity. Most meals consisted of cornbread or biscuits and soup beans if they were fortunate. If she had breakfast, she was lucky. When she did, it was what was left over from the night before. Hunger was a pain she grew used to. All her clothes were handed down from her older siblings or donated to her family by the church or school.

Life was hard, and her upbringing made her very resourceful. She never wasted anything, and she made a dollar stretch further than any person I ever knew. This was a very handy skill that was resourceful in her life. Because she was the baby of the family, she was very close to her mother, who relied on her for companionship and support. When her mother died when Mom was only fifteen, she was devastated. She had already met my daddy, who was forty years old at the time. Not long after her mother passed, she was pregnant with her first child, just before she turned sixteen years old. It wasn't uncommon back in those days, especially in Appalachia, for young girls to marry older men.

Although my parents were extremely poor, backward in their ways, and lacking in formal education, they made up for it with strong values, respect, compassion, caring, and love the best way they knew how. Daddy was older than the other dads on our street. He was a tall, strong, hard-working man with enormously long big hands that were cracked and worn from years of hard work. He had beautiful, caring blue eyes encircled with lines from years of hard labor and worry. He had a tender heart for his children, love for his family that was deep beyond measure, and empathy for the less fortunate. He'd buy watermelons and call all the kids on our street over and cut them open and share with everyone.

If he saw a beggar outside of a restaurant when he'd take us out to eat as a treat, he ordered another meal and took it to them and let them know he'd be praying for them. He was good natured that way, because he knew what it was like to go hungry. Even though we lived in the city, we raised chickens to eat, planted fruit trees in our small backyard, and grew a garden and canned food each year to help us get through the winter. He never wanted to see anyone, especially children, go hungry like he did when he was a boy.

He was very strict and a stern disciplinarian with a big heart. He didn't think twice about whipping us if we needed it. I was the most strong-willed, active child, a nonconformist and unwilling to bend against my determination to do things my way, no matter the cost, which meant much more discipline for me than my siblings. I was very headstrong and found myself many times at the other end of his switch. He'd say, "Angel (that's what everyone called me when I was young), don't you back talk me, girl, cuz I'll lay this switch to you again until the blood runs!"

I just kept mouthing and talking back, and sure enough, he'd whip me until I couldn't stand straight.

Mom would beg him, "Please, Walter, don't hit her no more!"

But I was defiant and wouldn't shut my mouth, and he'd say, "Faye, you stay out of this now while I'm disciplining this here child. She needs to learn to listen and walk the line. I need to put her in her right mind. Now, don't you interfere, woman, or you will ruin this child."

Eventually I gave in when my legs and back were covered in welts that felt like at any minute they'd burst open and bleed, and I didn't think I could stand another hit. My siblings, David and Jenny, hid behind the doorway, watching with eyes open wide, flinching with every lick, learning by my example of how not to get into my predicament. He'd stop, pull me close, and look into my eyes. "Now, child, this hurt me more than it hurt you! I love you, and I only whoop you cuz I love you, girl! You have got to learn to listen. You are going to have a hard time in life if you don't." It sure didn't feel like it hurt him more, but I wouldn't say another word. I hugged his neck and went on to lick my wounds. I knew he loved me, and I would understand his words in time.

My early childhood was replete with safety, security, love, and discipline. Rejection, feelings of not being loved or accepted, often found me in the lonely hours. I was often picked on, blamed, or shunned by my older brother and sister, as a pesty little sister, and I got on their nerves. Sometimes they would tease and say I was adopted, and since I didn't look like my siblings, I often wondered where I belonged. One evening, sitting at the dinner table for a home-cooked meal my mother had prepared, as she always did, Jenny and David began picking on me and telling me I was adopted. Daddy chimed in, "Yep, we found you in the garden behind a patch of cabbage. We felt so sorry for you, we brought you home. You were a poor, pitiful thing, you were." Pain welled up in my chest as they continued to taunt and tease me. I knew Daddy liked to tease, but this day it felt more painful, maybe because it went on for so long. I looked to my mom in hopes she would rescue me, but she was distracted, arranging the glass bowls of food around the table for our meal. I always felt that I was different, that I didn't quite belong in this family. My mother often coddled me and paid more attention to me, as if she had a secret that only she knew. I felt like my siblings resented me, maybe because I took up so much of my parents' time and attention being unruly.

Deep down I knew they loved me, but I was difficult, and they would poke at me when they could. They kept on needling me and making fun of me being adopted. I argued, "I am not adopted!" and looked to my mom for reassurance but got nothing. I finally ran into my parents' room, pulled a few items from my sock and panty drawer, then went into the dining room where my dresser was. I never had my own bedroom or shared a room in this house. I don't know why; I never asked. Jenny had her own room with a full-size bed that I sometimes slept in. My toys were in there, but it wasn't my room. David had a room with an extra twin bed that I often slept in, but I did not have a place that was my own. I then filled a brown paper bag with a few more items of clothing and proceeded to tell my family I was running away.

I visualized living out in the woods, hoping a fairy godmother would come down like in the story of Cinderella and rescue me. I was only six years old, but I was angry and hurt. I thought if I ran away, they would feel bad for running me off, and it would hurt them, and they would miss me.

As I was running toward the door, Mom told them, "Stop all this now!"

Daddy grabbed me and said, "Sit down, girl. You ain't going nowhere," in his strong, authoritarian voice. His large hand wrapped around my arm startled me and brought me to attention. Tears ran down my face, but this time without hesitation, I obeyed. I sat back down in my chair and I sulked. I felt unloved, unwanted, and as if I didn't belong, but I didn't say a word. I would carry this feeling with me throughout most of my life.

My parents weren't perfect. Daddy seemed more like a father figure to Mom. Someone who could provide a stable home and security, not a romantic partner who she was compatible with. They struggled with a twenty-five-year age gap, and I rarely saw them hug, kiss, or be very affectionate toward one another unless we were going out of town. Mom often complained, when Daddy came in from working hard all day at the body shop or in the garage, about him walking through the house with his dirty shoes on or leaving the bathroom sink full of dirt after washing up for dinner. Mom was a constant complainer and often criticized and ridiculed, but Daddy rarely argued or complained. If he got upset, it was for a good reason.

Daddy had a whole other life before he married Mom. And I think she put up with a lot she never talked about, especially early on in their relationship. She later told me Daddy was a rambling man and ran after women all the time when they first met. He had so many children from various women we lost count over the years. He and his first wife, Joy, had four children, my half-siblings Joyce, Ann, Bonnie, and Mary. They'd all come in from Lexington, Kentucky, and stay the weekends. Or we'd drive down there to their house and stay. Mom never seemed to mind when they came, but I often wondered, later in life, if it ever bothered her that Joy came with the kids and would even crawl up next to Daddy and they'd talk and carry on for some time. But to me we were just one big family.

CHAPTER 3

Things began to unravel in our world in the summer of 1977 just before I was turning nine. It was a hot and humid August day when a green AMC Pacer pulled up in front of our house. My three other siblings and I waited in anticipation to see what was about to occur. We were used to family dropping in on their trips from Michigan to Kentucky or my daddy's other children coming to stay, but this seemed unusual. Jake, our younger brother, was only three and was too young to remember the day that would begin the cycle that would change the destiny of our family's lives forever.

David, Jenny, and I just watched but didn't say a word. The woman who spilled out of the driver's side of that unusual vehicle was the oddest woman I had ever seen. My daddy didn't like her from the day she stepped out of that vehicle until the day he died. He said she was the ugliest woman he'd ever laid eyes on and even called her double ugly when she wasn't around. She was loud, boisterous, and arrogant in her manner. Time seemed to stop for a moment to notice the sight of this woman.

She had shoulder-length stringy blonde hair, well, at least most of it was. At the top, her roots were dark and had grown out about two inches. She wore wire-frame glasses that sat on her crooked nose and laid off to the left side of her face. Her lips were thin and ragged. She had dark-brown eyes and very thin ghost-white skin and was nearly skin and bones, but her overbearing personality took up the space her body didn't. She looked like the hippie women who hung out at a house around the corner from our elementary school that our parents told us to avoid at all costs, but we never knew why.

You could tell she wasn't just on vacation. Her car was loaded down with the weight of the luggage. She had a girl with her who was about my age. The girl had a fuller face and figure but was not overweight. Her dark-brown hair ran halfway down her back. She had brown eyes and light skin but not nearly as white as her mother's. She was a very attractive girl. Seductive in ways and developed well beyond her years. She was an only child, which was foreign to me, and spoiled rotten by her parents, which made her self-centered and flashy with a sense of superiority.

Skeptically my dad listened and hung on to every word that was uttered from Louise's breath. "I left Robert. I got my things together, put Stephanie in the car, and left Detroit, and I'm not looking back. I only need to stay for about a week."

She had called Mom a week before and asked if she could stay a few days until she figured out what she was going to do. I overheard my parents talking. "She needs help, and she is only going to stay a few days," Mom said, trying to convince my dad.

"Now I don't want no trouble from this woman. I won't tolerate it, Faye! We've got young'ns here to raise, and I won't put up with it," my dad said forcefully.

"There won't be no trouble. I promise," she said convincingly.

Somehow, I believed my dad had an intuition that this situation was not a good thing. She was my mother's niece, but they were the same age and grew up more like sisters in Harlan. She took up residence in our basement, which had recently been remodeled with a new bedroom, full bath, and family room.

The week turned into months, and our loving, quiet home became a haven of disruption, although us kids didn't know the extent of it because my parents were good about keeping things from us. My mother, who had always been the center of our lives, began to change. On the weekends, she and Louise would pack up her Pacer with Stephanie and me, leaving my dad with the rest of the children to tend to, and we'd go to Harlan. Jenny and David never seemed to mind being left behind. Daddy was their hero, and they clung to him. I believe they always felt I was Mom's favorite, and it wouldn't be until later in years I would learn why she favored me more. I was Mom's shadow, and I clung to her. She was my hero. Once we arrived in Harlan, though, Louise and Mom would drop us off at some old friend's house, and we would not see them again until the weekend ended, and I never knew where they went.

In the middle of the fall of 1977, we came home from school and learned that Louise and Stephanie had left for Harlan.

"Good riddance! I'm glad she is out of here. She was nothing but trouble," Daddy said.

And after that, life seemed to go right back to normal. At least for the moment. A few weeks later, when our uncle Junior, a very interesting character, to say the least, pulled into town, Mom and I were on our way for another weekend trip to Harlan. My mother had a colorful family, but Uncle Junior was by far the most extraordinary person I ever met. He was full of energy and a fast talker with a line of bullshit that would leave you in a whirlwind. He had a name for everyone except for the name they were given. He talked a mile a minute and never seemed to ever shut up. He was a short, overweight man whose personality and energy took over the room. He had long, straight, stringy brown hair and short, stubby hands. He wore a T-shirt that was too short to cover his large belly, which hung over the waist of his work pants, and a pair of worn-out tennis shoes. He was very anxious and in a hurry and rushed my mother to get her things together if she was going to Kentucky with him. I'm not sure why she always took me with her. I suspect it was to appease my father. He must have thought if she had a kid with her, she'd stay out of trouble, but as always, she would leave me with some stranger she used to know, and I wouldn't see her until we left to go back to Cincinnati.

For me, this was just another trip to Harlan, a town that seemed lost a hundred years back in time. I often wondered if the people down there knew a whole world with modern conveniences existed outside the county line. It was late fall, and the Kentucky bluegrass had faded to brown, yet there was a warm breeze in the air and the sun shined brightly in the morning sky. The miles that passed between Cincinnati and Harlan seemed endless, listening to Uncle Junior go on for hours talking about useless bullshit and me having to pee so bad, but he wouldn't stop.

"Now, Devil," he called me because he said I was no Angel, a name that would stick with me for a lifetime in my family, "we'd lose too much time, girl, if we stop again. You should have peed when we stopped the last time," he said firmly. "There is a Coke bottle in the back seat. Pee in that and pour it out the window."

I was horrified at the thought. I'd never heard of such a thing in my life. And how was that going to work? I would pee all over myself. Besides, Uncle Junior brought his twelve-year-old son Joey, and I wasn't going to pull my pants down and pee in front of him. I looked at my mother, thinking she would say something in my defense about how absurd that idea was, but she didn't. This wouldn't be the last time she didn't stand up for me.

Finally, the car came to a stop when we got off I-75 onto US 25 East toward Corbin. We must have finally needed gas or Uncle Junior thought this was a good place to stop before we made the last sixty-mile drive from there into Harlan. I slung the car door open and ran as quickly as I could to the restroom. It was locked. I ran to the attendant, and he pointed to a key hanging next to the register. I grabbed it and rushed outside again to the restroom, feeling annoyed it took so long for Uncle Junior to stop but grateful for this long-awaited opportunity. The gas station attendant filled up the gas tank and washed off the windshield, then back on the road we went.

Why we were in such a hurry to get to no place, I had no clue. But for Mom and Uncle Junior, they couldn't get to "no place" fast enough. They were going home. Not to a physical place but a place that brought back sweet memories, a place in their hearts where they belonged.

We pulled up to an unfamiliar house in a place called Sunshine; there was no evidence whatsoever as to why it would be called such a bright name. The houses were weathered, tired, and worn. About the same as the people who cluttered the sagging porches with ragged clothes and leather skin, smoking cigarettes they rolled from a can. When they smiled, they were missing most of their teeth.

When we got out of the car, the door to the house flew open, and my mom's niece Louise ran out onto the porch, with Stephanie not far behind. They hugged us and invited us in.

"Faye, you're a sight for sore eyes. We've got so much to catch up on. I figured Angel could stay here with Stephanie and we could go out later," Louise said.

Louise, Uncle Junior, and Mom began making plans for what they were going to do while we were in town, like three teenagers getting ready for a night on the town. Joey plunged onto the couch and turned on the television and began to watch *The Andy Griffith Show*.

Mom asked Louise, "How do you like Harlan?"

"I've found a good man, and he's got money. He treats me and Stephanie good, so I ain't got no complaints." She laughed an obnoxious laugh that filled the whole space.

As the early evening approached, Mom, Louise, and Uncle Junior were preparing to leave to go out. Joey was going to a friend of Uncle Junior's who had some boys his age to hang out with, and Stephanie and I were getting excited about the evening we had planned.

"You girls stay out of trouble and lock the door when you go to bed. We probably won't be back home until late. You girls have a good evening and don't let anybody in the house."

"We'll be fine, Mom. Have a good time. Be sure to come back and get me." I kissed her goodbye.

"We'll see you later. We are going to stay here with Louise while we are in town this time."

I was excited to hear this news because they had an indoor bathroom.

"Love you, Mom. Hurry back! I'll miss you."

"I love you too."

As soon as their car was out of sight, Stephanie turned up the music and said, "Let's get ready for our Friday night."

I was about to turn nine, but I felt like a teenager. I had never gotten ready for Friday night, but it sounded like fun. She pulled some makeup out from a dresser drawer. She put blush, lipstick, eyeliner, and mascara on, then helped me do the same. I had never worn makeup before. I was relieved she helped me and didn't make me feel bad about it. I looked in the mirror and was shocked to see how much older I looked. We fixed our hair and sprayed it with hairspray, something else I had never done before. Then we walked down to the little store and got some snacks for the evening and listened to a couple of boys who were on their porch whistle at us as we walked by. Something I had never experienced before. Later, after we got back from walking through Sunshine, getting attention from all the boys, we hung out, played cards and board games and listened to music.

The next morning, I woke to the familiar voice of Mom and Louise talking in the kitchen. Not long afterward, a car pulled up outside and blew the horn.

Mom looked at Louise as if to ask for approval, then looked at me and said, "Come on, Angel, I want you to meet my friend."

The window was rolled down on the passenger side of this old blue Buick. Inside sat a young man, a little younger than Mom, with big blue eyes and dark-brown shoulder-length hair that was parted and combed over to one side. His thick hands and stubby fingers were clasped around the steering wheel, and he had on a blue-jean coat with white sheeplike fur around the collar. He had a round baby face with a small black mustache neatly groomed above his thin red lips, which had a cigarette hanging out the side. He didn't look as worn and as weathered as some of the young folks I had seen in this town, but you could tell that he belonged here all the same.

Mom said, "Percy, this is my daughter Angel."

"Hi," I said with curiosity.

With a deep southern drawl and the cigarette moving as he spoke, he said, "Howdy, girl. Faye said you were a purty girl. You look just like your mama. You sure do look a lot older than nine. Are you sure you're not twelve or thirteen?"

I remembered the makeup I still had on from the night before, then smiled and blushed from the kind words this young, charming southern man had to say to me.

"Well, it sure was nice meeting ya. I hope to see ya again."

"Yeah, you too."

"Me and your mom are gonna run up the road here for a bit and meet your uncle Junior. I reckon he is gonna take you all back to Cincinnati here in a bit."

I looked at Mom with approving eyes as her tiny body slipped into the passenger seat.

"See ya in a little while. But don't be gone too long, Mom," I instructed.

"We'll be back in just a minute. Make sure you have all your things together because we are going to leave when we get back here, and you know your uncle doesn't like to wait. And make sure you go to the bathroom before we leave. You remember he doesn't like to stop."

"Okay, Mom."

I ran back into the house to get my things together, thinking, *He sure seemed like a nice friend. I wonder if he's friends with my daddy too.*

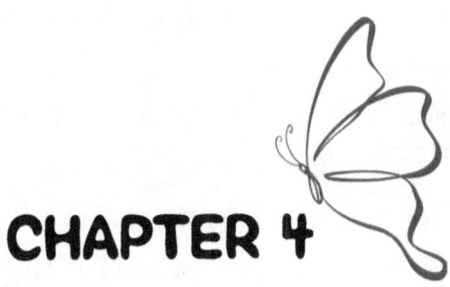

CHAPTER 4

Christmas was my favorite time of the year. Mom made peanut butter fudge and bought bags full of nuts to crack and eat. Putting up the tree was always special, and all us kids would bug Mom until she conceded. She put in a tape with a variety of Christmas songs in the eight-track player, and we'd listen to "Rockin' Around the Christmas Tree" and "Jingle Bell Rock," among others, to get into the Christmas spirit. I loved decorating the tree with all the ornaments. There was a special one I loved most. It was a small golden bell my kindergarten teacher, Mrs. Lynch, gave me years earlier when I was five, and she told me to ring it each year to remember her by. I loved her so much, even though she was the first teacher to give me a spanking for playing in the paint during story time. David, Jenny, and Jake would help put the ornaments on the tree, then put the icing on the limbs once the lights and ornaments were up. Jake was four and more in the way than anything, but we all helped him join in the fun.

My parents had come a long way from their childhood poverty in Kentucky and made a comfortable living. Since my parents didn't have much growing up, they always made sure we had plenty at Christmas. Daddy worked as an auto body repairman, and with the work he did in the garage as a side job, he brought in extra money. Mom sold Avon as far back as I could remember, but in 1977, she started selling Home Interiors, Inc. It was a home party business that specialized in selling home decorating accessories. She really enjoyed this new endeavor and saw it as her own little business. She was very talented at it and became an award-winning distributor. It was the perfect job for her. It allowed her the flexibility to be home, work around her family's schedule, and she was making a lot of extra money. It was especially true this year, and Daddy took her out and bought her a brand new 1977 Mustang hatchback, so she could get her merchandise out of her car easier when she went to do home parties.

Everything seemed normal this holiday season, just like every other year. Christmas Eve was always special. The guy down the street near the corner always dressed up like Santa Claus and came to our house and brought candy canes and asked if we had been good this year. After he left, we would open all the presents from our mom and dad. Then on Christmas morning, we'd run down the staircase to find the living room full of every toy a boy or girl could wish for, waiting for us from Santa. We hardly slept the night before in anticipation of what would be waiting for us when we awoke. But we knew something was wrong a few days after Christmas. Mom had gotten up early one morning before us kids had awakened and left to go to Harlan. When we came down the stairs, Daddy was sitting at the table with a pale and fragile look on his face.

"I made some rice for breakfast, and it's on the stove," he murmured.

Daddy usually made rice for us on Sunday mornings before we'd go to church, but I assumed he made it for us today because we were out of school for the holidays.

"Daddy, what's wrong?" Jenny asked.

"Nothing, honey," he replied with a long, tired sigh.

We suspected there was something more going on, but we were afraid to ask.

"Where is Mom?" I hastily asked when I saw she wasn't in the house.

"She took a trip to Harlan and won't be back for a few days."

I became very anxious and started to cry. "What do you mean? Did she leave me? She wouldn't have left me! Where is she?" I started to cry a heavy, hysterical cry.

"Now, girl, I don't have any patience for that this mornin'. Dry it up before I give you something to cry for."

I continued crying hysterically. I couldn't believe she left me. She never left me. I didn't think I could make it without my mother being there, and that was all I could think about. I felt abandoned, and I needed her. Right now. My thoughts began to race, my heart began to pound, and I began to sweat. *Will she come back to get me? What if she doesn't come back to get me?* I cried even harder.

"Dry it up, girl. I mean it. Not today." I couldn't hear him. I was too much in shock.

The room was spinning, and the next thing I remember was Daddy grabbing hold of my arm with a spatula in his hand, about to whip me.

"What do you know, girl?" he shouted at me.

"What do you mean, Daddy?" I cried.

"You're with her every time she goes down there. What is the name of the man she is seeing down there?" he demanded.

"What do you mean?"

"I mean it, girl, answer me now," he ordered, raising the spatula at me. I was in shock. Daddy had never acted this way and certainly never used a spatula before.

"I don't know what you mean, Daddy. I don't know of any man. What are you talking about?" I was scared and confused. *My mother is gone. She left me, and now my Daddy has gone crazy and is about to whoop me with a spatula, demanding I tell him about a man I have no clue about.*

"Girl, I know you know! You are with her all the time. She can't shit without you being right there with her. How can you tell me you don't know? You better not be lying to me."

My eyes grew big. My daddy rarely cussed. "I don't know what you are talking about, Daddy. I don't know about any man. I swear, Daddy, I mean it. Please don't hit me." My mind started reflecting and surveying every moment we had ever been in Harlan. *Was there a man? What man?* My mind raced, my countenance grew weak, and then … *Percy. But no, he was just a friend. Just a friend of Mom's. Right? Wasn't he? That's what Mom said, and I believed her. I pondered. No, what if he wasn't just a friend? No, don't mention it to Daddy. What does this all mean? If he isn't just a friend, Daddy will kill them both. Oh God, please don't let it be true, dear Lord, please.*

I could feel his long hand and firm, sweating grip around my trembling arm. I was scared to say a word as he fiercely gazed into my eyes. Then all of a sudden, tears began to stream down his face, and he gently let me go and hugged me to his chest. It felt as though his heart broke right beneath his ribcage as he held me and cried.

"I am sorry. I am so sorry, Angel. So sorry." As he cried, he held me, and I cried even harder.

I felt like I was betraying him, now that I remembered Percy, but he seemed to let it go, and I wasn't about to bring up something to cause him to get upset again, especially when I wasn't sure what was going on. I was distraught. I had never seen my daddy cry before. He was our beacon of strength, our provider, and our protector. He had never shown weakness or sorrow. Only firmness, power, and vigor. My mind was in a whirlwind, and I couldn't get enough air. I was sure I was going to suffocate. My body was numb, my face was on fire, and I couldn't feel my feet. My insides were churning, and I was sure at any moment I would throw up.

Then he said, "I love you! Everything is going to be okay." I felt the strength of his love and hope that our family would be okay, but deep inside, for the first time, I felt uncertain, confused, and insecure.

I don't remember much about those final days we were at Daddy's, except for the day we left, and I overheard Daddy telling Mom, "You take the younger two, and I'll take the older two," as if they were dividing up real estate or assets or something, not children.

They never argued in front us, ever, and this time was no different. They never told us they were divorcing or that our family was being split in half or why. No one discussed it or what lay ahead or how our family would work from this point forward. Maybe no one talked because they themselves didn't know. It just happened, and that was that. We were left to deal with our private thoughts and emotions on our own.

The day Mom, Jake, and I left was like any other. Daddy hugged Mom just like every other time when we left to go somewhere, although this time, the hug was a little longer and a bit more tender. My daddy loved Mom, and I know it broke his heart to see us leave. You could see it in his eyes. It was as if someone was tearing his heart from his chest, but he held back the tears. He didn't want us to see how hard this was for him. He just gracefully turned and walked back inside. He couldn't bear to watch us drive away.

I didn't know it then, but when we pulled out of the driveway to leave that day, the innocence of my youth would begin to quickly peel away, and I would never be the same.

CHAPTER 5

We moved into a two-bedroom upper flat in Norwood, which was about ten minutes away from Daddy. Louise, Stephanie, and Louise's new boyfriend, Bear came back from Harlan and moved in with us to help share the expenses.

I learned Percy was more than just a friend, and he was moving in with us too. Something that I was really uncomfortable about.

The house was a large older home on Smith Road, which was a busy main street that ran through Norwood. The street was lined with tall maple trees, and enormous older homes sat back off the road on moderate-sized manicured lots. The house we moved into had been converted into an upper and lower flat. The rooms were very large, unlike the small bungalow house I loved and had been used to. There were two bedrooms, a large living room, an eat-in kitchen, and a bathroom. Jake and I didn't get a room; instead, we slept on the two loveseats Mom brought with her when we left Daddy. Louise, Bear, and Stephanie used one bedroom, and at the end of the hall, to the right, was another large bedroom Mom and Percy would share.

At first, things were okay, although it was strange being in a new place without Daddy and my older siblings. It was hard to see Mom with a new man, and it took a while for me to get used to it. Percy tried hard to bond with Jake and me. He would wrestle with Jake and tell us stories about growing up in Harlan and let us stay up late when Mom was gone to work. He tried to be more of a friend at first, but soon that faded.

The drinking and loud music started right away. Neither of my parents ever drank. We were Christians and went to church every time the doors were open. Percy, Louise, and Bear would stay up half the night listening to David Allen Coe and Gary Stewart and drink nearly every night. Jake and I would have such a hard time sleeping. Jake cried, and I would comfort him by telling him a bedtime story to calm him, so we could get some sleep. I asked Percy to turn the music down because I had to get up for school the next day, and sometimes he would. Mom was always gone at night, doing her Home Interior shows and waitressing. Jake and I turned on the thirteen-inch black-and-white TV in the living room to try to distract and drown out the noise. It did little good, but we'd try.

One night after many nights of loud music playing and me asking politely for him to turn it down, I got upset. I went and turned the music down myself and went back into the living room to bed. Percy started yelling at me, and I told him not to yell at me.

"You're not my dad."

He reached to grab me, and I ran down the hall into the bathroom. He came after me and demanded I come out, or he was going to bust the door down and he would whoop me good with his belt. *Who the heck does he think he is? He's not my daddy, and he isn't going to whoop me.*

Where is Mom? I was afraid to come out, but I was afraid to stay in there. Percy was a big man, and he could bust the door in.

What am I going to do? I slowly turned the lock, and before I could turn the knob to open it, he pushed open the door so hard it hit me in the forehead and knocked me to the floor. I began to cry as he reached down and grabbed my arm and pulled me to my feet. In the other hand, he had his belt and began to hit me. At first the belt hit my legs and then my back and arms.

"I opened the door like you asked!" I screamed.

He continued to hit me. "When someone tells you to do something, you better listen, girl!" He screamed as he continued to swing the belt against my flesh.

"I'm gonna tell Mom!" I screamed.

"You go ahead and tell your mom. She isn't going to help you. I've been putting up with your smart mouth and attitude for two months now, and it's time it stopped. You understand!"

"Yes!" I said through my tears.

"What, girl? I didn't hear you."

"Yes," I murmured. I instantly hated him and wanted him to leave. I hated it here and wanted to go back home, where things were normal. I was in hell, and I didn't know how to escape.

"Now go to bed and don't get up again. I better not hear another word out of you tonight."

The next morning, when I woke, I told my mom what Percy had done.

"I don't want to hear it, Angel. You've got to learn to listen when people tell you to do things."

"But Mom, he keeps us up all night and won't turn the music down, and we can't sleep."

"Well, he is the parent here, and you need to listen to him."

"He's not my dad and he whipped me. Look at my legs and back, Mom. He hit me hard."

"You better get ready for school or you're gonna be late."

"I don't care about school. I'd rather stay here with you, Mom."

"No, you got go to school. Now go get ready."

I hugged her so tight. "I just want to spend some time with you."

"You know I have to work, Angel. Now go get ready for school."

I hated all these people and all these new rules and ways. This house was not a home. It was a zoo. People coming and going and staying up all hours of the night. People fighting, screaming, and hollering all the time. You never knew what to expect. And there never was enough money or food, but somehow, they could always afford beer and cigarettes.

By spring, two families trying to live under one roof had run its course, and Louise and Stephanie had moved back to Detroit, while Bear went back to Harlan. The downstairs flat became available, and it had three bedrooms, which would allow Jake and me to have our own room for the first time in our whole lives. Percy and Mom were doing better financially, and he convinced her to cosign for him a pickup truck. Soon after that, they got their income tax refund, and Mom took me out and bought me my first bedroom set.

I was ten years old and had never had my own room or bedroom, furniture, or anything that was all mine. She bought me a white canopy bed with my favorite character on the sheets and the comforter I wanted. I cherished these things and was so happy to have my own bed and my own room, where I could put my things where I wanted and not feel like I was intruding on anyone or having anyone intrude on me. Mom bought Jake a new twin bed and chest and a huge multi-colored, elephant-shaped toy box he begged her for. We finally seemed to be settling into our new life, and things seemed stable at least for the moment.

One afternoon when I got home from school, Mom was getting her things ready for a show she had that evening. "Hi, Mom, do you gotta work tonight?"

"Yeah, honey, I do. Could you help with Jake? I'm running a little late, and I'm not sure when Percy will be home. Could you make you all something for dinner and clean up for me?"

"Sure, Mom. When is Percy gonna be home?"

"I don't know, but it shouldn't be too late."

"Oh. I was just wondering because I met a friend at school, and she asked if I could come over to her house later, and I'd like to go."

"Where does she live?"

"Just around the corner and up two blocks. Can I go, Mom, when Percy gets home?"

"Yeah, it's okay with me, as long as you get the kitchen cleaned up."

"Of course, no problem! Thank you!"

At 7:30 p.m., Percy was still not home. He had never been this late coming home, and I was getting aggravated because I wanted to go over to my new friend's house. I was scared because our house was on a main road, and it felt big and creepy there at night, being all alone. I cooked dinner for me and Jake. I cleaned the kitchen and got Jake bathed and ready for bed. He watched TV, and I did my homework, wondering if Percy was ever going to get home. I called my friend and told her I wouldn't be able to make it. By 9 p.m., every creak, squeak, or crack

I heard made me recoil. I sat on the loveseat, hoping any moment an adult would come home, and I would feel safe. But hours would pass, and I eventually fell asleep in the living room waiting.

Suddenly, I heard the back door open and jumped. "Who is it?" I nervously shouted.

"It's me," Mom yelled. "Where's Percy?"

I ran down the hall into the kitchen. "He never came home from work."

"What do you mean?"

"I've been waiting for him all night because I wanted to go over to my friend's, but he never came home."

"Did he call?"

"I haven't heard from anyone except Aunt Jeanette, and I called her around nine o'clock because I was scared and I didn't know what to do. I fed Jake and got him ready for bed. He was good for me tonight, for the most part, but I told him you would come in and give him a kiss when you got home. He was worried about Percy not coming home."

"Well, where do you think he could be?" she asked in a puzzled tone.

"I don't know, Mom. How would I know?"

I could tell she was very concerned, and that made me concerned too. I began to wonder. *Maybe something happened to him on his way home from work.* I had never experienced someone not coming home from work before. This was new for me. I didn't know where people went if they didn't come home.

"Well, you better get ready for bed, so you can get up for school in the morning, Angel."

"Okay, Mom. I'm very tired. Be sure to kiss Jake. I promised him you would."

"Okay, honey."

The next afternoon after school, I came home to find Mom sitting in the kitchen, crying. "Oh my God, what's wrong? What's wrong, Mom?"

"Nothing, honey."

"Then why are you crying?"

"I'm just upset right now."

"What happened, Mom? You are making me scared."

"Oh, I'm just upset. I just got off the phone with Percy. He's in Harlan. Yesterday morning, we got into a fight, and he left. I thought he went to work, but he went to Harlan, and that's all, honey. It'll be okay."

"Oh. Is that what happened to him?"

"Yeah!"

"Oh, Mom, I'm sorry."

"It's okay, honey. I'm just upset. He didn't go into work yesterday, and he promised me when I cosigned for that truck he would make the truck payment on time every month, and he hasn't done it. And I can't afford to pay for it. I just don't make enough money on my own. I have good credit, and if he doesn't pay the truck payment on time, he will ruin my credit."

My mind began to race. I had never heard my mother worry about money before. I wanted to make her feel better, but I didn't know how to fix it for her. What did all this mean? "Why didn't he work yesterday, Mom?"

"He couldn't get up because he stayed up all night drinking and claimed he was sick. We got in a big fight over it because I need him to work every day in order for us to pay all our bills. This is the second time this week he didn't go in to work, and I was afraid he is going to lose that good job he has. He got mad because I was yelling at him and got up and left. I thought he went to work, but he left and went back to Harlan." She started crying hard. "I shouldn't have left your daddy. I was such a fool." She cried. I stood there in shock.

This was the first time I had heard Mom talk about my daddy since we left. "Call Daddy, Mom, and tell him we're gonna come back home!"

"I'd love to, Angel, but it's too late."

"What do you mean it's too late? Daddy loves you, Mom, and he will let us come back home."

"No, honey." she said with the most pitiful voice I'd ever heard out of her. "I have asked him, and he said it's too late."

How could it be too late? I wondered. *Could it ever be too late?* I didn't say anything because Mom was crying too hard. I just held her while she cried. But my mind was racing, and I wanted us to go back home and for things to be the way they used to be instead of the way things had become. I wanted to call Daddy right then and ask him why we couldn't come home and why it was too late. I just didn't understand. Mom wanted to come back; why couldn't we come back? It just didn't make sense to me.

"Go on, honey, and get your homework done. I just need some time to myself right now."

"Okay, Mom." I went into my room, put my books on my bed, and lay down and cried. *How can it be too late to go home? Why did Mom leave in the first place for this bum? What is going to happen now? Can we afford to pay our bills if Percy doesn't come back and work?* In the background, I could hear *Tom and Jerry* on the television in the living room. *I hope Jake couldn't hear Mom crying.*

I closed my eyes and fell asleep from the heaviness that hung over our lives.

Percy didn't come back for almost a week, and Mom was distant and not herself the whole time. The moment he stepped in the door, they started arguing.

"How could you leave and not tell me where you were going? And leave these kids here all alone, not knowing when you were coming back?" Mom said.

"Get out of my face, woman. Don't start on me when I walk in the door, or I'll walk right back out it."

"You shore have put me in a bad place, leaving like you did. You didn't pay the truck payment like you promised, and your job has been calling here every day looking for you. The bills are all due, and I don't make enough money on my own to pay everything. You know that. You promised when you moved in with me you were going to help me, and you haven't done much of that."

"Screw that job. I don't like that boss. He thinks he owns me. I'll get another one. And what do you mean I haven't helped you? I have helped you. I've been working."

"What do you mean, Percy? How can you leave that good job you have? Jobs like that don't come along very often. You better call them back right now and tell them you had a family emergency and beg them to let you come back. We need the money. You had a hard enough time finding a job in the first place. Please don't lose that good job." She cried.

"I'm not begging no-friggin'-body for my job. I'll get another job."

"Please, Percy, please don't get us in a bad place. I don't want to lose this apartment. It's the nicest apartment we can afford. You promised me you would keep this job and pay this truck payment every month on time, and not once have you done what you said you were gonna do. Please don't screw me on this truck."

"Woman, I'm not screwing nobody. You worry too friggin' much."

"Well, if I don't worry about things, nobody around here will. You better not ruin my credit now, Percy. I mean it. I am already working two jobs, and it's not enough. I need your help. You promised you would help me."

I spoke up. "What do you mean, work more? You already are never home."

"Well, Angel, since I don't have a man I can depend on, I had to work more to pay these bills."

"Yeah, Angel, she is right. She doesn't have a man she can depend on. I'm just a piece of shit, and I haven't done nothing to help her," Percy said sarcastically.

"Exactly!" Mom agreed.

"Woman, I've had enough of your friggin' mouth putting me down." He reached over and shoved Mom.

"Don't you touch her!" I screamed.

"You don't worry about it, Angel. You're a kid. Why don't you go outside and play."

"No! You aren't going to hurt Mom."

"I'm not gonna hurt your mom!" he yelled back at me.

"That's enough, Percy. I mean it!" Mom shouted.

"I ain't putting up with this shit. Get my stuff, Angel, and I'll leave for good. I ain't gonna be treated this way."

"Really, you want me to get your stuff?" I inquired incredulously.

"Yes!" he screamed. "Get my stuff and I'm out of here."

"Do you mean it this time?" I was getting tired of packing his things and him not leaving.

"Yes, get my stuff right now."

I couldn't get up fast enough. *Thank God, good riddance, as my daddy would say. Me and Mom could make it on our own. I could help her.* I ran and got a plastic bag like many times before, hoping this time it was for real, and went into their room and pulled all his clothes from his drawers. I could hear him and Mom screaming at one another the entire time I was filling the bag. *Maybe he will leave for good this time. We don't need him here hitting us.* I dragged the heavy bag into the kitchen and handed it to him.

"You are gonna miss me when I'm gone."

I looked around to be sure he was talking to me. *I would be thrilled if he left. He couldn't leave fast enough for me. I was very happy all last week when he was gone. Me and Mom were close again like we were before he ever came into our lives.*

"No, I will be happy when you are gone."

He shot me a look with daggers in his eyes. "What do you mean, girl?"

"Just what I said."

"You are a little smartass. Maybe I'll just stay to piss you off."

"No, don't stay here on my account."

"Oh, I get it. You all are ganging up on me, aren't ya?"

"I don't know what you're talking about." I glared at him.

He jumped from his chair, grabbed me by the arm, and pulled me into his face. "You better watch your smart-ass mouth, or I'll bust it for you. I'm sick of your smart-ass attitude, and I am going to knock you across the room. You hear me, girl?"

I just looked at him with an evil eye and snarled my face. He smacked me so hard, all I could see was white and all I could hear were bells ringing. Time seemed to stand still for several moments, and when I could see and hear again, he was screaming in my face, "I warned you, girl, not to be smart with me!"

"Percy, stop! Stop it right now!" Mom yelled out.

Tears were running down my face, and I didn't speak.

"Percy, that was uncalled for. She didn't do anything to you!" Mom screamed. "Let her go."

"Oh, I see you are going to let her get by with talking back to me."

They began to argue again. Then he smacked Mom across the room. I was flabbergasted. I couldn't believe what I just saw. He had yelled at Mom before, but he had never hit her.

I began to scream at him. "Don't hit Mom. Just leave! We don't want you here. Just leave."

He turned, looked me dead in the eyes, and said, "You bastard child! You don't even belong to Walter." My heart shattered and I couldn't comprehend what he just said. I stood stunned and in disbelief. My whole world was turned upside down. *What did he just say to me?* I shook my head, then looked at Mom, who was yelling at him.

"Why did you tell her that? You asshole!" When her eyes met mine, I looked for reassurance, but I didn't find any.

"Mom, what is he saying?" I cried.

"Get out!" She screamed at him as she hugged me while I sobbed. He grabbed the bag of things I had gathered for him, slamming the door as he left. But like always, in a few days, he would soon be back again.

CHAPTER 6

I hadn't seen much of Daddy, David, or Jenny since we moved. Daddy had come and gotten me a few times, but today he was coming to pick up me and Jake for the weekend. Mom made me promise not to ever tell him what I learned about him not being my biological father. She said it would break his heart. So, I buried that pain and carried it in my heart. Jake and I packed our bags, said goodbye to Mom and Percy, and waited on the front porch for Daddy to come.

When we saw his blue 1974 Ford LTD coming up the road, we raced to the edge of the sidewalk, where he pulled up to pick us up.

"Hey, Daddy! How ya doing?"

"Good, baby girl. How are you doing?"

"Good. Where are David and Jenny?"

"Ah, they're at home, getting their things packed. I'm taking you all on a trip this weekend to Kentucky."

"Oh, wow! How exciting!"

"Come on, Jake, jump in, little feller. You wanna ride up front here with your daddy?"

"Sure, Daddy!"

"Who are we going to visit, Daddy?" I inquired.

"I'll tell you more about it when we get on the road."

"Okay." It wasn't unusual for Daddy to take a spontaneous trip to Kentucky or Michigan. He liked to take off once in a while for the ride. I didn't think much of it and was excited about getting away. I was also excited about seeing David and Jenny. I missed them so much but rarely got to see them. They never came over to our house to visit. I never asked, but I didn't know why they didn't come to see us. I just assumed that was the way it was. We didn't know any families that had divorced before; we were the first in our neighborhood, so we just thought this was the way things were when families separate.

"Did you all have dinner yet?"

"No."

"Would you all like if I stopped by the Chili Bowl on Vine Street and pick up some of them delicious coney dogs and french fries they have there?"

"Oh, Daddy, could you? I haven't had a coney since we left home."

"No problem, darling. David and Jenny haven't had dinner either, and I'm as hungry as possum that's done without supper for days."

"Daddy, can we get ketchup for our fries, and will you make sure mine and Angel's coneys are plain? Cause we don't like nothing on our hot dog."

Sure thing, little man. David and Jenny don't like nothing on theirs either. I'll get you all fixed up right away."

The aroma from the bag full of coneys and fries filled the car and smelled so good, my mouth just watered thinking about them as we drove. They were the best hot dogs in the world. I could hardly wait to get to Daddy's to taste them. I hadn't had a treat like this in some time. When we pulled onto our old street, Jake and I asked Daddy if we could ride on the hood of the car the rest of the way to the house, the way we used to when he'd come home from work each day before the divorce. He smiled, pulled over, and let us climb up on the hood. I sat in the middle of the hood of the car, Jake sat between my legs, and I held him close with both arms wrapped around him to make him feel secure while the wind blew through our hair. Daddy drove very slowly up to our house and into the driveway.

Jenny and David ran out and hugged us. "Did Daddy tell you that we are going to Kentucky?"

"Yeah, he did."

"Did he tell you where we are going?"

"No, he said he'd tell me when we got on the road."

"How is school going, Angel?"

"Good. I got a lot of friends. One girl I like a lot. Her name is Diane. I hang out at her house a lot. Well, when I'm not watching Jake."

"Come here, little man. Let me see you." Jake ran and nearly fell as he jumped into Jenny's arms. "What have you been up to?"

"Nothing much. Just watching cartoons. Tom and Jerry are my favorite!"

"Did you bring any toys to play with?"

"Yeah, I brought my red fire truck and my cars and my GI Joe guys too."

"Good!" she said.

"Daddy got us coneys plain, the way we all like them."

"Oh, wow. That's good, cause we're hungry. Come on in and let's get the table set for supper."

It felt so good to be home again. I loved our little house. It was full of so many good memories. It was also good to see Daddy, Jenny, and David. They seemed to be doing well, considering all the changes that had occurred. The coneys were as delicious as I remembered. We sat in the dining room and ate together and listened to Daddy joke and tease us as he always would. Once the mess from supper was cleaned up, we all got our bags together and began loading up the car. It felt good to be going on a family trip like old times. Mom's absence was truly felt, but it was good to be with the rest of my family.

Daddy, Jake, and David sat in the front, and Jenny and I sat in the back and played cat's cradle with the yarn we had brought. We listened to Daddy sing songs like old times. "I got a gal, six feet tall. She'd sleep in the kitchen with her feet in the hall, umm hmm, umm hmm!" We'd laugh as Daddy sang his silly songs as David controlled the CB radio and listened to the truckers talk and keep track of the mile markers as we drove along, listening for any reports of bears, which Daddy told us was CB slang for cops. He asked David to alert him if he heard of any, because Daddy liked to speed to get to where we were going faster.

Jake had a hard time sitting still and occasionally jumped from the front seat to the back. He had brought his fire truck and cars and ran them across the edge of the back seat and down the armrest on the door and across the back of the front seats. He got on my nerves because I didn't have a lot of patience with him. "Jake, please sit down and stop jumping all over us," I'd demand.

Daddy looked back at me with a disapproving eye. "Leave him alone, Angel, he's just playing."

I turned and sulked and rolled my eyes at Jake as he smiled because Daddy stuck up for him.

"Angel we're going down to Evarts, just outside of Harlan. There's a pretty girl there that I want you to meet. Her name is Hazel. I met her thirty years ago when she was only nineteen years old at the ice-cream parlor in Harlan, and later, she became my housekeeper when I was married to Joy. She took good care of me and the kids when Joy would run off. We parted ways, and she married, and I hadn't heard about her until a few months ago when I learned her husband died, and I got in touch with her. She's got two girls about yours and Jenny's age. The older one's name is Melissa, and the younger one is Tina. They're her grand-daughters by her oldest son Don, but she adopted them when they were little, and they stay with her. She also has a nineteen-year-old daughter, Irene, and a twenty-year-old son, Herbie, who stays with her. She lives way back in the woods, and we can only drive so far, and then we have to park the car and take horses back to her house. She doesn't have any running water inside and only has an outhouse for a bathroom."

I was a little incredulous. However, since it was Harlan, it wouldn't surprise me. He smiled at me when we pulled up in front of her house, acknowledging he was just teasing me.

Within six months, Hazel, Melissa, and Tina moved to Cincinnati to live with Daddy, and our relationship with him would never be the same. Hazel was a very jealous, selfish woman and didn't want anyone getting too close to Daddy. We weren't allowed to talk with him alone or she would throw a fit and run into her room like a two-year-old and not come out until Daddy went in there and begged her to come out.

She worried we would talk to him about Mom. She couldn't stand the thought of him thinking about her because she knew how much my dad had adored her. Hazel also carried a great deal of hurt from Daddy leaving her years ago. As Daddy said, she was his housekeeper, but what he didn't mention, and we later learned was she was his mistress when his wife Joy would run off. She even got pregnant by Daddy but had a miscarriage, which devastated her because she thought the baby would make Daddy leave Joy for her. However, when Joy came back into town, Daddy shunned Hazel, which broke her heart, and this hurt was something she would never forgive or forget.

One evening Hazel bought Melissa and Tina some new clothes and a new baseball glove but didn't get me or Jenny anything. I asked "Hazel, why didn't me or Jenny get anything new? I need a new baseball glove too."

"Well, Melissa and Tina have money coming in from their daddy, and that money bought these things for them."

"Well, don't our daddy have some money too?"

"Umm, well, I don't know. I don't think he can afford to get you all anything, but my girls needed these things."

"Hmmm! Well, he had money when he was with my mom and could buy us things. Why doesn't he have any money now?"

"Well, umm … I don't know. I will have to talk to him," she replied, annoyed.

I walked away feeling hurt, wondering what had changed. Later Daddy was on the porch, sitting on the swing, and I sat down beside him.

"What's wrong, baby girl?"

"Daddy, Hazel bought Melissa and Tina some new clothes and a new baseball glove, but she didn't get anything for me and Jenny. She said you didn't have any money to buy us anything. Don't you have any money, Daddy?"

"What do you mean, girl? Let me see what is going on." He got up off the swing, and a few minutes later, I heard him and Hazel arguing in the house. Then suddenly, Hazel came running out of the house with a suitcase, yelling at Daddy, and looked at me and said, "You ain't nothing but trouble," and went off the porch, walking up the street.

I felt horrified. I just asked a simple question.

When she didn't return an hour later, Daddy and David went looking for her and found her on the train tracks, *supposedly* with her foot stuck in the tracks. They brought her home, and from that day on, she resented me and didn't want me around. A few days later, I went back home and rarely returned. I learned then, I could never ask Daddy for anything again. He never stood up for me or any of his children after this. She made it clear if he ever did anything like that again, she would leave and never come back. Daddy didn't like conflict and didn't want to be alone, so he gave in to her insanity and shunned and pushed his children away to keep the peace.

It broke all our hearts, but I think Jenny suffered the most. Daddy was her world and the only one she had to turn to. She had already lost Mom and now the only parent she had left was rarely available to her.

CHAPTER 7

In February of 1979, fourteen months after we left Daddy's, I was popular in school. I had lots of friends. I was getting good grades and had won a merit for the highest score in math for our fifth-grade class. One day I came home from school and learned Percy had gone to Detroit to visit his brother. While he was there, he was offered a job working for his brother as a roofer. Mom told me we were moving to Detroit.

"Why are we going there? I swear to God, Mom, this man does nothing but make my life miserable." I ran to my room and sobbed.

I couldn't think of leaving all my friends. How could this be happening to me? How could Mom allow this? I was devastated. I cried for days, but my tears would not change things. And quickly my nightmare became a reality. I wish I could have stopped time or convinced Mom somehow that leaving Cincinnati was a huge mistake. But I was ten and didn't know how to tell her what I knew in my heart was a mistake. If only I'd known then that she had no plan and that we were just packing up and going up there with no place to live and no certainty of a job lined up. That she had no money saved or any way of taking care of us.

I would have told her, no, begged her not to go. But I was a kid, and I didn't have any power.

I don't know if Mom ever said goodbye to Jenny and David. I don't remember saying goodbye to them or Daddy. David and Jenny didn't come around much. I think they resented Mom for leaving. Our family was like two ships on two entirely different seas.

The day we left Ohio, my best friend came by and hugged me, and we cried. She said, "We'll keep in touch," but I knew even at the age of ten, it would never be the same.

This was the beginning of the way my life would be. I would learn that moving and loss would be a big part of my life for many years to come. Mom didn't have the money to rent a moving truck, so we loaded what we could in her car and Percy's truck and left what didn't fit with my aunt Jeanette, with the hopes we would return soon to retrieve them. We left Ohio with no home to go to, only a few dollars, no assurance of any jobs, no plan, and with a bum, who was a liar, an alcoholic, and a con artist who was known for his instability and uncertainty. I often wondered what my mother was thinking.

I couldn't understand what happened to her to turn our lives upside down and make the poor decisions she made. Maybe meeting Daddy so young and having so many kids starting at age fifteen took its toll on her. Maybe Percy made her feel young again. She must have been so blinded by his love, any good sense that she should have had she lost in her desire and devotion to this dead-end dream and deadbeat man that she was running after.

CHAPTER 8

We arrived in Detroit in the spring of 1979, and I was ten years old. It was cold and dreary with no signs or evidence that spring was approaching. The snow piles that had been shoveled off the roads to make way for the traffic still lingered along the streets. A dark gray cloud hung densely over the sky, which brought a feeling of sadness and loss. Perhaps these feelings were coming from within me. Everything about this city felt foreign and unfamiliar to the only place I had ever called home. When we left Cincinnati, the sun was shining, buds on the trees had started to bloom, along with the flowers, and spring was arriving. I felt like we had landed in a dark place on the wrong side of time.

The "big job" Percy so eloquently sold my mother on leaving the comfort of our home to come to Detroit for a grand new beginning was over before it barely began. We had packed up our entire life and left my daddy and my two other siblings, all my friends, and the only life I had ever known, to come to a place that felt like the wrong place to be. We had given up everything we had to come here for another disappointment. But it seemed like we had no means or way of turning back now, and we had to make the best of it. All but three of Mom's ten siblings who were still alive lived in the Detroit area.

We stayed with Mom's sister Jackie for a few weeks. Then we moved in with Uncle Junior and his five kids into a small bungalow house with three bedrooms in Detroit. My mother had always been a good house-keeper. She told me her mother always taught her, when a man came looking for a wife, he wanted one that knew how to keep up a house. She said her mother told her if the man threw his hat under the bed and it came out dirty on the other side, he knew she was no good and would take off running.

So, when we arrived at Uncle Junior's house, it was shocking. I was like a fish out of water, and I tried not to show it, but I was afraid to sit down anywhere. The couch was soiled with food and drink stains. There were dirty dishes piled up for days in the kitchen sink, with an odor lingering throughout the house. Everywhere you looked was cluttered and dirty. Dusting didn't appear to have ever been done. The toilet, bathtub, and sink were black with dirt rings round them. The laundry area had clothes piled up higher than I was tall, and the garbage was running over and laying all over the floor. The walls had holes that had been knocked into them and were dingy and dirty, full of handprints and stains. The floors were filthy and looked like they had never been cleaned. But nobody seemed to notice. I would learn later and see that almost every house my uncle and his family moved out of was either burned down or condemned.

We were excitedly welcomed by Uncle Junior's loud and gregarious personality. It seemed as if the kids barely noticed our arrival at first, as they were all involved in some kind of wrestling, running and throw-ing things through the house to recognize their new guests. But after a while, they came to greet us, and the laughter and greetings went on for a while. Uncle Junior offered Mom and Percy his oldest son's bedroom at the back of the house. He said Jake and I could sleep on the couch. I cringed at the thought of it, but at this point, I was feeling grateful to have a place to stay, and I hoped it wouldn't be for long.

When I arrived in Detroit, other than smoking cigarettes occasionally, I was still very innocent to most adult things in life other than the financial struggle, the drinking and carrying on, and some abuse I had endured and seen with Percy. Over the next four weeks in this house of chaos and craziness, I got an education in life on the other side of the tracks.

Until my parents' divorce, my childhood seemed perfect, at least to me at the time. While I did find out later there were a lot of secrets and pain under the surface, as a young child, I felt secure, in large part because I was able to be a kid and not worry about adult things, including bills, money, and the stressful things of life. I also wasn't living below the poverty line, and life was predictable and stable. Compared to what I would face after my parents' divorce and all the chaos, insecurity, poverty, abuse, and upheaval, I felt like my early childhood was pretty darn perfect.

Moving here with my uncle's family was far from anything I had been accustomed to. School seemed like an option to these kids, and rules were vaguely defined, unless you managed to do something that would rattle my uncle, and then you might experience a plate full of food flying across the room, headed straight toward the wall where the kid was sitting who caused the rattling.

The first time this happened, I screamed in shock and fear. Over time, these crazy, unpredictable responses became more commonplace and were somewhat entertaining, not in a funny way, but more in an unbelievable, outrageous way. You could tell by the response that the kids feared their father, but they also loved and admired him and were always happy when he was at home, which wasn't a regular thing or something they could count on.

My uncle was a volatile, rambling man who didn't sit still long enough to let much grass grow under his feet. He seemed to live life on his own terms, and he didn't let anyone get in the way when he had his mind set on what he wanted. My aunt Mary loved and supported him, and she put up with and endured a lot of heartache and hell being his wife.

Within a few weeks of arriving here, Mom managed to get a job working as a cashier at a local restaurant chain on Michigan Avenue in East Dearborn. She worked in the afternoons and didn't get off until 1 a.m., which left Jake and me alone in the evenings with my aunt Mary and the kids. Aunt Mary worked the first shift at an automobile manufacturer and had to get up during the wee hours of the morning, so she was often in bed before 8 p.m. Uncle Junior and Percy were off rambling in the city, and us kids were left unsupervised.

The weekends were always active. Other teenagers who were friends of my uncle's two oldest children, Joey and Julie, would come over or would pick them up to go riding around the city. Julie would invite me to come and hang out. I was always eager to go and grateful to be invited. My little brother Jake was young, only four years old, and my uncle's younger sons were around his age, so he stayed back and played with them. I was young too. Really just a baby, but here in this life, I was growing up fast.

The car was loaded down with teenagers. Seatbelts were not required, and no one bothered or even thought to wear them. We rode down

Michigan Avenue, which was filled with an array of nightlife and stunning bright lights I had never been exposed to before. On the corner of Michigan and Livernois, scantily clad women stood on the corner in high heels and outrageous outfits, offering their services to those who passed by. There were all kinds of commotion as we approached the area. Horns were honking, men would hang out the window and yell obscene or outrageous things to the women. You could see women getting in and out of cars, and I wondered what was going on and was confused by the spectacle.

I innocently asked the question, "What is going on here? Why are these women waiting on the corner dressed like this?"

They all laughed at my lack of knowledge and made fun of me. "You hillbilly girl, you don't know nothing, do you?"

I sank down in the seat, feeling embarrassed, because it was true, I didn't know much about this life.

Someone replied, "They're whores!"

I still shook my head. "I don't know what that is either."

"Are you kidding me, Angel?"

"No, I don't know."

"Oh my God! You really don't know anything! You've got a lot to learn."

The song "My Sharona" came on the radio, and Julie turned it up and blasted the sound through the speakers. We all sang along and cruised up and down Michigan Avenue for endless hours, taking in the scene. There was a boy named Jade in the car, a friend of my cousin Joey's, sitting next to me. He was about twelve years old. I had met him a few times at the house. We were all dancing and singing in the car. Some of the girl passengers in the car had rolled the windows down and were hanging out without their shirts on. Horns from the cars nearby were honking, and just like with the hookers on the corner, guys were calling out giving a lot of attention to the girls. I was the only girl in the car that hadn't joined them, except the driver.

After a while, they started pressuring me into taking my top off and joining them. I didn't want to do it, but the pressure became relentless, and I had already felt stupid and embarrassed earlier. So, I gave in. I took my shirt off and hung out the window and felt like a teenager and part of the crowd, something I longed for most all my life. I had never done anything so crazy. Hanging out the window half-naked felt freeing, rebellious, risky, and fun. When the song ended, I pulled myself back inside, and Jade pulled me into him and kissed me. I was caught off guard and didn't know what to think, say, or do. This was so random and unexpected. My heart started beating fast, and I felt it flutter with passion, excitement, and confusion. When he pulled away, he smiled at me, and I felt intoxicated. I quickly put my shirt back on and blushed; then we rode through the city holding hands.

When we returned to the house, it was after 11 p.m. It was quiet, and Aunt Mary and the younger kids were sleeping. Mom was still at work, and Percy was out with Uncle Junior, and there were no clues to when they would return. Julie pulled out a bottle of vodka and some orange juice from the refrigerator and poured us all a drink. At first, I refused. I was only ten. I had never drank before, except for a hot toddy my dad had made me with whiskey, when I was very sick, and it was awful. The pressure I felt earlier from them was back, and before long, I gave in. Not long after I had my first drink, we went out on the back porch, and someone lit up a joint and gave it to me to smoke, and without a thought or resistance, I smoked marijuana for the first time. It felt like an initiation into the big kids' club, and I felt like I had become a part of it.

That night I became a teenager at the age of ten.

CHAPTER 9

About a month and a half after moving in with Uncle Junior, Mom finally had enough money, and we were able to move out to our own place. I was so happy to finally have my own bedroom and space again. She had also managed to scrape up enough to go back to Ohio and retrieve some of our things she had left behind at my aunt Jeanette's house. The thing I was so grateful to see most was my own bed. Jake and I slept on that dirty couch at Uncle Junior's, him at one end and me at the other, listening to the mice gnawing and scurrying about in the framework beneath the cushion. We laid and watched cockroaches climbing on the walls and ceilings, struggling in fear, and got little rest. I learned to appreciate things in a much different way than I ever had. The comfort of my own clean bed, free from the anxiety and worry over the bugs, the mice, the mess, the chaos, and the crazy, brought feelings of comfort. But this wouldn't last long.

Over the next six months, my life would continue to change and evolve into a different crazy and chaos, sprinkled with a new normal. Jake was five years old and not ready for school yet. Since Mom worked evenings, she could stay with him during the day, but at night she'd leave him with Percy to take care of, but most of the time, as soon as she left for work, he would leave Jake for me to tend to. I cooked us dinner and took care of chores, then we left to walk the streets of southwest Detroit. Uncle Junior and his family only lived five blocks away, and we often went there to hang out. I enjoyed this because Jake had kids his age to play with, and I hung out with Julie, and we smoked cigarettes and listened to music.

I hadn't seen Stephanie and Louise since they left Norwood and moved back to Detroit. Louise met a new man named Doug, and they all lived about a mile from our house. Soon after moving into our new place, Stephanie and I began hanging out, and I stayed with her often on the weekends. I was sleeping on a pile of blankets on the living room floor the first time it happened. It was the middle of the night, and the house was very quiet except for the air blowing through the vent. I hadn't met Doug yet in the few times that I had stayed in the past. He came in late and turned on the television. Then at some point he got down onto the floor where I was and began to massage my back, running his hands down my legs and over my panties touching my private areas. It startled me, and I abruptly woke up. My mind was racing, and my heart was beating fast. Sadly, this wasn't my first experience with sexual abuse.

It took me back to when I was five years old and my dad's close friend Leo, who often visited, used to come up to Jenny's room at bedtime and rub and gently tickle our backs and help us fall asleep. Then over time just as I would start to fall asleep, Leo would begin to rub my legs. In time, those rubs would grow longer, and eventually his fingers would slip under my panties.

The first time Leo touched me this way, I jerked away and reacted with surprise, and he calmed me and assured me it was okay. "This just feels good. It's just a little tickle," he responded, then he put his index finger to his lips and said, "Shhhh, this is our little secret."

I didn't say a word and lay there really still. This went on for years until my parents divorced.

I tried wiggling away from Doug, but he moved closer and pulled me into him. I continued to move around and finally got up and went to pee. I took my time in the bathroom and got a cup of water and drank it very slowly. When I returned, he was gone. I lay back down and pulled the covers over my head, breathing a sigh of relief, praying he wouldn't return. Thoughts were ruminating in my head. I thought about Percy and the creepy things that had just started happening with him too since we moved into our new place. He often came into the bathroom to pee when I was taking a bath and would linger in there, watching me through the mirror.

It was very uncomfortable, but Percy justified it by saying, "You're just a kid, and besides that, I have seen many women naked in my life."

I didn't care how many women he had seen; I didn't want him to see me. It felt weird, and I didn't like it. And I wasn't just a kid; I had already started to develop and had even started my period the year before, even though I was so young. I wondered while I lay there trying to go back to sleep if most older men were creepy like this and if this happens to all girls. My heart sank into my stomach as I tried to erase the thought from my mind.

The next day, I got up as if nothing ever happened and never said a word to anyone about Doug touching me. The incidents continued and became more frequent. He would leave twenty dollars in my panties after touching me, or "petting me," as he would call it, perhaps to justify his behavior. Doug was a predator, and I was perfect prey. He continued to groom me, earning my trust by giving me money, buying things for me that we couldn't afford, and doing things for me that no one else did. It was our little secret, but it all came at a price.

Stephanie and I walked through the neighborhood. She told me about her new boyfriend, Daniel, and how hot he was. She confided that they had begun having sex just a few weeks before. I looked at her with shock because she was only eleven years old. She noticed my expression and said, "Oh, it's no big deal! You have a lot to learn, girl!" I had so many questions turning inside my head, and she was happy to share the details. I wondered what would cause her to give up such a precious gift at such a young age. I was taught your virginity was very valuable and you were supposed to keep it until you were married, because men wouldn't want you if you'd been with other men. I didn't say a word. I just listened and took it all in. Soon she moved on to a new conversation as the thoughts lingered inside my mind.

The one-way sign on the side street had graffiti written on it, but I could still make out what it said as we turned the corner onto Stephanie's boyfriend's street. It was a hot and humid day in southwest Detroit, and the steam from the heat that hit the blacktop street rolled off and staggered in the air. As we were walking, I looked up and saw a teenage boy coming out onto the porch of a red brick house, one of many that lined the street. He was gorgeous. His hair was golden blond and shoulder length. It was straight until it got to the ends, where it lay in waves. His eyes were sea blue, and when he smiled, I felt my heart skip a beat. He didn't have a shirt on, and his hairless chest was chiseled and his abs were defined. "Who is that?" I asked Stephanie with delight.

As we approached him, Stephanie barked out orders. "Don't say anything stupid, Angel." Feeling her arrogant dig at me and feeling hurt from her words, I fell back behind her and let her take the lead. She called to him, "Hey, Charlie, what's going on?" He nodded his head, greeting us, but didn't say hello. They made small talk for a few minutes, and I listened intently, blowing smoke from a cigarette, trying not to seem too interested. "This is my cousin Angel." He looked me up and down and glanced back at her. "Angel, this is Charlie. He's Daniel's cousin."

Cautiously trying not to say anything to be criticized for, I said, "Hello, it's nice to meet you."

He raised his chin in a cocky way, nodded his head, and took a drag off his cigarette then blew the smoke from his lips. "Hey." He nodded toward me.

"We are on our way to Daniel's; we'll see you later," Stephanie called out as we walked away. "He's weird," she said as I turned back to drink in one last glance.

As we walked down the street toward Daniel's house on the cracked and broken sidewalk along rows of houses that were in different stages of disarray, some even abandoned, half burnt down and falling apart, thoughts of Charlie spun in my head. His bare chest, his tight jeans, and his cocky silence engulfed me.

"What are you doing?" Stephanie called out to me in her bossy way.

"Nothing!" I said defensively, having been startled from my thoughts.

"Well, hand me a cigarette."

I pulled a cigarette from my pack and lit it, annoyed that she had interrupted such a pleasant thought and thinking how rude she could be but never having the courage to say anything. I sucked in the smoke and allowed it to roll around my tongue. Blowing it out, I handed the cigarette to Stephanie. As we walked down the uneven pavement, I wondered why no one cared about the neighborhood or took care of their houses. Detroit had a smell that lingered in the air … a smell of factories, poverty, and River Rouge. It looked like a war zone. Vacant lots lined the block full of trash where houses once stood, and other lots were littered with half-burned-down abandoned houses. No one bothered to come back to tear them down or put the time and energy in that was needed to rebuild them. They were just left broken, tattered, abused, and alone, as if no one ever cared for them at all. My thoughts wandered back to Charlie and how cute he was. *Hmm, it would be nice if he could be my boyfriend someday.*

CHAPTER 10

Things were quiet with Mom and Percy while we were staying at Uncle Junior's, but it wasn't long after settling into our new place that things heated up again. It was like a roller coaster ride. You never knew what you were going to get. I hated being there and mostly stayed in my room to escape. Percy and Mom fought most of the time over money and him not working, him staying drunk, sleeping all day, and never helping her out. Or worse, when he stole the rent money from her purse or siphoned the gas out of her car and put it in his truck so he could run around after other women all night while she was at work.

When he wasn't around, she confided in me how hard things were and cried about how hard he made things on her. This made me resent him even more. She seemed like a little kid sometimes, so vulnerable and unsure. I felt sorry for her and wanted to fix it, but I didn't know how. I was only ten. I helped her keep the house clean and cooked when she didn't have time to do it. As time went on, she relied on me more. Mom always paid our bills first before anything, even food, but she often didn't make enough to pay everything. She'd have me call the electric or gas company when our bill was overdue, and they were threatening to turn off our service, and asked them to work with us and set up a payment plan. I did my best to help her when I could, but I felt resentful that she put up with Percy and wouldn't make him leave for good. He kept our life in turmoil, and I never understood why she put up with it.

Within a few months of moving into our new place and Percy rarely working, no matter how hard Mom begged him, I came home to find her crying and learned that her Mustang and Percy's truck had been repossessed.

"I just don't understand why he won't help me. I do everything I can to work and make ends meet, but I need his help. All he ever does is pull me down. What am I going to do now without a car?"

I felt so bad for her, and I didn't know what to say or do. I never knew your car could be taken from you like this, and I was feeling the loss of it too. "I don't know, Mom. Why don't you make him leave? Our life is so much better without him."

"Oh, Angel, you just don't understand."

I shook my head and thought, *no, Mom, I really don't.*

Mom picked up more hours and worked more. I helped as much as I could and dealt with the regular fights and struggles, they were constantly in. I started having trouble getting up in the mornings for school because I was so tired I couldn't wake up. Mom yelled at me for not getting up on time, and I couldn't figure out what was going on. Not only was I waking up late and groggy, I often found my panties missing and couldn't recall why I didn't have them on. One month, I had my period for an entire month and was cramping and in pain. I told my mom, and she took me to the doctor, but they couldn't figure out what was wrong with me. We never figured out what the problem was, but

Percy's creepiness and the way he constantly watched me made me very uncomfortable. I avoided him as much as I possibly could, but he was always creeping around.

One night after pouring myself a glass of juice, I left it while I went to the bathroom. When I returned, he was hovering over it. "What are you doing, Percy?"

He seemed startled and nervous.

"Oh, nothing, Angel. I was just going to take a drink of your juice."

"Well, there is a whole pitcher I just made and put it in the fridge. You can get your own glass," I said with attitude. I took the juice and went into my room and noticed there were white specks of something floating around in it and wondered what it was. I didn't drink it. I poured it out and went to bed. Later that night, I woke up with Percy in my bed lying up against me, breathing heavily on my neck. He was rubbing my stomach with one hand and his other hand was in my panties, and he was fondling me. "What are you doing in here, Percy? Get out! Get out right now!" I could smell the alcohol on his breath and pushed him away from me.

"Oh, I heard you yelling. You were having a bad dream, and I came in to check on you and comfort you so you could go back to sleep." He jumped from the bed and left. I shuddered as he left my room.

The next day, I went to Mom. "I need to talk to you about something, and I don't want you to be mad at me."

"Well, what is it, honey? What did you do?"

I told her about Percy being in bed with me and rubbing on me and the juice and the many times I woke up to my panties missing. "Mom, I think he might be putting drugs or sleeping pills in my juice at night.

I don't know what is happening. This might explain why I sleep so sound and can't get up in the morning."

"Oh, Angel, there is no way that Percy is doing anything to you. If he was, you would know it, because it would hurt."

"Mom, he was in bed with me, and it was creepy and made me feel very uncomfortable. It just isn't right. It is really weird, Mom!"

"Well now, Angel, I don't think Percy would do anything like that."

I was embarrassed in the first place to tell her about these things, and when she didn't believe me, I felt confused and devastated and even questioned myself about what I had experienced. Even though weird, creepy things continued, I didn't go back to her about it anymore. I couldn't stand Percy. I sat and wondered how I was ever going to get away from him. I hated my life and was angry and resentful at Mom for not protecting me and for putting up with this deadbeat man. These feelings only grew stronger with time. I just couldn't understand what kind of spell this man had on her that she would continue to keep him around.

I was desperate to get out of this situation, but I had no idea how to escape. This went on for the next couple of years. I just tried to stay clear of him as much as I could and hoped he would leave or Mom would throw him out.

In May 1981, right before finishing the seventh grade, I ran into Charlie while hanging out with Stephanie. She had dated him for about a month but wasn't compatible with him, and they broke things off. He asked me if he could have my phone number, and I said yes. I was so nervous and excited.

"Oh my God, Steph, can you believe he asked me for my number?"

"Yes, I told him you liked him and encouraged him to talk to you."

"I am so nervous. He is so cute, but he is a lot older than me. I wonder if he cares."

"Well, you don't look or seem twelve. You actually seem more like you're fifteen, and he is a bit immature for almost sixteen; it should be fine. Besides, age doesn't really matter."

I drank it all in as we walked with my head in the clouds, looking forward to the hope that he might call me. I thought back to the first time I saw him and the many times I thought about him over the past two years, and I felt my heart flutter inside.

My life at home was miserable, and thinking of Charlie made me happy. Six months earlier, we had moved to Dearborn, Michigan, to get away from Percy again. Mom took on an extra job cleaning at a motel on the weekends, and I went to work with her to help her clean, but no sooner did things settle down than he sweet talked his way right back into Mom's life. This was a never-ending cycle. He was like a recurring nightmare that never ended.

Our life was so much better when he was gone, but she couldn't shake him loose, and it infuriated me. His creepiness and sexual behavior toward me grew worse. He would watch me through the vent in the bathroom while I showered, and I could see him peeking in on me. He continued to come into the bathroom when I was bathing to look at me when I was naked. I often woke up with him feeling on me and touching me in inappropriate ways, and I would yell at him, "Leave me alone and get out of my room!" But it never stopped. I never felt safe and eventually took some money that I earned cleaning the motel rooms and put a lock on my bedroom door. Over time, I grew distraught and felt hopeless.

This man brought so much pain and torment into our lives. He whipped me and my little brother Jake, beat me down at every turn, preyed upon me nearly every day to the point I didn't even feel safe to go to sleep in my own bed at night or take a shower without him creeping around upon me. Every time he came back into our lives, he tore my mother down, mesmerized her from her own good senses, drained her of the little bit of money or resources she had to provide for us, causing us to lose our home and have to move, lose our vehicle, go hungry, and live in constant chaos. I was desperate to get out of this situation, but I had no idea how to escape this never-ending hell. I would sit and think of ways to get rid of him, but going to jail and living with the guilt of killing someone wasn't something I could ever do and certainly I couldn't live with.

When Charlie came into my life, I had been through so much, and I was looking for someone to just love and rescue me from the constant turmoil of my life. I felt alone and broken and in need of a savior. He was alone, broken, and in need of a nurturer. It was the perfect storm. We talked on the phone every day for hours until Mom yelled, "Get off the phone Angel, so I can use it!"

Once school ended in June, he'd call later at night, once Mom had made all her calls, and we'd talk all night. Often, I fell asleep on the dining room floor next to the wall phone with the phone in my hand, because neither one of us wanted to say goodbye. When he told me he loved me, I thought my heart would jump out of my chest. I was so happy for the first time in forever.

He lived five miles from my house, and our parents rarely would drive us to see one another. All I could do was think about him, and I wanted to be with him every opportunity I could. His dad lived in Dearborn, and he came to stay with him sometimes, so we could see each other, but that wasn't very often. So, I walked several times a week, five miles each way, to see him, or he'd walk to come see me.

Within a month of our relationship, he started pressuring me to have sex. Even though I had been fondled, violated, and abused in sexual ways, I was a virgin and scared, but I also didn't want to lose him. I knew I was taught to wait for marriage to have sex, and I struggled to give in. But he told me he was a virgin too and wanted to share this experience with me. That made me feel special, something I didn't feel very often, and I finally relented.

After we had sex for the first time, Charlie looked at me and said, "Guess who is pregnant."

"Who?" I said naively.

He smiled at me, and instantly I knew he was insinuating that I was pregnant.

"Oh my God! What is my mother going to think?"

I hadn't thought about birth control before having sex. It never crossed my mind. From that point on, he began pressuring me to get pregnant. He talked about how wonderful it would be and how we would always be together. At first, I was reluctant and thought he was kidding. But soon it was obvious to me that Charlie wanted me to get pregnant. The pressure continued, and he talked about it all the time. He was always disappointed each month when I got my period. I could feel his disappointment, and I wanted to please him and make him happy. He was the only bright spot in my life. For the first time since my parents divorced, I felt loved. I wanted to run away with this man and live happily ever after. I rationalized in my mind. My grandmother married when she was thirteen, and Mom and Dad got together when she was fifteen. *Maybe if I get pregnant, it will be my way out.*

By the time I was thirteen and in the final few months of eighth grade, I was pregnant.

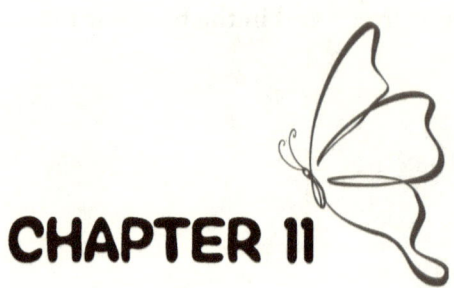

CHAPTER 11

"Mom! Get someone, please! Mom! *Get someone!* I am dying! I am going to die, Mom! Ow … ow … ow! Oh, it hurts so bad! Whew … ow … whew! Charlie, get someone, get someone now to help me. Please! Oh my God! Please! Help me someone, please!"

"Angel, the doctor was just in here. They just checked you, honey."

"But I am dying, Mom. Can't you see? Tell them I am dying."

She left, and a moment later, she returned with a nurse. The nurse looked at the monitor and watched the contractions. The pain was so intense and rapid, every two to three minutes apart.

"I am dying, do you understand? It hurts so bad! Help me, please!" I begged.

"This is the hardest labor I have seen in a long time. She's having contractions as if she's ready to deliver, but she is only dilated three centimeters," the nurse told Mom.

"Is there anything you can do for her?" Mom asked as concern filled her eyes. The nurse looked at Mom and left the room. I worked on trying to breathe through the pain, but it didn't help. The nurse returned with cold rags for my head and ice chips for me to eat. Mom gently wiped my head to try to calm me. "It's okay. Just breathe. The contraction should be over soon." Mom tried to encourage me, but it didn't help. Between the labor pains, exhaustion fell on me, and I slept until only moments later I awakened to the unrelenting agony, and back into the pain cycle I went.

I am finally going to have this baby today. I hope he is going to be okay. I hope I am going to be okay. Endless thoughts swirled through my head. *I hope it's a boy. Charlie wants a boy so bad to carry on his name. I love him so much. I just want him to be happy.*

I could see him pacing back and forth in the room. He looked like a lost puppy, completely out of place. I could tell he was uncomfortable, but he didn't leave. He came and stood by my bed and held my hand and let me squeeze his during the contractions. Then he'd take a break and move away to give himself some space from all my pain. I took comfort in knowing he was with me and appreciated him standing by my side.

The pain rattled through every nerve in my lower back, abdomen, and pelvic floor like stabbing pains from a sword piercing my body. Endless hours passed, and I remembered what everyone told me, *it is going to be painful.* But I never imagined it would be this bad! I cried and screamed and begged for mercy, but none would come. I begged, "Please give me something for pain. I can't handle this pain, it is too much! Please!"

"Honey, I am sorry. I checked with the doctor, and the baby's heartbeat is unstable, and we can't give you anything. Concentrate on relaxing. Just breathe."

"I can't fucking relax. I can't!" I screamed. Sitting next to my bed, my mother looked at me in disappointment.

"She is only trying to help you, Angel!"

I was in too much pain to take on her disapproval. The torture felt as though it would never end. Many times, throughout the night and way into the next day, the labor pains were so intense that I wasn't sure I would survive it. It was the longest night of my life and the closest thing to hell that I had ever experienced. *I will never do this again. I will never have another child. There is no way I can go through this again.*

The contractions started coming faster, and I couldn't stop pushing. I had dilatated to ten, and the baby was crowning.

"She's ready. We are going to take her to the delivery room now." The doctor said as they rolled my bed out of the room. Charlie kissed my head as I was leaving and smiled in relief that the time had finally come for the arrival after sixteen hours of agony.

In the delivery room, I sat on the side of the bed and tried not to move as they gave me an epidural shot in my spine. My body was automatically pushing without my effort.

"You got to be still, honey."

"I am trying. I am trying!"

They managed to get the needle in and laid me back on the bed. Nearly instantly, I couldn't feel anything from the waist down. Within a few minutes, at 4 p.m. exactly, the doctor announced, "It's a girl!"

She was beautiful and perfect. Her skin was like velvet, and she had a light dusting of blonde hair that covered her tiny head. She weighed six pounds and four ounces, and she was a bundle of beauty.

The nurse placed her in my arms. "You can hold her for a few minutes, then you need to lay flat for the next twelve hours. You'll get to see her again tomorrow."

"What? No one told me that." I looked down at her and took in as much as I could before they took her away.

While I was in the recovery room, they rolled her out in a small bassinet to meet Charlie and my mother. Later, Charlie came in to see me. His big blue eyes were shining. "She is so beautiful, Angel. She is so tiny; I can't believe how perfect she is."

"They only let me hold her for a moment," I said sadly.

"She looks like me," he bragged as he puffed up his chest. Then he looked at me with care. "I was so worried about you. Whew, it was tough to see you go through so much pain!" He kissed me on my forehead. He had a childlike silliness and immaturity about him and could be so loving, tender, and sweet. But I also discovered he had a dark side that I often dismissed out of naiveté.

"I never dreamed it would be that hard, Charlie."

He nodded in agreement and smiled. He was happy. I had never felt more joy in my life than I did in that moment. He never said a word about her not being a boy, at least not at this time, and any thought I had about wanting a baby boy disappeared the moment she was born.

All through the night, I longed to hold her. Before the sun began to rise, the nurse came in. "It is time to get you up for a walk. I'll take you down so you can see your little baby girl." Excitement filled my heart. I couldn't wait to see her. My movements were slow from pain between my legs and in my back as we walked down the long hallway to the nursery. When we arrived in front of the large window, another nurse inside pulled a small bassinet over to let me peek in through the glass to see her. She was wrapped tightly in a pink blanket. She had a little cap on her head and was sleeping peacefully. My heart fluttered with love and delight, and I couldn't wait to hold her.

I turned to the nurse. "When will I get to hold her?"

"In a couple of hours, I will bring her into your room."

Joy filled my heart, and I couldn't wait. It was like Christmas morning after a long night of anticipation.

When they brought her to me, I held her close, and my heart changed forever. I never knew you could love someone so much. I pulled her sweet face close and rubbed her cheek to mine. Her soft, precious skin felt like the petals of a rose. Her little nose and small mouth were drawn up like a miniature pink bow as I counted her tiny fingers and toes. I swaddled her and tried to feed her, but it took some effort as she attempted to navigate the nipple of the bottle. "Lea Nicole, you are so beautiful and perfect! You look just like your father, and he is so pleased and proud of himself." I thought of him as I gazed at her, lost in time.

In that moment, I had no idea the next two and a half years would bring as much emotional pain as the labor of birth had brought physical agony. I didn't understand the lifetime of heartache I would endure being a mother or that this little girl would be one of my greatest teachers.

CHAPTER 12

It didn't take long for the reality of motherhood on top of the reality of everything else I was dealing with to set in. Only a few days after bringing her home from the hospital and the fanfare of the newness had worn off, the enormous responsibility of taking care of this little human's every need became a reality. I ignored the wet stickiness of the milk that leaked from my breast and had soaked my pajama top as I was startled awake from the baby crying. I yawned and jumped from the bed to attend to her.

Charlie was still living at home with his parents, sound asleep without a care in the world. His life hadn't changed much at all, and here I was having whiplash over the extreme changes my life was going through. There were bottle feedings all through the night, diaper changing, more crying, staying up trying to comfort her when she was fussy, and feeling like this was more than any one person could handle. And nothing I did soothed her. He never asked how I was doing or if I was tired. And I was exhausted, overwhelmed, and I didn't know what I was doing. I had just turned fourteen and should have been thinking about what jeans

I was going to wear to school the next day, but I was knee deep in the responsibilities of a little baby who needed so much.

It helped that she was so beautiful and sweet. I am sure that's why God makes babies that way. So cuddly and soft. *I love dressing her in those cute little outfits, tiny little caps, and snuggling with her, but I am so tired. If I could just get some sleep. No one gave me instructions, but I am doing the best I can. You'd think they would've given me an instruction book to tell me what to do, but they just gave her to me like I knew what I was doing. They didn't even ask me any questions. They just put her in my arms, and off we went. I just want to sleep for one night. How am I going to do all this all by myself? Charlie is at home with his mom, and Lea's needs never end.*

The early morning sun was peeking in as I peeled back the curtain and rocked the baby. I glanced out the window and saw my friends from junior high, who I hadn't seen since I got pregnant in the eighth grade, filing into the high school across the street from my house. They were hanging out on the ballfield, talking and gathering to share the latest gossip of who was dating who, who the stuck-up girls were, and which guys were the hottest, I imagined. I lingered for a moment then saw Heather, my best friend before all this, talking and laughing with a new set of friends. I pulled the curtain shut. *I don't miss any of that. I hated school anyways.* I tried to convince myself as I envied their freedom and the life I left behind for Charlie and this little baby. Mom helped me when she could and gave advice when the baby wouldn't eat or when she cried after I had tried everything. Sometimes she would take her to give me a break, and I appreciated it. But Charlie made things hard. He didn't like my mother. He didn't seem to like women; he didn't actually, seem to like anyone. *I don't know why he was so mean sometimes. He doesn't mean to be. He is really sweet sometimes.*

I looked out the window and saw Charlie pull into the driveway. *Oh good, Charlie is finally here. Maybe he can help me with Lea. She's been fussy and crying all day.* I pulled Lea from the crib. "I've tried to rock her, Charlie, but it hasn't helped. I tried to feed her; she doesn't want it. I've checked her diaper, and it's dry. I've done everything, but nothing is working. My nerves are frazzled, and I don't know what else to do. I need to smoke."

I handed the baby to him. He rocked and cuddled her for a few minutes. That seemed to work. He put her back into the crib and turned on the musical mobile, gave her a pacifier, and came into the dining room to smoke a cigarette with me. Within a few minutes, she was screaming again. I quickly jumped up from the table and ran into my room to check on her. Just as I entered my bedroom, I remembered I had the cigarette and was about to turn around, but Charlie was right behind me and kicked me with his boot right between my legs, hitting me right where the stitches were. I doubled over, screaming in pain.

Mom came running and began yelling at Charlie, who was attempting to attend to Lea to calm her down. "What is going on? What happened? What did you do, Charlie?" she yelled as she came to comfort me and to try to calm the baby.

Charlie began screaming at her, "Faye, mind your own business, and don't you dare touch my baby. I don't want you to kill her the way you did your first two children!"

Those words hit us both like a freight train. Mom recoiled, and her eyes welled up with tears.

I screamed at Charlie, still crying from the physical pain I was in. "You asshole! You know she didn't kill her babies. That is not true, Charlie. You need to leave right now. Get out of here, Charlie! I mean it!"

"I am not fucking leaving!" Charlie shouted.

"Stop this, both of you!" Mom cried.

"Don't you ever touch my baby." Charlie pointed his finger and shouted at Mom.

Mom shook her head at Charlie in sadness and pain. I am sure the memories of losing her first two children to death from unfortunate circumstances flooded her mind and she was crushed.

Instantly I looked at her and saw her eyes filled with pain and disappointment. "Charlie, you need to leave right now!" I shouted.

"Oh yeah, you want me to leave? Okay, I will leave, but don't expect me to come back." He ran out the front door, and I gathered myself as my mother helped me off the floor.

"I am sorry, Mom. He can be so mean sometimes. I know he didn't mean it."

"Angel, I don't know about Charlie. I just don't know how someone can be so mean." She shook her head and hugged me, then turned away crying and went into her bedroom. I walked away feeling horrible that Charlie had hurt her so deeply.

How could Charlie be so cruel? Why did I share such private information with him about such a painful, awful thing that happened to Mom? She was only fifteen when she had her first child, Walter Jr. He was sickly, and the doctors in the coalfields of Kentucky couldn't figure out what was wrong with him. He only lived a few days. Her second child, Kimberly, was born a year later and died of pneumonia when she was only three. I can't imagine how devastating that must have been for her. It wasn't something she ever talked about.

I imagined Charlie's words were like daggers in her heart. I could feel her pain and helplessness. It hurt when he told her she could not touch our child. It was like he took pleasure in causing pain. *How could he say she can't touch our baby? Lea is my child too, and Charlie isn't going to keep Mom from holding her and helping me. She is the only help I have right now. Why does he have to be this way?*

I was so angry, hurt, heartbroken, and torn in every direction, but I had no time to think about that. I was in pain, and the baby was still crying and needed me. The pain between my legs was throbbing. I pulled an ice pack from the freezer to place in the area while I rocked Lea and she cried. I was completely shocked and baffled at why he kicked me. He had hit and shoved me many times, but he had never done anything this severe before. I glanced down to see that Lea had finally fallen asleep and took a deep breath of relief. I enjoyed these rare quiet times and took in every second.

By late evening, my anger began to diminish, and my mind began to race. *I wonder where Charlie is. Did he mean what he said? He has done this so many times, but he always comes back. But he hasn't yet. What if he doesn't come back?* I began to cry. *Maybe I shouldn't have sent him away. I love him so much. I just can't lose him. What would I do without Charlie? I just don't get why he has to be so mean.* Feeling desperate over the whole situation and the day's events, I decided to break down and call him.

"Hi Dottie, is Charlie home? He was upset when he left here hours ago, and I was wondering if he has gotten home yet?"

"No, Angel, he's not here. I haven't seen him. You two need to quit this fighting, now that this baby is born," she scolded me.

"I know, Dottie. Can you have him call me when he gets home? Please?"

"If I am still up, but I am getting ready to go to bed. Mitch has to work tomorrow, and we don't have time for all this nonsense," she said, annoyed.

"Okay. Thank you!" I hung up the phone feeling defeated.

As bedtime neared, my mind raced, and I felt helpless. There was nothing I could do. Just wait. *Surely, he will call me before the end of the night*, I debated. Just as I was about to go to bed with worry, the phone rang.

"Hello?"

"Hey."

"Charlie, I have been waiting all night to hear from you. I was worried."

"You told me to leave."

"I know. I am really sorry. I just couldn't take it all. You have no idea how hard it is when the baby has been crying all day. And then you kicked me, Charlie. I just needed it all to stop. Why did you do that, and where have you been?"

"I needed to drive around and think about things. Angel, you know we talked about not smoking around the baby. Why don't you listen? Why did you go in there with that cigarette?" he demanded.

"Charlie, I forgot. I am sorry! I didn't mean to. My nerves were a wreck, and it is my bedroom and I have smoked in there for years. I didn't even think about it. I was just trying to get to the baby to calm her. And just before you kicked me, I remembered and was about to turn around, but you didn't give me a chance."

"Yeah, but you should have known better. If you wouldn't have done that, I wouldn't have kicked you."

I started crying. "You have no idea how much you hurt me today. And you were awful to my mother, who was just trying to help me."

"That fucking baby killer. I don't want her touching my baby ever again, and I mean it, Angel!"

"Charlie, that's awful. She didn't kill her babies. Can you imagine if that happened to our baby, how awful that would be, Charlie?" We argued until I was completely depleted. I hated arguing, but he was so hurtful and provoking that I couldn't stand not defending myself. Somehow it was always my fault. I could never win.

"Charlie, I love you. Please calm down. I just want things to be better. I really appreciate you calling me back so I didn't worry all night. Lea is crying again and needs to be fed and I have to go. Please call me back tomorrow."

"No, we are going to talk about this, right now!"

I tried to stretch the cord from the wall phone closer to my room so I could peek in on Lea, but it wouldn't reach. "Okay, Charlie, I hear you. The baby is crying, and I have to go. I hear you, you don't want Mom to touch our baby. I love you, Charlie. Get some sleep."

"Angel, I mean it, you better listen to me."

"I will," I lied sadly, exhausted from arguing. I didn't want him to leave us, and I was so tired and wanted to end this long day of hell. "I love you and I hate when we fight. I am sorry! I know you didn't mean to hurt me."

"I really didn't, Angel, but it's your fault. You've got to listen. I love you too. Give Lea a kiss from me, and I will come by and see you both tomorrow."

"Oh good. I can't wait to see you. Good night, Charlie." I hung up the phone feeling defeated. *Why does he want to start a battle with Mom over our baby? It makes me so sad. It's not fair.* And an even deeper part of me that I didn't want to listen to wondered how I could so desperately love someone who would act and treat me this way.

I got a bottle ready for Lea. *Why does he have to make things so difficult?* I shook these thoughts from my head as I took Lea in my arms and fed her until she fell asleep.

Three months before Lea was born, Percy returned again, and the quiet in our house returned to chaos. Once again, his drinking and loud music blasted throughout the house. I came in and asked him politely several times to turn the music down, but he refused. Out of frustration, I came back again. "Can you please turn the music down, Percy?"

"No, it ain't that loud."

"Yes, it is. I am trying to talk on the phone, and I can't hear."

"Don't you talk to me that way, girl!"

I reached over and turned the music down, and he smacked my hand away and turned it back up. "Why can't you just turn it down some?" I asked.

"You are not going to back talk me, girl."

"I don't know why you keep coming back here. No one wants you here anyway. You always make things worse when you're around."

His eyes narrowed, and he jerked his belt from his pants, then grabbed my arm and began whipping me across the front of my body, hitting me in the face, arms, and belly.

I screamed, "You are going to hurt the baby!"

He continued hitting and pushing me. I ran to my bedroom and locked the door. He banged and pounded on the door so hard trying to get in, it shook the walls.

"Let me in this door right now," he screamed and began kicking the door until he busted the door frame, and it flew open. He pushed me, backing me into the corner and continued to hit me across my shoulders, torso, and back.

"Mom! Mom, please come help me!" I shoved him, trying to fight back, but he continued to hit me.

"Percy, stop!" she shouted.

"Woman, she ain't going to talk to me like that. I ain't gonna put up with it. I don't care if she is pregnant," he said sternly.

"Angel, why don't you listen? You just don't know when to keep that mouth of yours shut, do you?" she scolded me as he continued to hit me.

I flung my arms, trying to defend myself, then raised my foot and kicked him as hard as I could and managed to get away from him. I looked at Mom and shook my head as I ran out the back door.

When I got a couple of blocks up the street, I stopped to catch my breath as I trembled, trying to think what I should do. I then ran to the police station and made a report. I used their phone and called my best friend, Heather, and she and her mom came to the police station and got me and let me stay at their house overnight. The next morning, I knew I couldn't return home. I called Charlie and told him I had to run away. I stayed at a friend's house for a couple of days, then Charlie sneaked me into his dad's basement, and I stayed there a few nights. I heard the police were looking for me, and when I decided to return home, after many years of dealing with Percy's abuse, social services got involved. Percy finally left for good, and I was very happy.

Not long after Lea was born, Mom realized the little two-bedroom house where we lived in Dearborn was too small, especially after my older sister Jenny, who lived with Daddy after the divorce, came to live with us just before Lea was born, to get away from the years of emotional abuse and shunning she endured with Hazel. Me, Mom, my younger brother Jake, and older sister Jenny moved into a three-bedroom house in Detroit. It was in a rundown area near Livernois and Michigan Avenue, where years earlier, when we first moved to Michigan, I had my first experience of the big city. The area had only worsened since then, but it was what Mom could afford on a waitress's salary, and it gave us a little more space.

Not long after moving in, Mom met a new guy named Ben. From the beginning, we didn't get along. I was headstrong, angry, and having had put up with so much with Percy, I had an attitude toward people who tried to tell me what to do or ridicule me on how I screwed up my life by dropping out of school and having a baby so young. *Why can't people see how much Charlie and I love each other? We belonged together, and age doesn't matter. Who cares that we are young? We are going to make it. No matter what.*

"Charlie is a punk, and he isn't going to stick around," Ben antagonized me.

"You don't know him like I do. He loves me, and he would never leave me. We are going to get married, and we are always going to be together," I argued.

"Oh, he will be off with some other girl before you know it. If he doesn't already have one."

My heart sank. "You don't know nothing. He loves me. He would never do that."

Just before Lea turned six months old, Ben asked Mom to move in with him in the suburbs but told her I wasn't invited.

"Angel, I am going to let you and Charlie move in together. You can have the living room sofa, your bedroom set, the washer and dryer, and I'll give you $200 to get started," Mom said.

"Are you serious?"

"Yeah, I am going to give you what you want."

I was stunned, but happy that I was going to be with Charlie and in charge of my own life. But at fourteen, as a young mother in an abusive relationship, I had no idea the world I was getting ready to step into.

CHAPTER 13

Right after we met, Charlie turned sixteen, quit school, and tried to find a job. But he couldn't find anyone who would hire him, with no education, skills, or work experience. Two years later, when his older brother, Randy, heard we were moving in together, he offered Charlie a job pumping gas at the station where he worked, making minimum wage, which was $3.35 an hour in 1983. We found a nice apartment a mile from where I was living with Mom for $265 per month. The first six months, even though we didn't have much, was like a honeymoon. I was so happy to be with Charlie; it was all I ever wanted from the day I first laid eyes on him.

While Charlie worked, I stayed home with Lea. There rarely was enough money to make ends meet, but we did our best. As time went by, things continued to be difficult financially. The struggles with money began to create a strain, and we started fighting more. Charlie was hard on me. He ridiculed me at every turn. He loved to argue and debate, and I hated conflict with Charlie and often shrank in fear and did what

I could to avoid it. I was always under a microscope with him questioning everything I did. He was also very jealous and controlling.

One evening, we were in the grocery store. I went to reach for a package of pork chops at the same time another man went to reach for it, and we both laughed.

Charlie looked over and began yelling, "You whore! You want to fuck this guy, don't you?" He looked at the innocent stranger. "You want to fuck her, don't you?"

"Hey dude, I don't know what your problem is. We just reached for the same package of meat at the same time. Chill out!"

"Charlie, stop it! Let's go!" I demanded. I pushed the cart full of groceries aside, grabbed Lea, and pulled Charlie by the arm out of the store. All the while, he was screaming at this man, who stood stunned with the other customers watching us leave. "What in the hell is wrong with you?" I shouted as we got outside. He shoved me and pushed me into the car, then squealed the tires as we pulled out of the parking lot, racing up on the car in front of us so quickly, I thought he was going to hit them. "Charlie, slow down! You are going to kill us!" I shouted. He kept on driving erratically, scaring the shit out of me as I continued to scream. "Please, just stop and let me and Lea out of this car, right now! We will walk home!"

Ignoring me, he continued to drive recklessly. My heart was racing. "I don't understand why you have to act like that?"

"I could see the way you looked at that guy. You wanted to fuck him, didn't you?"

I just shook my head. I didn't have anything to say. I knew if I kept quiet and let him yell, he would eventually stop. I held Lea on my lap and pulled her close to my chest to try to shield her from his angry words and his craziness. She was crying, and I rubbed her back and rocked her, trying to comfort her.

As we pulled in front of our house, he reached for a cigarette from the pack in his shirt pocket and lit it. I jumped out of the car and ran into the house. I got Lea settled into her crib and then lay down on the bed and cried. I didn't have anywhere to go. I was completely dependent on Charlie. I didn't have anybody. *I wish he could just be normal.* I cried.

After a while, Charlie came in and jumped in the bed and hugged me. "I am sorry, Angel. You know I love you. I didn't mean to get so mad, but I can't think of you being with anyone else." He hugged me and started poking at me, throwing pillows, tickling me and playing like a little kid, until he got me to smile and relent to his charm, pushing the crazy and chaos he created out of my mind for the moment. He kissed me, and for a week or so, things would be better.

We moved three times in the first year, until we found an affordable place to live. Charlie's brother heard of a place near his work that included all the utilities and was only $185 per month. It was a nicer place and in a better neighborhood in Dearborn, just on the border of Detroit. One afternoon, Charlie's dad brought over some dinner, and we sat on the couch and ate while visiting with him. Charlie had been sick and was lying stretched out on the couch, propped up with some pillows. I was at his feet at the other end. "Angel, can you get me a napkin?" he asked, just as I had taken a bite of food. He pulled up both legs and plowed both feet into my side, knocking me and my food onto the floor.

"What the hell, Charlie?" I cried.

"Did you hear me? Get me a fucking napkin!"

"I was going to as soon as I swallowed my food," I cried as I ran into the kitchen to get the napkin for him.

"Well, you didn't respond." He started screaming and yelling at me and threw his plate at me as I returned to the living room. I moved just in time to miss the plate as it flew past me and hit the wall and broke all over the place.

His dad, Chuck, got up. "I am not going to stand by and watch this, Charlie! This is ridiculous. Why are you acting like this, son?"

"This is none of your business, Dad!" he shouted.

Chuck shook his head, looked at me, shook his head again, and walked out the door.

Charlie continued to yell, then went into the kitchen and busted up several of our dishes.

"Please, Charlie, don't. Please calm down. I just didn't hear you. I was happy to get you a napkin."

He continued through the house, finding things that he knew I cared about, and smashed them.

My oldest brother, David, who was a country boy and an outdoorsman, took a special class and hand-made a beautiful cloth doll just for Lea. Her hair was blonde, made from yellow yarn, and her eyes were stitched in blue. The doll looked a lot like her. I loved this doll, and it meant a lot to me because he had made it for her, and Charlie knew it. It was sitting on the mantle near the front door. He saw it and walked over and took his lit cigarette and put it out right between the doll's eyes, burning a hole through its forehead.

I screamed, "You asshole! What kind of fucked up are you! That doll belonged to Lea!" I looked down, and she was crying. I picked her up, hugged her, wiped the ashes from the doll's forehead, handed it to Lea, and took her to our room and put her in her crib. I went back into the living room and begged him to stop. The more I begged, the worse it got. Hours went by before he grew tired of tormenting me. I was completely spent.

Loneliness and isolation had become my life. I didn't have any friends. I didn't have any money. I was too young to drive. I was completely dependent on Charlie. I rarely saw Mom. She was also in her own world, and I wasn't a part of it.

By the summer of 1984, only a year after we moved in together, Charlie, lost the job with his brother because of his hot-headed, cocky attitude.

"Please, Charlie, go ask Randy for your job back."

"Fuck that. There is no way I would ask that fucker for my job back. There ain't no way I am crawling back to him."

"Charlie, we can't pay our bills without that job. What are we going to do?"

"Don't worry about it. I will figure out something."

Another week went by without a job, and finally, out of desperation, I called Mom to ask if she could help Charlie get a job at the restaurant where she waitressed when she lived in the area. Within a week, he had a job. He worked the evening shift and didn't get off until 1 a.m. but seemed happy with his new job.

A month later, the phone rang in the middle of the night. I was startled and jumped up to see who was calling. Charlie was on the phone and appeared nervous when he saw me.

"I will! Yes, I will! I promise. I hear you. I will take care of it. I promise. Okay, *okay!* I will! Bye." He hung up the phone and looked up at me.

The energy in the room shifted, and I could tell something was wrong. My heart began to sink. "What's going on, Charlie? Who was that?"

"Let's talk about it tomorrow. It's late." He looked over at the clock on the mantel.

"What do you mean, tomorrow? What's wrong? It's two o'clock in the morning. Who is calling here at this time?" I asked with panic in my voice as my heart began to race.

"Angel, I don't want to talk about it tonight. We can talk about it tomorrow."

"Who was on the phone, *Charlie*?" I demanded.

"It was your sister Jenny."

"My sister? Why is she calling you?"

"I don't know, *we can talk about this tomorrow!*" he insisted.

"Charlie, you are making this worse. What is going on?"

He got up and lit a cigarette and left the room.

I picked up the phone and called my sister back. "Jenny, what is going on?"

"Didn't Charlie tell you?"

"No? Tell me what? Please tell me what is going on?"

"You need to ask Charlie."

Charlie returned and grabbed the phone out of my hand.

"Who is that?"

"It is my sister!" I yelled. "What in the hell is going on?"

"You better tell her, Charlie." Jenny was still talking when Charlie grabbed the phone from my hand and hung it up.

"Why won't you tell me what is going on, Charlie?" I began to cry.

Charlie took a deep breath, looked at me, then immediately looked down. "There is a girl at work. Her name is Elaine, and we have been talking."

I felt like the world was shattering all around me. Time seemed to immediately stop. "What did you say?" I couldn't comprehend what he was saying to me. Every ounce of blood in my body seemed to drain out of me. "What do you mean, talking? Are you cheating on me?" I screamed. "How could you do this to me? How could you do this to our daughter?"

"No, I am not cheating! We are just talking!"

"Just talking, Charlie? I don't understand!"

He tried to come toward me, and I pushed him away. I expected him to hit me back, but he just wrapped his arms around me to pull me into his chest to confine me. A million questions flooded my mind.

"Are you sleeping with her?"

"No."

"What is going on? Are you going to keep talking to her?"

"I don't know. I don't know what I want." He pulled away from me.

"What do you mean, you don't know what you want? What is going to happen to me and Lea? Don't you care anything about us? I got that job for you. How could you do this to me?"

He turned away and sank into the couch with his head in his hands. I expected him to yell, but not saying anything was worse. My mind raced. I never dreamed he'd do this to me. We were supposed to be together forever. I felt like I was going to die from the pain in my heart. My mind was swimming in disbelief, and my body was in shock. I sobbed and he tried to pull me toward him to calm and comfort me with a hug.

"No, don't come near me." I shouted. "I don't want you to fucking touch me!" I went and lay down in my bed alone and cried until the sun came up.

I got up just after 6 a.m. I got Lea up, got her dressed, and put her in her stroller. I needed to get out of the house, away from him, and try to get my head together. I didn't have anyone, but I knew Charlie's dad, Chuck, cared and had compassion for me. He always got up at 5 a.m. I walked six blocks to his house, pushing Lea in the stroller.

"Angel, what are you and the baby doing here so early?"

"Chuck, I had to get out of the house. I found out last night that Charlie is talking to a new girl." I began to cry. "She's a hostess at the restaurant, and they have been seeing each other for a couple of weeks. I don't know what I am going to do."

He came over and hugged me and tried to comfort me. "That damn boy. I don't know what to do with him." He shook his head. "I am sorry to hear this. Maybe you two can work it out, Angel."

"I don't know. I have no idea what is going on. I am so mad and so hurt." I cried.

Lea looked up at me. "Mommy's crying?"

"I am sorry, sweetheart. Mommy is just feeling sad today. Come into Papa Chuck's living room and get you some toys."

We played on the floor, and I talked to Chuck. Talking helped, and it felt good to have someone who listened. I stayed all morning and tried pulling myself together enough to walk back home.

I was exhausted, confused, heartbroken, and clueless about what I was going to do or where I was going to go. I couldn't go to Mom's. I wasn't wanted there. I had no money, no job, no car, no driver's license. I had nothing and nowhere to go. All I had was Lea. I looked down at her sweet face and walked around in front of the stroller and hugged her. Not only was my world devastated, although she didn't know it, so was hers. I just held her and cried. *What am I going to do?* I turned the corner and headed back home. Charlie had no idea where we were. I had no idea how he would respond when we came in, and a part of me didn't care.

When I came in the door, Charlie was angry and asked where we had been. He tried to start an argument but soon shifted and began telling me how worried he was, how much he loved me, and that he wanted to work things out. After hours of talking and him professing his love for me, I felt hope that things would change, and maybe this was just a wake-up call that we both needed to shift things in our relationship.

CHAPTER 14

Over the next month, every day was a roller coaster ride of emotions. Charlie would profess how much he loved me and how he wanted to work things out, but night after night, he wouldn't come home on time, and things continued to deteriorate. We fought, made love, and fought even more. He lied and played games, but nothing ever changed. One morning after another fight, he said he was going to the park to meet Elaine to break things off. After about forty-five minutes, Charlie didn't return. I was so tired of the fighting and uncertainty. The park was only a couple of blocks away. "Come on, baby, let's go for a walk."

Lea smiled as I put her in the stroller and began our walk toward the park.

The sun beat gently on our faces as a cool breeze ran through the busy morning streets. As I entered the park, I could see Charlie with this girl, straddling a park bench, facing each other. She was running her fingers through his hair and caressing his face. Parked next to his old white

Maverick was a red Corvette, Charlie's dream car. I studied Elaine as I waited in the distance. Her hair was blonde and flowed in waves and hung to her shoulders. Her skin was porcelain white, and her eyes were as bright as her smile. She wore designer pants and leather brand-name shoes. It was apparent she came from money. I looked down at my old, worn-out shoes and saw the pink footies peeking out through the holes. My T-shirt was wrinkled and tattered, and my shorts were old and ragged. I instantly felt the sting of poverty and the feelings of being less-than. A bitter reminder from the days when every six months, I was always the new girl at school and was bullied because I couldn't afford the nicer things the other kids wore.

My heart sank at the sight of them, and tears welled up in my eyes. Charlie was running his finger down Elaine's face so intimately and sweetly. She smiled with innocence and blushed at him. I remembered back when we first met and he used to be so tender and gentle like that with me. Long before Lea and the responsibilities of life set in.

Elaine must be a breath of fresh air for him. A new adventure or challenge that intrigued him, and I am old to him, tired and no fun. I had no idea if this was true, but in the moment I lingered there, I could see and feel it. It was difficult to watch, but I stood there for several minutes to take it all in.

My hands were sweating, and my jaw was tight. I needed to witness this with my own eyes and drink in the pain, so I could muster up the strength and courage to leave. I had to watch to confirm what my soul had known for some time but my heart did not want to believe. When he leaned in and kissed her and pulled her into his chest, time seemed to stand still as my heart shattered. *He has lied and lied and lied to me. He keeps hurting me, and I keep staying. How could I be so stupid? She doesn't even know what she is getting into. He seems so loving and sweet, but she hasn't learned yet how his love brings pain, and it stings quite deep.*

My mind raced, and adrenaline rose up in me. I wanted to fight and yell at him and cuss her out and call her a homewrecker, but I was so exhausted from the weeks of this craziness. I wiped the tears from my eyes and gathered up as much strength as I could. I took a deep breath in and walked quietly with the baby in the stroller up to the bench where they were sitting. I wanted Elaine to see me and the baby and the lives she was destroying.

"Hey, Charlie!"

He jumped when he heard my voice. "What the hell are you doing here?" He reacted in surprise.

"I guess I should ask you the same question. I can see you aren't here to break things off, like you said," I said sarcastically as I glanced over at Elaine. She immediately looked away. "I am going to start getting some boxes so I can move out. I can see clearly this is all just a game." I looked at Charlie as tears began to run down my face. I waited long enough for him to see the hurt in my eyes, then I walked away. He didn't say a word. I knew at that moment I had to leave. Nothing was going to change. I was a fool, and this was tearing me apart.

What I didn't realize then was Elaine coming into Charlie's life was the greatest gift that could have happened to me, by helping me leave this toxic unhealthy relationship.

The weeks that followed were difficult. Charlie and I fought every day. He didn't want me to leave. At least that is what he said. "Angel, you know I love you, and I can't live without you and Lea here. Besides, who is going to have you anyway? You have a lot of baggage." As he looked down at Lea.

His words cut deep. I had done everything for him. Given him everything I had, and he treated me like a piece of white trash. I felt like trash, and I wondered if he was right. A few hours later, to add more salt to my pain, Elaine pulled up in her dad's red Corvette to pick Charlie up, and off he went without a word. He was spending money on her we didn't have, spending time with her instead of us, and it hurt to watch. He wanted to date Elaine, and he wanted me to stay and put up with it. And for now, it was what I had to do. I began looking for a job. I had to have money to get out and to get my driver's permit. I didn't know where I was going to go, but I knew if I had money, I could figure it out.

I finally called Mom and told her what was going on. "I tried to tell you, Angel, this wasn't going to work out, but you wouldn't listen. What are you going to do?"

"I don't know, Mom. I have put in applications everywhere, but no one has called me. I am sure it is because I am fifteen."

"Well, let me talk to my old boss at the restaurant in Allen Park, where I used to work. He called me last week and asked me if I would come back to work for him, but I told him I was working at a restaurant near the airport. I might be able to get you in there, but you will have to tell them you are eighteen years old."

"Okay, whatever I must do. I can't stay here much longer."

The next day, I asked Chuck if he would drive me to fill out an application. Her old boss hired me on the spot.

"You can start next Monday on the evening shift, training as a waitress."

"Thank you, sir! I appreciate the opportunity."

My aunt Sissy lived nearby. She stayed up late at night and told me she could watch Lea for me. She needed to earn a little bit of money, and it would help her too. She only would charge me sixteen dollars per week.

It was nearly nine miles one way to work. I didn't have a car or anyone who was willing to drive me there every day, but I had a job, and it was the only one I could find at age fifteen. I wanted out of this situation so bad; I was willing to walk to work. Walking those long miles, then working a long eight-hour shift, and sometimes having to walk the nine miles home if I didn't get a ride, change rattling as I took each step through the dark, busy city streets from Allen Park to Dearborn, were some of the most educational moments in my life. I made my mind up with each step that my life wasn't going to be this way forever. It was humiliating to ask people at work for a ride or call my mom or sister and be told no, they couldn't help me. I was determined I wasn't going to be stuck depending on someone else and having to ask others for help, then feeling rejection when they said no.

I wasn't going to be beaten up, mistreated, and cheated on ever again. Seeing my mom going through this with Percy and ending up in a worse situation, I knew I wanted more for my life than this. I thought about all the humiliation and rejection I felt, being poor and treated like white trash most of my life. I thought about all the hell I had been through in this relationship and having hardly anyone to turn to. I thought about all the struggles I had been through after my parents divorced when I was nine, and I knew for sure this was not the life I wanted to live. I didn't know how I was going to get out, how long it was going to take, or how things were going to change, but I knew in my soul that they were. I was determined to do better. I knew from my own experience and from watching Mom, who only had an eighth-grade education, who had been beaten down by the man she left my dad for and started out life as a teen mom too, that this was a hard life. *The only way out is to get an education, and when I get on my feet, I am going to figure out what I must do and do it.*

Nearly four weeks had gone by since I saw Charlie and Elaine at the park together. So much time had passed, I think Charlie believed I wasn't leaving. I didn't talk about it, because I didn't have anywhere to go, and I knew it would only start an argument. I just worked and saved my money. I figured when I got enough saved, I would find a place and move. It was difficult being there with Charlie. He was unpredictable and moody. The more independent I became, the more jealous he was.

One night, he was home when a guy from work dropped me off out of courtesy so I didn't have to walk.

"Who the fuck is that guy? You are fucking him, aren't you?" Charlie shouted at me as I walked in the door. He grabbed the door out of my hand and slammed it behind me.

"Charlie, don't start. He is just a cook at work who was kind enough to give me a ride. I am tired. Please leave me alone." He started shoving me around and yelling at me.

"You are a fucking whore."

"Stop, Charlie, please don't do this tonight. I am exhausted."

"Tell me who that guy is. I am going to beat his ass. Tell me, Angel, I mean it."

"No, he is nobody. He was just nice enough to give me a ride home."

He pushed me against the wall and punched the wall near my head, and I screamed.

"What the hell, Charlie! You are the one seeing someone else, and you are acting like this. I don't want to do this tonight!" I shouted.

"Now look what you did, Angel! You made me bust my hand up."

I got away and went into the bathroom to take a break from his rage. I could hear him pacing outside the door, waiting for me.

Lea was sleeping, and she woke crying from the noise of us arguing. I came out of the bathroom and headed for her room to comfort her. He followed me, continuing to yell. "It's okay, baby. Shhhh, go back to sleep." I patted her back and put my other hand up and waved Charlie to leave the room to keep from waking Lea. I stayed with her for a few minutes until she fell back asleep. I took a few breaths and tried to calm myself. He was waiting for me outside the door when I came from the bedroom. "Come here, Charlie, let me look at your hand. I will get some ice. Go sit down in the living room." I went to the refrigerator and pulled the ice tray from the freezer and got a towel from the drawer and filled it full of ice. I pulled another rag from the drawer and ran it under warm water. I was so tired of fighting him. "Let me see your hand, Charlie." I sat down on the couch next to him, took the warm rag, washed off the blood, and put the towel full of ice on his knuckles. "There, that should make it feel better." I took a deep breath as he took comfort in my nurturing.

He pulled me close and hugged me. The way he usually did after his violent outbursts. I took in the hug as a sign of relief the chaos had ended, at least for tonight. He kissed me on the head, and I rubbed my cheek into his. "I'm going to bed, Charlie. I am exhausted." As I walked away, I knew he wasn't ever going to let me leave in peace. I called my mom.

"Mom, Charlie just left for work. We had a big fight last night, and I am afraid he is really going to hurt me. Even the neighbor said something to me this morning about all the noise and said she could hear me screaming and was worried about me. She told me she almost called the police. I need to get out of here soon. I know Ben doesn't want me there, and I know we don't get along, but is there any way you can talk to him and see if he would let me come and stay with you, just long enough for me to get enough money together to get my own place? I have been working hard, but I don't make a lot, and I haven't been able to save much. Things here with Charlie are bad. He almost punched me in the face last night because I got a ride home from a guy at work. I need to get out of here before he really hurts me. Please, Mom, ask Ben if I can stay with you."

"Well, Angel, I don't know. You know I tried to tell you, but you were hard-headed and wouldn't listen to me, and now look at where you are."

"I know, Mom, you were right. I am sorry. I hate to ask. I have been trying to save and get out of here, but I just haven't been able to make enough money."

"Well, I don't know. I will have to see. You know, if you would have listened to me, you wouldn't be in this shape."

"I know, Mom."

"Well, if you come back here, you know you would have to go back to school."

"Really? Um, school?" I sighed.

"That's right, Angel, you need to get back in school. And we ain't going to be putting up with no bull crap with Charlie coming around here starting no trouble."

"Okay, Mom, I hear you. Can you ask Ben? But don't call here. I will call you when Charlie isn't home. I will have to move out when he is at work. He isn't going to let me leave without a fight."

"Okay, now you heard what I said, right?"

"Yes, Mom! I heard you. Please ask him."

"I will talk to Ben tonight, and I will let you know."

I hung up the phone. *School? How is that going to work in my life? I barely have time to do everything I am doing now with work and taking care of Lea. But I have to get out of here. I can't take this anymore*, I mumbled to myself.

Later in the week, I called Mom to check in.

"Angel, I talked to Ben, and he ain't happy about you coming back here, but he agreed to let you come, as long as you understand you have to follow the rules and go back to school. Do you understand me?"

"Oh my God, yes, Mom! Thank you so much! I promise I will!"

I had enough money saved to rent a small moving trailer. Rob, the cook from work, agreed to help me move, even though I told him how unstable Charlie could be. "I am only taking my bedroom furniture, Lea's crib, and our personal belongings. Everything else Charlie can have," I told Mom and Rob as they began carrying things out to the trailer. I was a nervous wreck as I threw things as quickly as possible into the boxes, worrying Charlie would come home early from work and find Rob there helping me move out. We packed and carried things out as fast as we could. The last item I took was the stereo Charlie had bought me the summer before, which had sat on the mantle. It was the only thing he had ever bought me the entire time we were together, and it was something, as a young girl being poor, I always wanted. The stereo had a clock with blue lights that could easily be seen when you walked into the dark living room from the front door. I took one last look around as I took the stereo down from the mantle and closed the door. Sadness and fear filled my heart as I walked away. I knew Charlie wasn't going to be happy when he walked in the door, but it was long past time for me to leave.

Sure enough, at 2:30 a.m., the phone at Mom's house rang. Charlie called multiple times that night, wanting to talk to me, but Mom made it clear to Charlie she didn't want him calling here, especially at this time of the night. He stopped calling. I crawled back in bed and managed to sleep more soundly than I had in a very long time.

CHAPTER 15

It was difficult being at Mom's. I had been on my own in my own house, making most of my own decisions and taking care of myself and my child for nearly two years. Lea was about to turn two years old. It was hard moving back in with my siblings, Mom, and Ben, who didn't like me. From the very beginning, Ben was cold and rough toward me. He picked at me and made comments or complained about my parenting, and just about everything I did. I tried my best to ignore and stay clear of him as much as possible. When I moved in, they gave me my little brother Jake's room, and he had to sleep on the couch. I felt like I was in the way. I wasn't comfortable there, but I was happy to have a place to stay. I did as Mom asked, and I went and enrolled at the local high school. I was now two years behind my graduating class, nearly sixteen years old, starting the ninth grade. I had been an adult for the past two years, and the other students were still kids, passing notes and worried about the Friday night football game, when I was working full time, taking care of a baby, trying to save to get my own place and a car.

Within a week, I knew this wasn't going to work. I went to the principal's office and talked with my guidance counselor and told her about my situation.

"Oh, my. I didn't know you had a baby. Yes, I can see how it would be difficult with trying to find a sitter, making it to class, and working on top of it all. Well, there is a teen-parent program nearby to help kids in your situation go to school. There is a bus. It can pick you up and take you there each morning. They have daycare, and you can bring your daughter to school with you. Would you like me to get you enrolled over there?"

"Absolutely, it sounds perfect for me."

I started school there the next week. Even though I didn't want to go back to school, this was better than the local high school, where I didn't fit in.

Lea snuggled into my chest as we rode the bus to school each morning. She loved her teacher, Ms. Vicki, who took good care of her while I was in class. She also enjoyed learning and having other kids her own age to play with. There were about forty students at the school. Mostly all girls, but there were a couple of boys who attended. It was very informal and accommodating for the students. They offered a student smoking lounge, and we called our teachers by their first names. The principal, Diana, was an angel. She showed so much love and respect to all the students and was like a mother hen who looked after us.

There was a lady I waitressed with who lived near Mom's and offered to drive me to work if I helped out with gas money. I appreciated her help.

Within a few weeks of moving to Mom's, I got my learner's permit. I needed to practice driving. But no one would help me. "Angel, now you are too nervous to be driving. I don't think you need to get your driver's license just yet."

"Mom, I have to get my driver's license and a car. I can't depend on other people to get me to work."

"Well, it makes me too nervous to drive with you. Maybe your sister will let you drive with her."

Reluctantly, Jenny let me practice a couple of times, but she was gone a lot with work and preparing to go into the US Army Reserves. "Angel, I am going to be leaving after your birthday in November for boot camp. If you want to buy my car, I will sell it to you for a hundred dollars."

"Really, Jenny?"

"Yes, it's not worth much more than that, and I am not going to need it. I plan on buying a better car when I get back home."

"Oh my God, it is perfect. I definitely want to buy it. I will get the money to you here in a few weeks." I was so appreciative. Excitement rushed over me. *Things are working out for me. This is all so perfect.*

As someone who had already faced so much restriction and poverty, I saw owning a car as the key to my freedom and success. Having a car meant so much to me because not having one caused so much pain in my life, and I was determined to never be without one ever again. The car was a 1971 Chevy Chevelle. It was light blue and had rust around the fenders. The front-right bumper was tied on with some wire and a coat hanger. The front seat was broken and wouldn't slide up any closer to the gas and brake pedals, so I had to buy a chair cushion to place in the driver's seat so I could reach the pedals.

But it ran.

Because I rarely had any practice, I didn't put in the required hours in for driver's training, but enough time had passed, and I was eligible to take my driver's test. Mom wouldn't let me use her car, and Jenny wasn't available, so I asked Charlie's dad, Chuck, if he would let me borrow his car for the driver's test at the Secretary of State, and he agreed. I was a nervous wreck. I messed up a few times during the test, and it was evident I wasn't ready to drive, but I think the lady testing me was so scared she passed me so she didn't have to get in the car with me again. "Ma'am, your daughter needs a lot of practice, but I am going to go ahead and pass her," she told my mother. And with that, I stood in front of the camera and got my picture taken for my official driver's license. *Freedom at last.*

Charlie called me at Mom's a lot when I first left, begging me to come back. I was short with him and dismissive. I wasn't going back to that hell. I was getting on my feet, and after a while, he stopped calling. I imagined he was preoccupied with Elaine, and I was happy without him and all the craziness he brought in my life. Dottie and her husband, Mitch, loved Lea and kept her for me often when I worked. I also took her down to stay the weekend from time to time. Charlie moved back in with his mom, and he saw Lea when she was there.

One Sunday when I came to pick Lea up at Dottie's, Charlie came out. Many months had gone by, and I had changed a lot since leaving him. I was in school; I had a job and was making money. I bought new clothes and nice shoes. I wore makeup, something he didn't like me to wear when I was with him. I was talking with a guy named John. It wasn't serious, but he made me feel good about myself. This was the first time I saw Charlie in a while.

"Hey, Angel, what are you up to?"

"Not much, Charlie. Just working and going to school."

"Oh yeah? You look very nice."

It stunned me. He was so nice and sweet. *Who was this guy?*

"Thank you, Charlie," I said with surprise.

"Hey, I heard you were seeing someone. Is that true?"

My heart sank. I wasn't sure if he was going to start an argument. "Where did you hear that?"

"You know I got friends around."

"Hmm," I replied. I didn't want any trouble, and I wasn't sure where this was going.

"We should have dinner sometime and talk."

"I don't think so, Charlie. What do we have to talk about?"

"I'd just like to catch up, Angel," he said softly as he smiled, and my heart melted.

He was such a charmer. So childlike in ways and adorable to look at. I knew he was a snake, but he had a way to mesmerize me. "I will think about it, Charlie."

"Come on, Angel, I want to talk to you. I miss you. I made a mistake. We need to talk. Think about Lea. We need to work things out."

"Where is all this coming from, Charlie?"

"I miss you so much. Please think about it."

"I will."

I took Lea from Charlie's arms.

"Goodbye, Daddy!"

"Goodbye, darling. Daddy loves you." He kissed Lea's cheek and brushed up against me as he pulled away. He looked at me and smiled, knowing I felt his touch. "Angel, please, let's talk soon."

I shook off his charm and put Lea in the car and drove away. I smiled inside at the thought that he was missing me; then I shuddered at the thought. *Get your head together, girl. That guy is no good for you. But maybe he has changed like I have*, I pondered.

That Christmas, Charlie was sweet and poured on his best charm. The phone rang. "Hey Angel, what does Lea need for Christmas? And is there anything you need?"

"No, Charlie, I am fine. Lea could use some new clothes, and she likes dolls, books, puzzles, and any kind of learning toys."

"Okay, I will see what I can do. When are you going to let me take you out to dinner?"

"Hmm-hm." I nervously snickered. "I don't know, Charlie. I am not sure that is a good idea," I replied in a firm tone.

"Oh, come on. It's just dinner. I miss you, and I just want to see you," he pleaded.

I didn't respond.

"Okay, maybe just a Coke or I mean Pepsi, that's what you like?" he corrected himself.

"I will think about it, Charlie. We have Christmas at Mom's on Christmas Eve. If you want to pick Lea up on Christmas Day, that would work fine. You can keep her overnight, and I will come get her the day after Christmas."

"What about her birthday? She turns two on New Year's Day."

"Yeah, I know. I have to work that day. I planned to have cake with her with my family on Saturday before her birthday. I work on New Year's Eve too. If you want to pick her up then, you can keep her overnight and have her on her birthday."

"That works great. Thanks, Angel! And let me know about getting together. I miss you."

"I will let you know, Charlie!"

Over the next month, Charlie kept pressuring and begging me to have dinner or take some time to talk with him. It seemed to be bothering him to think I was with someone else and my life was going well without him. I had always been a doormat and given in to him, and he didn't know how to take this new behavior from me. I held my ground and was firm, and he didn't seem to know what to do.

"Angel, please, meet with me. I love and miss you so much. I made a huge mistake, and I am willing to do anything to work on things. I promise things will be different. I have grown up since you left. Please come talk with me."

A part of me knew this was not a good idea, but my heart yearned for things to be better. Things must not be going so well for him, I imagined. I loved him and I missed him, and I wondered if things could work out. *What if we both just needed some time away from each other to grow up some?* I wanted so badly for Lea to have a family and for her parents to be together, but it had to be a healthy environment. Not like it was before. I could never go back to the craziness. I wasn't happy at Mom's. I didn't like the rules, and Ben was constantly giving me hell at every turn. A part of me felt like I had to talk with Charlie or I'd regret it for the rest of my life. I finally gave in.

"Okay, Charlie, I will meet with you."

We decided to meet at a park and talk. I didn't want anyone to see us together. I opened the door to his car and slid into the passenger seat.

"Oh my God, you look amazing!"

"Thank you, Charlie."

"Thank you for coming to talk with me. I have missed you so much, Angel. I am sorry for everything that happened in the past. I promise if you come back, things will be different."

"I don't know, Charlie. Things were bad, and you were mean to me. And your temper is awful. And what about Elaine?"

"I have changed. I promise things will be better. I don't care about her. I only love you. I couldn't see it before you left. But I know now I can't live without you."

"Are you still with her?"

"Not really. We still talk, but all I can think about is you. I left my job at the restaurant, and I don't work with her anymore. I got a job working at a self-serve car wash, and I am making more money now. Things will be better."

"I don't know, Charlie." I hesitated.

"Please give me another chance! I promise you won't regret it."

"If I even consider coming back, you'd have to promise you will never ever hit me again. Never, not ever!"

"Oh, I promise. I will never hit you again. You didn't deserve it, and I was wrong for getting so angry."

"Where would we live, Charlie?"

"I have talked to Mom already, and she said you could come live with us. With the money I am making and with what you are making, we could get a place of our own pretty quick."

"At your mom's, Charlie? She doesn't like me."

"Angel, I am her baby, and she just is overprotective. You know that."

"Yes, I know, but she doesn't like me, and she makes me feel like a terrible mother."

"I will talk to her and tell her to take it easy on you. Please! Please come back! I will do anything to get you back."

"Oh my God, Charlie, I just don't know. It all sounds good, but I just don't know. Mom will kill me."

"Well, you don't have to tell her. I could come and move you out while she is at work."

"I don't know, Charlie." He pulled me in and kissed me so passionately my heart melted. I loved him so much. The pull I felt around him was so strong it took my breath away. It was like an obsession that mesmerized me. Was this really love? At the time, it was the only love I really ever knew.

I felt confused, excited, scared, and uncertain. *What am I doing? Can this really work this time, or am I crazy for even considering this?* It was like Charlie had a spell on me. I was sixteen years old, and he was my first and only love, and I couldn't imagine ever loving anyone this much, ever. Things with John were not great. He didn't care about me. I was just another girl to him, and he wasn't Charlie. Charlie felt comfortable, like an old pair of jeans. I drove away with a thousand thoughts and emotions swimming through my heart and mind.

CHAPTER 16

As I rushed to pack up my things, I knew this was going to break my mother's heart and any trust she had in me. But I also knew I didn't want to fight and argue over Charlie. I loved him so much and just felt like I was doing what was best for me and Lea. He seemed different, more mature, and I wanted to give it another chance. I knew if I didn't, I'd regret it for the rest of my life. Charlie and I rushed and packed up my things on the trailer he rented. I also knew this seemed crazy. I recognized that I'd been doing the very same secretive and frantic packing just months earlier when I left Charlie, like I had so many other times in my life when we had to move so often, when things went awry with finances, and we were trying to survive or escape Percy. But I pushed all of that out of my mind.

He seemed so happy, knowing I was coming back, and that made me feel important. I had a lot of mixed emotions. I had been free to be myself for the past six months. I was independent and had my own money. I had nice clothes and felt good about myself. I had grown up a lot. I hoped Charlie did too and that things would be better this time.

I definitely had some doubts, but the love and hope I felt was much stronger. Every time I carried out a box and my eyes met Charlie's, he smiled at me, and my heart melted. It felt so good to feel his love and attention, the way I felt when we first met. It was like a whole new beginning, and I was excited.

At first, things were amazing. Charlie showered me with his love and attention, but I wasn't the same girl I was before I left him. I had grown up, was more independent and self-reliant. Charlie didn't like the new me at all. Over the weeks, he became more and more jealous and paranoid. He hated the fact that I had my own car and I wasn't completely dependent upon him for everything.

Every time I went to work, he questioned every minute I was away. He accused me of cheating on him and started verbally and mentally abusing me again. He'd hide my keys to keep me from going to work. We began fighting again, and I started walking on eggshells in fear. Within the first month, all the promises he made were broken, and he was meaner and crueler than he had ever been.

One day, while we were staying at his mom's and she and Mitch were away, we got into a huge fight over me wanting to go to the store, and Charlie hit me. I reminded him he promised he wouldn't ever hit me again. He began taunting and making fun of me.

I told him, "That is it! I am leaving!"

I began packing up my things.

I went into the bathroom to get some items, and when I turned around, he was coming through the door with Mitch's double-barrel shotgun. He backed me in the corner between the wall and the toilet, and I knew at that moment he was going to kill me.

"Oh my God!" I screamed a blood-curdling scream. Lea was right beside me, and I grabbed her and pulled her in my arms to shield her. "Please don't hurt me! Please!" I screamed as I braced for him to shoot me. I begged him for my life. "Please Charlie, I promised if you put the gun away, I won't leave."

He just stared at me for what felt like forever.

"Do you promise?"

"Yes, I promise! Yes! Please!" I cried.

He shouted, "You're a whore, and I know you want to go to the store so you can call John. One dick isn't enough for you, is it?"

"Charlie, stop, please! You are scaring me and the baby. You know I love you!"

Lea began to cry, and I pulled her in closer to my chest.

"You are never going to fucking leave me again. Do you hear me?"

"Yes, I hear you, Charlie. I hear you! I am not going to leave you. I love you too much." I cried.

"I am never going to let you leave me. Get it through your head. You hear me?"

"Yes, I am sorry. I was just upset. I hear you! Please, put the gun away. Please!" I continued to beg for my life, and finally he put the gun down and he ran to me and began kissing and hugging me.

"I love you so much, Angel. You know how much I love you. I just can't live without you, and I can't let you leave me ever again."

I wish I could have said what I was feeling in that moment. *You mother fucker, you are never going to ever make me feel this fucking low, vulnerable, scared, and deflated ever again. You fucking little, little mother fucker. I do not deserve this, you piece of shit, you little, little pathetic man. No one will ever fucking hurt me this fucking bad again. Not ever ever ever a-fucking-gain.* I was enraged, but I was not safe to express it at that time. Yet, I knew with every fiber in me I was never going to be in this situation ever again in my entire life.

I knew instantly I had made the worst mistake of my life coming back to this asshole.

Whatever love I had for him died in that very moment, but I knew I couldn't leave. I felt like a prisoner in a cage again, but this time it was worse. He had never tried to kill me before. This was new territory. My mind was shattered, and I was in shock. I couldn't believe what had just happened. I needed a cigarette. I hugged Charlie and kissed him. "I love you! Thank you for not hurting me!" I said so he would feel assured, and I could get away from him. "I need a cigarette, Charlie." I pulled away from him and took Lea into the living room and got her some toys to play with. I turned on the cartoons. "Sit down here and play, sweetie. Mommy loves you! Let me get you a snack. You have been a very good girl."

I pulled a cigarette from my purse and went into the kitchen, got Lea some pretzels and took them to her, and went back into the kitchen and sat down at the table and smoked. My hands were still shaking, and my nerves were shattered. *I don't know how, but I have got to leave. How will I ever get away from him? Why in the hell did I ever come back? Why did I trust him again? I am so stupid. What kind of fool am I?* I took in the smoke of the cigarette and felt some relief. I knew I couldn't leave, not today at least, but I had to leave. I just didn't know when or how. I was terrified for my life and was so angry at myself for ever coming back. *What in the hell was I thinking?*

I knew in my heart I was leaving at the first opportunity I could get, but when you are poor and have few options, you have to weigh all of this in your mind very carefully and navigate leaving. Often you have to be manipulative to stay safe. I was hypervigilant about surviving. I had learned a lot about this surviving Percy and watching my mom put up with his shit.

For now, I was stuck, but I began plotting my escape again.

The week before, Charlie and I had rented an upper flat and we were getting ready to move in. But after this happened, I didn't want to move into the new place with him. I wanted to leave, but I knew I couldn't. It wasn't safe. In the weeks that followed, things were better, as they often were after his outbursts. We moved out of his mom's and got settled into our new place. It was like that. Charlie would be so awful and beat the shit out of me, verbally and mentally abuse me, and have me so shaken and scared I would become submissive.

I was strong. Very strong. I had been through a lot before I met Charlie, but I was vulnerable, and he knew how to break me down. He didn't like the fighter in me; it pissed him off, and he would challenge me, and he worked hard to break me down. I was so emotionally hurt and needed to feel love so desperately, and he knew it and he knew how to manipulate me. He'd apologize and tell me how much he loved me and how sorry he was for hitting or hurting me, and then for no reason, something, a little thing would happen, the door slammed, the dishes weren't clean, dinner wasn't made, or it wasn't what he wanted, and he would explode and go into a tirade.

It was like living in a war zone and never knowing when you were going to step on a land mine. It was awful being stuck somewhere you didn't want to be, living in fear and not knowing if or when you were ever going to get out or if you were going to survive. It was pure hell. It helped that it wasn't bad all the time, but the uncertainty of not knowing when things would explode kept me on edge, and I was a nervous wreck most of the time. It was hard to concentrate or focus on anything.

When I got back with Charlie, I stopped going to school because he didn't want me to go. That was another mistake I made. I had a lot of support at school. Diana, the principal, was a huge advocate for the students. I knew if I could get away from Charlie and get to the school, they would help me. I had already burned the bridge with Mom, so I didn't have a lot of options.

One night Charlie came in and started on me again, accusing me of being out with someone else. We got in another huge fight over his jealousy, and he hit me in the nose. Blood was everywhere, and I was crying. We fought for an hour, and as usual, it eventually died down, and things were calm when he went into the bathroom. I immediately saw this as an opportunity. I didn't even think. I just grabbed my keys and Lea, and I ran out the door and down the steps, jumped in my car, and drove off as fast as I could. My aunt Sissy only lived a mile away, so I drove there. Mom just happened to be there visiting when I walked up to the door with blood still smeared across my face.

"What in the world happened, Angel?" They both gathered around me. "Get in here and sit down," Aunt Sissy instructed.

I told them everything that happened over the past several weeks, including the incident with the gun, and they listened in shock.

"I told you, Angel."

"Mom, stop! I know. I am stupid. I made a huge mistake going back. He promised things would be different. I'm sorry! I just don't want to hear it. It doesn't help!"

"I know, honey. I am sorry. You need to go right now to the police station and have him arrested. That is the only way you're going to get this to stop."

"Oh, you are right. I never thought of that. Do you think it's the right thing to do?" Fear came over me.

"Yes, it is the right thing to do. You go right now, and we will take care of Lea."

"Thank you so much!"

I got into the car, with blood still on my face and hands. I felt hope as I drove to the police station. *This is my way out. They will arrest him, and I can go back while he is in jail and get my things. Yes, this will work,* I assured myself. I parked my car, feeling nervous, and went inside. I waited fifteen minutes until a police officer became available. I sat and tried to clear my mind. I lit one cigarette after the other, smoking to try to calm my nerves. I worried about what Charlie would do if I had him arrested. *Would this make things worse for me? No, this will scare him, and he will leave me alone. I don't know where I will go, but I will sleep in my car if I have to. I can't go back there. This is the right thing to do.* I felt sure.

A tall, white officer came out and called me back into his office. "All right, ma'am, give me your name, the address of where the alleged event occurred, and the name of the alleged assailant, and tell me what happened."

I started crying as I told him what happened that evening. I also told him about Charlie pulling the shotgun on me at his mom's house several weeks before. I told them I was scared to leave, but after the fight tonight, I was afraid he was going to really hurt me.

The officer listened. Then he looked at me and cocked his head sideways and said, "It sounds like you have left, but you keep going back."

"Well, yes, I did leave, and I did come back, but he promised …."

"Yeah, yeah, ma'am" he interrupted me. "We hear this all the time. There isn't anything we can do for you here. We know how this goes. We'll arrest him, and you'll be in here in a few hours, bailing him out."

"No, sir! No, I won't. I promise. I have to get away from him. He is going to hurt me."

"Ma'am, we see this every day. You are going to have to work it out. There is nothing we can do for you."

"But … but …"

"You heard me, ma'am," he insisted.

He made me feel like a piece of white trash. I took a deep breath in, gathered my purse, and walked out of the police station feeling defeated. I drove back to Aunt Sissy's house feeling hopeless. I had no idea what I was going to do now. I didn't think about that when I ran out and left Charlie. I just left. I pulled up in front of Aunt Sissy's house and went inside and told them the police wouldn't help me.

"What? Are you kidding me?" My aunt and mom both said in their own way, in surprise.

"No, I am not kidding."

Aunt Sissy got a warm washcloth and brought it to me to wash off the blood. Just as I finished wiping my face, there was a bang on the door. I looked up, and it was Charlie. I began to shake.

"He found me."

Aunt Sissy answered the door. "Now, we ain't going to have no trouble here, Charlie."

"I know. I just need to talk to Angel. Please. I don't want to cause any trouble." He sounded so sincere and humble. Aunt Sissy looked at me, and I went to the door and stood with the screen door cracked and talked with him through the door while he stood on the porch.

"What do you want, Charlie?"

"Come home, Angel. I am sorry."

"Yeah, I have heard that a lot, Charlie! You promised you wouldn't hit me."

"I know. You just make me so mad. If you wouldn't make me so mad, I wouldn't hit you. You know I didn't mean it. Let's go home and talk about this."

"It is not my fault, Charlie. I don't want to come back to that. I am afraid you are going to hurt me."

"Please, just come on. Let's go home!"

Lea came over to the door. "Daddy!" she exclaimed.

"Come here, baby." She ran to him, and he pulled her up into his arms. She smiled and kissed him. She loved her daddy.

"Come on, Angel, let's go home!"

"No, I am not going home tonight."

He looked at me and stared for a minute. Then he turned and ran with Lea in his arms and jumped into his car and took off.

I stood there stunned. *What the hell just happened?* "Shit!"

I turned and looked at my aunt and mom, who were just as stunned as I was. I started crying. "I am so tired of fighting with him! I just hate him."

"You got to go home, Angel. You need to go back and get Lea. You go back home and act like you love him, and in a couple of days, when things settle down and he is gone to work, you pack up your things and you leave," Mom instructed.

"Where am I going to go?"

"I don't know, Angel. You sure have made a mess of things. We will just have to figure that out when you get out of there." She and Aunt Sissy built me up and gave me the encouragement to go back.

"I am scared to go back. I am afraid he is going to hurt me."

"I think if you make him feel loved and make him believe you aren't going to leave him, he won't hurt you, Angel."

"I don't know, Mom, but I don't think I have any other choice." I was scared, but I put the key in the ignition, and I headed back to our flat.

I pulled up in front of the house and took a deep breath. I had no idea what I was getting ready to return to. My legs were shaking as I walked up the step. It had been a long day and was nearly midnight.

"Oh my God! I knew you would come back for her! Thank God!" He ran to me and pulled me into his arms. "Come here. I am sorry. I know it is hard for you to believe me, but I didn't mean to hurt you."

"I know, Charlie. I know."

"You just do everything you can to upset me, and it makes me crazy, Angel."

It took everything in me to pretend I was okay. That everything was okay and that we were going to carry on. I was not okay. I was shattered and a shell of the person I was eight weeks earlier, when I first returned to this relationship, believing things would be better, only to discover they were worse than ever. It took every ounce of energy I could gather to act the part that was needed to get through this until I could get an opportunity to leave for good. And I wondered if I was ever going to be able to leave. I was scared, and I felt lost. I remembered what Mom and Aunt Sissy told me.

I pulled Charlie close to me. "I love you. I know you don't mean to hurt me. I will try to do better and not make you mad." I kissed him, and he pulled me into his chest and held me so close I felt smothered.

He had put Lea to bed, and the house was quiet. He picked me up and carried me into the bedroom and undressed me, and we had sex. It took everything in me to lie beneath him, but I engaged and played the part. I felt like I was going to throw up before we finished, but I gathered my strength and made it through. I got up and cleaned myself up and went and smoked a cigarette.

"Are you coming to bed, honey?"

"Yeah, in just a minute, Charlie. I just wanted to smoke."

"Okay, I love you!"

"I love you too!" I said. I knew he was worried, and he didn't trust me not to leave, especially after today. I put the cigarette to my mouth and pulled the smoke into my lungs, feeling sick to my stomach over this situation I had put myself back in. *I can't do this much longer. Not much longer at all.* I climbed into bed, and Charlie put his arm around me. I snuggled up close to make him feel secure and lay awake and wallowed in my thoughts. I felt enraged like a caged lion. I didn't know how I could stand being here for another second. *How would I get through another day? He works in the morning. As soon as he leaves, I will pack mine and Lea's clothes, and I will leave. I don't know where I will go, but I will figure it out.* I felt some relief and hope in those thoughts. I was exhausted as I let those thoughts sink in, and I drifted off to sleep.

"Good morning, Charlie. It's time to get up and go to work," I said pleasantly the next morning as I nudged him to wake up.

"No, I am not going today. I am too tired after yesterday."

"What do you mean, you aren't going? We need the money, Charlie."

"I don't care. I am too tired. I am not going in."

This wasn't like Charlie. He never missed work. Anxiety and impatience came over me. I knew he was staying home to watch me and make sure I didn't leave. My hopes of leaving today began to fade. I didn't have to be at work until 5 p.m., and I had hoped to get out of here and figure things out before I had to be there. We didn't have a phone because we couldn't afford it, so I figured Charlie would have to go out to call his boss, but he didn't. I didn't want to push him, in fear of provoking him. He got up and made his coffee, and I got Lea up, fed her breakfast, and played with her on the floor with her toys. She loved being close to me and loved sitting on my lap. I cuddled her close to me, and we got on the couch and watched *Sesame Street*. She followed along with the characters and repeated the letters and numbers and sang, while I was lost and overwhelmed in my thoughts. *Maybe I can tell Charlie I am going to go to school today. I have to get out of here. I just don't want to be here for another minute. I don't think I can pretend I am okay, when I am not. I want to leave. I just want to get out of here. How can I leave? He isn't going to let me leave.* My mind was racing.

I could feel him watching me while he drank his coffee. I sat and pondered and wondered what to do. I was so angry and tired of all this. Nearly four years of hell with this man. If he was a normal person, we could talk and agree this wasn't working out and this relationship was toxic, and we needed to end it. But he wasn't normal. That approach would never work. The longer I sat there, the angrier I became. I hated feeling trapped, controlled, stuck, miserable, and unhappy, but I knew if I upset him, he would hurt me. I felt afraid. I felt angry at myself for coming back and for all the mistakes I had made. I sat and thought about all I had been through and evaluated why I was in this situation. *Why have I stayed? Why did I come back? I thought things would be different, I really did.*

When you live with a man who beats you, you walk on eggshells trying not to provoke him. Doing things to try to please him, never knowing for sure what might set him off. I learned to watch my words and to be careful of my actions. I had to think through things before I did them, to make sure I didn't make a mistake, knowing the consequences full well if I did. At first, it's like a game or figuring out a puzzle, and over time, you learn how the pieces fit together, and you try not to get them out of place.

It was like a list of things to do.

Make sure the house is straight.

Make dinner.

Make sure the baby doesn't make too much noise.

And of course, don't talk back or get out of line.

Do what he says.

Have sex when he wants.

Don't act like you enjoy it too much or he'll think you're fucking someone else.

Don't have an opinion.

Don't get too close to the guy looking at the pork chops in the meat aisle.

Make sure no guys look at you when you are walking with him down the street or at the gas station or at the store or as a matter of fact not anywhere because of course he'll just know you're fucking them too.

And on top of it all, be everything and do everything he wants, and everything will be just fine.

I guess that was my problem. I didn't live up to his expectations.

As I sat there on the couch, holding Lea and watching *Sesame Street*, I tried to put the puzzle pieces together and understand my life with Charlie. I was still so young, and I had never been with anyone else. I had experienced a lot of rejection and felt unloved. I was vulnerable and needy and clung to Charlie. I think he felt like he owned me ... like I was his property. I had been beaten down by most people in my life, and I wanted so badly to be loved and accepted. In the beginning, he was so attentive and enamored of me. I had never felt so much love in my life. I didn't think I could live without him, and I became a doormat and did everything I could to please him.

Over time he began to take advantage of my vulnerability and would use his love to manipulate me. He would use his words to beat me down and make me feel worthless. I tried so hard to make Charlie happy. I just couldn't. It didn't matter what I did; it was never good enough. He made me feel bad about myself, my ideas, my dreams and aspirations. He put me down and ridiculed things I did or the way I did them, and I could never win or do anything right. Over time I began to believe him, and my self-esteem was shattered. It was hard for me to see up from where I was. I couldn't understand why he was like this.

What is wrong with him that makes him so mean? Did he know when he was a little boy, cute, innocent, and sweet, that he'd grow up to be a monster? Did he know he would need to dominate women and have power and control over them to feel important? What happened in those early years that made him feel so insecure and powerless? I wondered if he was scared of me and the only way to keep me caged was to bully me, beat me down, keep me broken, dependent on him, and make me think I was worthless without him.

While I was thinking about all of this, Charlie sat in the kitchen, drinking his coffee. I could tell he had something on his mind. He came through the house and sat down next to us on the couch. He tickled Lea, and she laughed. "Good morning."

"Hi, Daddy! Me watching Cookie Monster" she said in her sweet little voice.

"Yes." he replied.

We played with Lea and engaged with her while she watched television. There was an awkward silence between us. I was trying to pretend I was happy, but I wasn't, and it is hard for me to hide my emotions.

"Are you going to go call your boss and let him know you are not coming to work today? You know you can't lose that job, Charlie!"

"No, I don't have to call him. He's never around anyways, and I work alone, so he probably won't even notice I didn't come in today."

"But what if he does, Charlie?"

"Then I will tell him I was sick, and I didn't have a phone to call him. It will be fine, Angel," he replied harshly.

Disappointment set in. It aggravated me. I couldn't stand being with him. I wanted to just grab my things and leave. I sat quietly, thinking and focusing on Lea. I played with Lea for a while, then fed her lunch and put her down for a nap.

Afterwards, I decided to go get cleaned up and start preparing for work to give myself something to do. I resolved I would have to wait until tomorrow, when he went back to work, to make my escape. I was sad and disappointed, but I had no other choice. Charlie followed me into the bathroom.

"What are you thinking, Angel? I know you are up to something."

I just looked at him. I was afraid to say anything. I knew whatever I said would be wrong. A flood of emotions was running through me, and I wanted to just scream.

"Tell me what you are thinking, Angel. Tell me right now! What are you cooking up inside your little head?"

"Nothing, Charlie!" I tried to push past him to get away, but he pushed me up against the wall and was up in my face. It felt like the day he had me pent up against the wall beside the toilet when he pulled the shotgun on me, and I started to shake. "Stop, Charlie. I mean it!"

"What are you going to do?" He bit back at me.

"Why are you doing this, Charlie? Why?" I started to cry.

"You are up to something! I know it!" He shouted so loudly at me it startled me.

I trembled and shoved him, and he nearly fell into the tub, and it gave me enough room to run out.

He came after me and grabbed my arm. "What the fuck did you do that for?"

"Charlie, you are scaring me. Stop, please! You promised you wouldn't do this anymore!" I struggled to get out of his grasp and began to run to find my purse and keys. *I need to get out of here before he hurts me again.*

He grabbed my purse and slung it out of my hands. Then he hit me so hard it knocked me onto the hardwood floor in the dining room, which was vacant except for a small toybox that sat in the corner. He smacked me in the face, then grabbed me by my hair and slammed my head against the floor, banging it into the hard surface again and again. I was afraid he was going to break my skull. He was so enraged, I was afraid he had lost all control. I didn't feel safe. I was swinging my arms and pushing him back, trying to get him off me so I could get away from him. "Please stop, Charlie, please!" I cried, but he wouldn't listen. "Charlie! Charlie stop!" It was as if he was in a trance or out of his mind. He didn't drink or use drugs. He just needed power and control over me, and when he felt he was losing it, he came undone and would go crazy to get control back over me. It made him feel powerful. I could taste the blood running from my nose and lip. My head was pounding, and I could feel my face beginning to swell.

He was on top of me, yelling, "You bitch, what are you going to do now?"

The coolness of the hardwood floor where my head rested brought comfort.

As he yelled and called me names, I lay there thinking about how I could ever get out of this mess and be free. The thought of being stuck here in his prison brought panic and anger. *I can't do this anymore. Am I going to be able to escape this time? I have lived in his prison for years, and I just want out. I left and survived. Why in the hell did I ever come back? Why did I believe his lies that things would be different this time? I wanted to believe him. I wanted things to be better. I wanted the fairy tale I had dreamed about, but this is a nightmare that is never going to change. Because I had left him, he punishes me every chance he can. He will never let me forget the pain I caused him.*

I knew if I didn't figure it out soon, one of us would end up hurt or maybe even dead. Many times, out of desperation and having no way out, I wished he was dead. I worried that it was the only way I was going to get out of this situation. And it scared the shit out of me.

He continued to shout at me and was knocking me around and slapping me across my face, to make sure he had my attention. I shouted, "Please, Charlie, stop this!" I could hear the door to Lea's room squeak as she opened it and ran from her bedroom, awakening from her nap by the rumble of his voice and screech of the scream that came reactively from my lips. Her blankie wrapped in her arms and snuggled up to her body for comfort.

Her blonde hair lay in curls and bounced as she approached me and began to plead, "Please, Daddy, don't hit Mommy! Why are you hurting Mommy?" She ran and lay down beside me and gently rubbed her tiny hand across my face to wipe the tears that fell down my cheek. It broke my heart for her to see this. I wanted so badly to jump up and take Lea and run out the door and leave and never look back.

I stopped fighting him as I pulled Lea into my chest. He looked at her and stopped hitting me. He got up and started pacing, rummaging through the house, throwing my stuff everywhere, kicking it across the floor, shouting, and calling me names. I didn't get up to try to stop him this time. I didn't care anymore. I was so sick of this. None of these things meant anything to me. I was just empty, numb, and tired of fighting. I just wanted out. I cringed as he walked closer to my body, curled up in a fetal position, lying still on the floor, holding Lea and thinking of how I could get out of here. I could see a spider crawling across the floor, making its way to its well-spun web, oblivious to the fear I felt or the pain I was in. I wanted to flinch, but I kept still. I didn't dare move, in fear of him hitting me again, but just as the thought left me, he kicked me in the back with his boot. Instantly my body coiled up in reaction to the pain, and I couldn't control the movement that naturally occurred as my body tried to protect itself.

"Get the fuck up, Angel, and get this fucking house cleaned up."

I screeched out in pain and pulled Lea closer to my chest. *I have to get out of here. If I don't go now, I may never get out.*

I gained enough strength to pull myself up from the floor. I knew if I didn't leave now, he was going to kill me, if not today, someday, someday soon. I began picking my things up and straightening back up the house back up from his tirade as he demanded. I noticed my purse and keys were lying on the floor near the door, where he knocked it out of my hand. Just as he went into the kitchen, and I was several feet away from him, I grabbed Lea and my purse and ran for the door, stumbling down the stairs of our two-story flat running with Lea in my arms as fast as I could. Immediately, he came running after me, grabbing my arm the final few steps at the bottom of the stairs. I pushed him backward as I went out the door and got a few steps ahead of him.

I ran and got in the car. My hands were trembling as I fumbled with the key, rushing, trying to get it into the ignition before he got to me. Lea was crying.

"It's okay, baby. We are going to go for a ride."

Just as I got the car started, he ran to the passenger side and found the door unlocked and jumped inside. My heart sank. He began trying to grab for the key, but I put the car in drive and drove off with him in it. *If I can just get somewhere in public, he won't hurt me in front of other people, or at least they can help me.* I didn't know where I was going. I thought quickly, *I can take him to his mom's. She only lives a few miles away, and I can drop him off. She can calm him down, and I can leave.* She would tell him to stop acting this way.

He slammed his fist into the dashboard and was shoving me all the while I was driving, trying to get me to pull over. I feared he was going to wreck us, but I was more afraid of stopping.

"Charlie please stop! You are going to wreck us!"

"You need to pull over! Right now, Angel!" he shouted.

I was so scared, my foot was shaking so bad, I could barely keep it on the gas pedal. I drove as fast as I could to get to his mother, even hoping I would get pulled over by the police so they could see they made a mistake not pursuing the complaint I made just the day before, but the police weren't coming to rescue me. I finally got to his mother's house. I jumped out of the car, leaving Lea behind. Blood, snot, and tears were running down my face, and I was hysterical. I banged on the door as hard as I could.

Dottie ran out. "What in the hell is going on?"

"Charlie has gone crazy, and he won't calm down. Please help me!"

She shook her head. "Now, I am sick and tired of this fighting going on. You all need to get it together! I don't know about the two of you. Why can't you stop all this foolishness and figure this out for this baby?"

Charlie was her baby, and she always sided with him.

Charlie ran up on the porch with Lea in his arms, blaming me. "It's her, Mom, she's trying to leave and take my baby. I am not going to let her do it again." He began screaming in my face.

Lea was crying and reaching for me, and I tried to get her out of his arms. She was scared, and I wanted to comfort her, but he kept pushing and shoving me away. I just wanted to get her out of his arms and leave. I was done with all this. I just wanted out.

At some point while we were arguing, Dottie went back into the house. Then suddenly, Mitch rushed out on the porch with a double-barrel shotgun, the same gun that weeks before Charlie had pulled on me. He pointed the gun at me. "Get the hell off of my porch!" he shouted.

I was in shock, and my mind raced. I wanted so bad to grab Lea from Charlie's arms, but I knew if I did, he would shoot me. I ran off the porch, screaming for my life. Mitch continued to chase me with the gun. I ran as fast as I could and got into my car, trembling. I knew any second, he was going to pull the trigger, and I would be dead.

I somehow managed to get the key into the ignition and got the car started as Mitch was staring me down while I pulled away, leaving my baby girl crying for me in Charlie's arms. I felt like I was in a nightmare I couldn't wake up from. *This can't be happening*, I thought as I drove as fast as I could to get off their street. I didn't know where to go or what to do. I was a nervous wreck and in shock over everything that had happened this morning. I knew going to the police was a waste of time.

I drove in a trance, trying to get my thoughts together and figure out what to do. *I don't have anywhere to go.* I sobbed as devastation rose up within me. *My poor baby girl. Oh, I should have stayed quiet. I shouldn't have run out of the house. All this wouldn't have happened.* I blamed myself, just like Charlie did, adding insult to my injuries. *What am I going to do? I have nothing. I don't even have my uniform for work. I have no money, no friends, and nowhere to turn. I burned all my bridges.*

My mind raced as I drove aimlessly farther away from Dottie and Mitch's house, trying to calm myself down, but I just couldn't. I remembered school. *Yes! I can go to the Teen Parent Program. They will help me! They will help me for sure!* An ounce of hope came through my tears as I drove onto I-75 South toward the school.

CHAPTER 17

I don't remember much after getting onto I-75. My mind was off in another world, trying to gain some insight about everything that had happened over the past several hours but not being able to put the puzzle together. I was shaking when I pulled up into the school parking lot and parked. I ran right into Diana's office, crying so hysterically I startled her. She jumped up from her desk and guided me to a chair. I began to hyperventilate, trying to tell her what had happened.

"Slow down, honey, slow down!"

I was in full crisis, and I couldn't slow down. I couldn't breathe, but I wanted so bad to tell her what had happened. Within a minute, there was a whole team of people surrounding me, trying to help me calm down.

The school nurse, Judy, came over to me. "You are hyperventilating, Angel. I am going to give you a paper bag to put over your nose and mouth. Just breathe slowly, and this will help you catch your breath."

I did as she instructed, breathing as my mind raced. I was terrified, in shock, and a complete emotional mess. I felt like I was going to pass out. I felt supported having all these people around me attending to me. The kind of support from others I had never felt before. I took comfort in knowing, at this moment at least, I was safe. It took a while for me to settle enough to tell them what had happened with Charlie beating me up and me running out of the house with only my life, and all the things that happened afterward, ending with Mitch chasing me off of the porch with the gun. They were all in shock hearing my story.

"Oh my God, that is awful, Angel. We need to call the police and tell them what happened," Diana said.

"Don't bother. They won't help me. I went to the police yesterday to file charges against Charlie when all this started. They pretty much laughed at me and told me there was nothing they could do."

Diana shot a questioning look at me and shook her head. "Sherry, do you think Legal Aid can help?" Sherry was the legal advocate at the school.

"Yes, let's call and see if we can get you an attorney and get things rolling, so you can get custody of Lea right away. Are you feeling up to making that call right now?"

"Yes, if I could just have a few minutes. I need to smoke a cigarette and get something to drink, and I will come back, and we can call them."

As I stood up, Diana hugged me. "You have been through a lot, girl. Go take care of yourself and come back, and Sherry will help you get Lea back." I stayed engaged in her hug for a long while. I didn't want to let go. I felt so alone, rejected, worthless, and unloved. I needed to feel someone in this world cared about me. It felt good to feel her strong, nurturing hug. I cried as she held me, and she was in no hurry to let me go. "You are going to be okay, honey. I am sorry you have been through so much," she said.

"Thank you."

When I arrived at the smoking lounge, I pulled a cigarette from my purse and lit it. Feeling the relief from the nicotine, I plopped onto the couch and stared out the window. I sat there, still coming down from the adrenaline and chaos, still in shock from the near-death experience, and the fear penetrated me from the day's events. I began to sob tears of terror, sadness, and disbelief. I still couldn't believe what happened. It just didn't seem real. I would have never dreamed Mitch would pull a gun on me. I don't even understand what happened to make him do something so extreme. I know things with me and Charlie were at their worst, but I could not comprehend why he pulled the gun on me. It was just so out of character for him to do something so crazy. Perhaps this is what had to happen for me to finally recognize this relationship had to end and there was no going back this time.

I thought about Lea and how she was screaming for me as I ran off the porch, leaving her in that craziness. I cried and felt terrible about all she had witnessed through the hell of this crazy relationship. I lit another cigarette and shook off those thoughts. *I have to get myself together and figure some things out. I am lucky I got out with my life. I may not have much else, but at least I have that.*

When I returned to the office. Marion, the school social worker, Sherry, and Diana were waiting in her office for me. "Where are you going to stay tonight?" Diana asked.

"I don't know. I haven't thought any further than right now. I don't have anywhere to go. I burned a lot of bridges going back to Charlie, especially with Mom."

"Well, work with Sherry on getting an attorney, and Marion and I will work on seeing what options there are for a place for you to stay."

"Thank you. I appreciate it so much!"

Sherry gave me the number, and I called Legal Aid and made the first available appointment, which was in a few days. I was scared, thinking about getting the courts involved. I was afraid they'd take Lea from me and give her to Charlie because he was almost twenty and was in a more stable situation than I was. I told Sherry about my fear before I called, and she reassured me the courts tended to favor the child being with their mother, especially since Lea has been in my care since her birth and in light of all that had happened.

I spoke with the Legal Aid clerk, and she gave me hope but said she couldn't give me any legal advice. She did say it was going to take a couple of weeks to get a court date, and I could speak to my attorney about that when I came to meet with him. My heart sank when I heard this. "A couple of weeks?" Lea had never been away from me more than a couple of days when she had visits with Dottie and Mitch. I felt sad as I hung up the phone.

"What is your situation, Angel?" Sherry asked.

"What do you mean?"

"Are you an emancipated minor?"

"What does that mean?"

"Well, I guess that answers that." She laughed. "It's a court order by a judge freeing you from parental power and making you an adult and in control of yourself legally. Since you have been on your own for the past two years, it shouldn't be hard to get done. It would be easier if your mom would sign the documents to release you. Do you think she would do that?"

"I don't know, maybe, but I don't see why not. She isn't involved in my life much. I would like that, Sherry."

"All right, I will work on the paperwork and get it back to you tomorrow."

"Thank you so much!"

"In the meantime, hang in there. You are going to get through this. You have been through more than most adults, and you are very mature for your age. I admire your strength." She smiled.

Wow, I had never had an adult say such positive things about me in my life. "Do you think so?"

"Oh, my goodness, Angel. You are an incredible young woman. Yes, I absolutely mean everything I just said. You are a fighter and a survivor. You are going to be okay."

"Thank you! I appreciate your kind words. It means a lot."

"You are welcome, honey."

When I got back to Diana's office, she and Marion were waiting for me. "Well, Angel, I have some hopeful news, but we must work out some details, and it is going to take a couple of weeks. There is a new group home for teen mothers nearby. It is for emancipated minors, and the minimum age limit is seventeen years old, but I am going to work with the board of directors, which I am a part of, and tell them your story and see what I can do to get you in there."

"Wow. What is it like?"

"It's a nice place. It's an old store that has been converted into a group home, with a large living and dining room, a kitchen, two bathrooms, a play area and meeting room, and six bedrooms. There is room for six girls, and we have one room available. You would have your own room with a twin bed and crib or twin bed for Lea. It would be a great opportunity for you."

"Can I keep my job? I want to keep working."

"Well, none of the other girls work, but I think having a job is a positive thing, and I don't want to take anything away from you. We would rather you just focus on school, but I am sure we can work with you. You are required to go to school, and there are household chores and duties that you share with the other housemates. Are you an emancipated minor?"

"No, Sherry and I just talked about that. I am not, but she is going to get the paperwork to me tomorrow, and I will do what I need to get it taken care of right away."

"Great. Well, Marion and I will work on seeing what we can do to get you into this program. Where are you going to stay tonight?"

"I don't know. Let me call Mom. Maybe she would let me stay at her place until I get into this program, but I don't know. I also need to call work. I am supposed to be there in an hour, but there is no way I can get myself together to go in."

"Yes, you have been through a lot today. You can use the phone in the front office to make whatever calls you need. Let me know if you have a place to stay tonight."

"Okay, I sure will."

The janitor pushed the mop across the floor of the empty hallway, and Diana lingered in her office, finishing up the last of her work for the day as she waited for me to complete the call with my mother. I poked my head in her office. "Well, Mom isn't sure if I can come there, but I called my cousin, and I am going to stay with her for a couple of days." I was grateful my cousin Louise let me come stay with her, even though it meant that I would have to be watchful for Doug, who I hadn't seen in years. I knew he would be creeping around once he knew I was there.

This has been a terrible day, but I have a lot to be grateful for. I thought about Lea, and my eyes welled up with tears. *She doesn't understand what is happening, and I know she is missing me as much as I am missing her. Charlie is such an asshole.*

I reflected for a moment, then turned up the radio to hear Elton John singing, "I'm Still Standing." I laughed and smiled through the tears that were running down my face. I listened to the lyrics of the song and sang along at the top of my lungs with the windows rolled down, letting the wind blow through my hair. I thought, *Yes, I am still standing.* I breathed in the cool spring air and felt a taste of freedom, for the first time in a very long while.

CHAPTER 18

I stood in the courtroom, dressed uncomfortably in a navy-blue skirt and plain light-blue blouse with buttons up the front and ruffles on the sleeves that I picked up at Goodwill, along with a used pair of navy-blue high-heel shoes that were a half size too big. My attorney recommended I show up in court looking nice for the judge. Charlie walked in wearing blue jeans with a collared shirt tucked in his pants and a new pair of shoes I am sure his mother bought him.

He and Dottie slid onto a bench across the aisle on the opposite side of the courtroom. Charlie gazed down at the floor, avoiding eye contact with me. His attorney went to a table at the front of the courtroom and chatted with my attorney. My palms were sweaty and shaking, and I was wrestling with my nerves as the bailiff announced promptly at 9 a.m., "All rise" when the judge entered the courtroom.

I was feeling hopeful but uncertain. Although my attorney assured me in most cases the judge sides with the mother, and he felt sure I would win the case, it still was all so intimidating and scary. Our case was called first, and my attorney walked confidently toward the center of the courtroom and approached the judge to present my case. Charlie's attorney argued that Lea was in a more stable environment with Charlie and should remain in the custody of Charlie and his mother, Dottie, who was retired and had plenty of time to tend to the needs of the minor child.

My heart sank, hearing these words. I hung on to every word that was said like my life depended on it, because at least as far as my heart was concerned, it did. When it was all over, the judge ordered Lea to be returned to me that afternoon by 3 p.m. at my mother's house in Taylor. He gave me full custody and ordered every-weekend visitation for Charlie. A smile came across my face, and joy leaped up in my heart. I hugged Mom, then my attorney, and looked over at Charlie, whose eyes were piercing me. I knew that look. I finally won an argument, and he didn't like it. The victory landed hard for him and well for me, and I could not wait to see Lea, who had been kept from me for nearly three weeks.

Later that afternoon, Charlie pulled up and got Lea out of the car. She ran with her arms wide open and jumped into my mine, nearly knocking me down. Her arm squeezed around my neck, nearly choking me while hugging me with all her might. We loved each other so much, and it seemed to make Charlie so mad to see how happy Lea was to see me. I thought, *It is really sad that Charlie wouldn't be happy to see Lea so happy. But I knew for Charlie, it was all about being right, being the most important, and winning, and for him this was none of these.*

"Mommy, I missed you! Why didn't you come get me?"

"Oh honey, I have been trying ever since I left, and finally today, I was able to get you back. I missed you so much!" My arms held her tiny body close to my chest as I ran my fingers through her curly hair, kissing her soft face. Watching over her shoulder, Charlie glared at me and snarled with disgust, then climbed into his car. I knew this was far from over. He wouldn't let me win this easily. I pulled Lea close to me, enjoying the smell of her sweet skin as I watched him drive away. I felt sad, compassion, even love for him, not the kind of love where I wanted him back, but love for what I hoped could have been. Loving thoughts, though he nearly killed me three weeks earlier.

Mom and Ben agreed to let us stay with them for the next week until our room was ready at the Teen Parent Home, and I was grateful. I tried to stay out of the way and not make any fuss or disrupt their lives in any way. I was humbled and trying to comprehend everything that was happening so quickly and chaotically in my life. I just wanted peace and not to fight so hard to just be myself. I was exhausted from this hell and feeling uncertain about the future. The past year had been a nightmare, and I was ready to move forward.

Even though I missed Lea so much, the past three weeks had been a relief. I didn't have Charlie on my back, and I wasn't constantly walking on eggshells trying to please him. I didn't have the never-ending responsibility of a small toddler's every need to tend to or the pressure of life that was so hard when you're poor, alone, and not having much support or anyone who could even remotely understand what I was going through. I left all my friends and a different life behind when I decided to get pregnant and quit school at thirteen. I was a teenager who became an adult instantly when this baby was born, and my life had never been the same.

I looked around my mother's living room at the pictures of my older sister, Jenny, at her prom hanging proudly next to her graduation picture. I felt the sting of a life I missed out on.

Even Ben would remind me how I screwed up my life and that boys my age weren't interested in me. "There aren't any teenage boys out there who want to be saddled down with a girl who has a baby! And if they are interested in you, it is only for one thing," he'd say in a condescending way.

I felt like my life was over and I would be alone like Charlie said. "No one is ever going to want you!"

What is going to become of me? I thought about the poverty I had lived through after my parents' divorce and all the hell that I had endured. I thought about the blocks and blocks of run-down houses in Detroit with single mothers on welfare, waiting around with more month than money, waiting for a welfare check and food stamps. I didn't want to end up stuck there. It is a hard place to get out of. I was proud of my mother for working so hard and teaching me the values of a strong work ethic. She always worked, and even though she didn't make much on her waitress pay without any child support, she did the best she could to make ends meet with what she made.

She taught me a lot during those difficult times when we were hungry and didn't have much to eat. She could stretch a dollar and a meal to keep us fed enough to get by. Although there were times when we were hungry and didn't have much, we always knew she was doing her best. She learned from her own upbringing and being poor the value of hard work and a dollar. But I didn't want that for my life. I wanted more, but I wasn't sure how it was possible for me.

I lay awake thinking about the events of the day and feeling relieved to have won the case and to have my baby back. I cradled Lea, who was snuggled up next to me, sleeping in my arms in the small twin bed that belonged to my younger brother, Jake, who agreed to sleep on the couch again, so we could stay in his room. I was exhausted but couldn't sleep. My thoughts drifted back in time. I reflected on my life and the decisions my parents had made. *What would my life be like if Mom had never left Daddy or Daddy would have taken us back when Mom asked, and we were still in Cincinnati? I had such a good life back then. I certainly wouldn't be in the situation I am in now. Things would be so much better.*

CHAPTER 19

Icouldn't move back in with Mom and Ben; they made that very clear. Mom agreed to sign the papers to emancipate me, and even though I didn't want to move into a group home, I didn't have any money or any options. Being emancipated meant that at sixteen years old, I was legally an adult and responsible for myself. Something I had really been since my parents divorced at age nine. The reality of it all set in as I watched my mom sign the papers. I reflected on growing up so quickly and being left alone in a world full of vultures who were ready to pounce on me and take advantage of my innocence without any protection. I reflected for a moment on the loss of my childhood and how it was abruptly stripped away so quickly before I was ready or prepared. Tears welled up, and quickly I wiped them away.

I turned my thoughts to gratitude for being accepted into the Teen Parent Home and to have a safe place to stay, but I was apprehensive and unsure. I was exhausted, overwhelmed, and had been through a whirl-wind of hell. I hadn't had time to even process or comprehend it all, and here I was, moving again. Being at the Teen Parent Home took some time for me to adjust. I was sixteen years old, in the ninth grade, with a two-and-a-half-year-old child and an ex-boyfriend I was still dealing with, who made my life crazy. I was the youngest girl in the home, and unlike them, I had a job, a car, and had lived on my own as an adult with my boyfriend for the past two years. Although we had things in common, most times I felt out of place. I was used to having my own place and doing things my own way. Even under the heavy weight of Charlie, I still did most things day to day on my own schedule.

We each had our own room with a twin bed, a crib, a counter with a chair and a mirror to use as a vanity and a desk, a small closet, and a window. It was cozy, and I appreciated having a place to retreat when the heaviness of being with so many others became too much. I moved in at the end of the school year and looked forward to the summer off to get settled in before school began again in the fall. There were a lot of rules at the house. Chores to do, meals to help prepare, clean-up duties, and activities to participate in, including house meetings. These took priority, and you couldn't leave the house until everything was taken care of. We also helped each other with childcare when needed. I hoped this would be the right place for me to get on track and head in a better direction.

At first it felt good to be around other people who were going through some of the same struggles I was and to have some support. They did a lot to create a family atmosphere and help us learn life skills. They provided grandmother-age volunteers who came each day to help care for our kids while we did our chores, homework, or took some time to ourselves or engaged in activities in the program. It was the most support I had gotten since Lea was born. They encouraged me to quit my job so I could focus on myself, and I complied, but it wasn't long before

I struggled waiting on a check and having a lot of month left without any money. I hated being broke and feeling dependent on someone else for my day-to-day expenses. So, within a couple of months, I went back to waitressing at night on the weekends, and my aunt Sissy took care of Lea when she wasn't with Charlie and Dottie.

Charlie's every-weekend visitation with Lea began after I moved in, and almost every time I took her to drop her off or pick her up, he would bully me and start a fight. It didn't take anything to set him off, and he would jerk my hood open and pull the distributor wires from the distributor cap, punch or kick my car, or do something to create chaos and hell, leaving me a mess and Lea crying. On the weekends Charlie had Lea, I felt relieved to have some time for myself. I never got to be a teenager, and I enjoyed just feeling the freedom of not having someone needing me every moment of every day. It helped me to feel a little more normal. By the end of the summer, things at the Teen Parent Home grew more uncomfortable. Six teenage mothers and their babies brought about drama and conflict. And Sandy, the house mother, tended to add to the drama.

Having been on my own for two years as an adult, it was hard moving into a place where I was treated like a child. I didn't like the rules, and I didn't fit in. I also didn't want to go back to high school. I didn't attend enough during the first year at the Teen Parent Program to gain any credits, so I was still in the ninth grade and would be twenty years old before I graduated. High school seemed hopeless and a waste of time. I worked late nights, and getting up at the crack of dawn to go sit through classes that I had no interest in was not high on my priority list. Things with Charlie were a never-ending war. He hassled me when he didn't have Lea and gave me a hard time at every turn. I felt like he was never going to leave me alone in peace. I started sleeping more and withdrawing socially. I struggled to get out of bed many days and wasn't in compliance with the rules in the house. The tensions grew, and I began to hate being there.

The long summer faded into fall, along with my hopes the Teen Parent Home was going to work out for me. I lived in a dark hole and cried for no reason. Day after day, the darkness grew, and I felt like the sun had given up on me too. *What's wrong with me? Why do I feel so bad? I want to get out of this bed, Lea is crying, and she needs me, but I just can't. I can't do anything right. It's just all too much. Lea always needs something from me. I try so hard. I do everything I can, but I can barely take care of myself. I have nothing to give. I am a terrible mother. Charlie is right. She deserves so much more than I can give her. I love her so much. Why? Why? Why, God?* I pulled the covers over my head to drown out Lea's crying. *If I just stay here under the covers, maybe it will all just go away. Maybe I can pretend I am little again. That Mom will come in soon and check on me and pamper me with her love and attention, the way she did when I was sick. Maybe then I would feel better. I just want it all to go away. I am so tired of hurting and trying to figure it all out. Maybe if I wasn't here, everyone would be happy. Especially Charlie. He would get what he has wanted all along. There is no way out of this. There is just no way out.* I crunched up the tissue I had in my fist and wiped my eyes and nose. "Come here, baby, get in bed with Mommy. Shhh, stop crying."

"No, Mommy, let's get up. I want to play!"

"I know. Mommy is just so tired. Let's just lay here for a few minutes, please? We can just snuggle." I pulled her close to me and hoped she would lie still for a few more minutes. *Maybe Mom could help me. If she could take Lea for a little while until I can get on my feet and get my own place, maybe then things would be better.*

The next day, I went to my mom and told her how I was feeling. I asked if she would help me and take Lea for a little while until I could get on my feet, feel better, and get my own place.

"Why do you want to leave that Teen Parent Home, Angel? You can't be happy with nothing, can you? I ain't got no time to take care of Lea. I got to work, and if you can wait a couple more years, she will be in school, and things will get easier. You ought to be happy to be at that place. Now you made your bed. I tried to tell you not to run after that boy. But you just wouldn't listen. You're hardheaded. You don't listen to nothing. Now, Angel, you better listen to me. You need to stay at that Teen Parent Home and do right."

"Okay, Mom! Just forget about it! I will figure it out myself!" I said in disappointment. I got my purse and walked out the door.

Later when I got back to my room, my inner critic showed up and started beating the shit out of me. *What is wrong with me? Why can't I get it together? Why can't I be normal and do the right thing? I must get this idea out of my head. I have to try harder.* Yet, the feelings of hopelessness, overwhelm, and exhaustion from fighting Charlie felt endless. I needed space to breathe without all the responsibility, judgment, criticism, abuse, and hell I was going through week after week, dealing with Charlie and the turmoil that ensued over Lea. I felt like I was choking to death and stuck in an endless hell I couldn't escape. I just wanted to run away from it all. I lay awake all night, thinking of how to get out of the hell I had created for my life.

Suicidal thoughts flowed in and out. *It is all my fault. How could I be so stupid? It would just be easier if I wasn't here. My mother is right, I made this bed and now I need to lie in it. Nobody cares about me. Why did I get pregnant so young? Why did I listen to Charlie? Why? I had no idea what I was getting into, and I have just made a mess of my life. It would just be better for everyone if I disappeared. No, stop it, Angel! That's a terrible thing to do. I surely will end up in hell.*

I shook myself, trying to escape from the terrible thoughts. *What am I going to do? There has to be a better answer.* I cried, feeling hopeless as I lay and pondered and racked my brain, trying to think of a solution. *Maybe I should just give in and let Lea go live with Dottie and Charlie. Maybe everyone would be happy then. That is all they want anyway. If I am gone, he will leave me alone. He just wants her. That is all I was good for to him. Maybe it is the best thing for Lea. Maybe it is the best thing for everyone. I can't imagine dealing with this for the next fifteen years of her life. This is horrible for everyone. She deserves better than this. She wouldn't have to deal with me and Charlie fighting all the time. He will never give me any peace. Ever! And they have so much more than I have to give her. Dottie and Mitch are retired, and they have more time and money to take better care of her. Surely, she would be better off than with me. I am such a mess. This is such a mess! Why, God, why did I get into this mess so young?* I sobbed and sobbed.

They will never give her back to me if I let her go, but I am so tired of fighting. My thoughts were endless and rapid, and with each one, I felt more destroyed and more certain. *Would she hate me? She is almost three. Would she even remember me?* I sobbed. *Will she understand that I can't fight this kind of crazy? It isn't healthy for her to see this all the time. It is absolutely toxic. I would come back for her someday when things are better.*

Yeah, for sure, I would. When I am stronger. When my life is better. When I am better and have more to offer her. Surely, life has to be better for her than this.

I packed all of Lea's things neatly, putting love and care into every item, then placed them in the car. I pulled her close to me and hugged her very tight, kissing the top of her head. I opened the car door, and she climbed into the front seat, bouncing and bubbly excited to go for a ride. Lea was so bubbly, bright, and full of energy as we drove along. Her blonde curls bounced as she wiggled around in her seat. Her blue eyes sparkled as we talked and laughed like we always did on our drives. It was like any other day, but it wasn't.

We loved each other so much, and she was my little shadow. My heart hung heavy. A myriad of emotions assaulted me with each mile. Conflict, fear, doubt, shame, and uncertainty suspended densely in my heart and mind. I felt lost, alone, and hopeless, desperate for relief, and this felt like the only answer. She had no idea of the destination. Neither of us knew the gravity or ramifications that would follow the decision that this tattered sixteen-year-old single teen mother was about to make.

Lea sat close to me and snuggled up next to me while I drove. When we arrived at our destination, I parked the car in front of the house. She cocked her little head sideways. "Mommy, why are you crying? she asked in surprise.

I pulled her in close to me and held her. "I just love you so so much, sweetie pie!" I whispered through my tears.

"I love you too, Mommy!" she said in a happy, reassuring voice, trying to cheer me up.

She had no idea the gravity or impact of this moment and how it was going to change the trajectory of both of our lives forever. I pulled away, just far enough to see her tender little face. "You are going to live with Daddy and Grandma now. Mommy has to go away for a little while, but I promise, I will come back and get you someday." I hugged her tight, trying not to fall apart in front of her.

Her brow furrowed, and she looked at me in confusion as she wiped away my tears. "Mommy, don't cry." She tenderly tried to console me, and I felt my heart fracture into a million tiny pieces.

I pulled her close as she laid her little head gently on my shoulder. I took a deep breath and sighed, trying to pull myself together. I took her in my arms, shifted her to my hip, and pulled the bag full of all of her belongings out of the car onto my other arm as we walked up the steps to her paternal grandmother's house. They were anxiously waiting for my arrival. I am sure they thought I wasn't coming. I hugged Lea tight, kissing her cheek, smelling her hair, and taking a deep breath.

I handed her to her grandmother Dottie, then walked away sobbing, leaving her motherless and both of us broken-hearted.

CHAPTER 20

After a week of tears, guilt, sorrow, and hopelessness, I was driving around aimlessly for hours before work. I looked over and saw a sign for a palm reader. My desperation to find answers leaped up inside of me, and I immediately pulled into the parking lot of the little shop. The sign on the window read "PALM OR CARD READINGS TODAY $5." I dug through my purse and found a five-dollar bill.

My thoughts swirled as I envisioned hope and better days ahead. I yearned for things in my life to be better and not so painful and hard. I also had hoped Lea would be okay and eventually we could be back together when things were better. The door screeched as I opened it. The shop billowed with the smell and smoke of incense burning as I stepped inside. There were shelves full of dusty books on tarot reading and the occult. Having been raised in a Christian home all my life, I felt a bit out of place yet filled with an intuitive knowing that this was a divine appointment.

A thin blonde older woman reached her weathered hand to pull back the curtain from a small room that set off from the main lobby. "Good afternoon, young lady, how can I help you today?"

"I was hoping I could get a card reading. The sign outside said you're offering them today for five dollars."

"Yes, we sure are. My name is Helen. Come on in. Let's see what we can find out for you." The warmth of her smile and the sparkle in her green eyes brought immediate comfort as she beckoned me into her space behind the curtain for my reading. She shuffled the cards. "What is it that you want to know?"

As tears welled up in my eyes, I looked up at her and asked, "Do you think anyone will ever love me?"

She said, "Oh, honey, I am sure you will find love in your life. Whatever in the world has ever made you believe you are unlovable?"

"Well, ma'am, I have been in a toxic relationship for the past four years that was pretty abusive, and he told me no one would ever love me and that I would never find anyone who would have me. To be honest, I have felt rejected by most everyone all my life, and I just feel alone. I am ashamed to tell you, but I also recently gave up custody of my daughter, because I felt like it was the best thing for her … well, and for me too. Do you think she is going to be okay? I hope I can get my life together and things will turn out for me and for my daughter. I've been feeling hopeless and not sure how to go on."

She looked at me with compassion in her caring eyes. "Oh, honey, I am sorry. You have been through so much. I am sure you will get through all this. There is an amazing book you must read by Dr. Wayne Dyer called *Your Erroneous Zones*. I think this book will help you, and

I suggest you seek out a counselor. I think you could benefit from the support. You're an incredible young woman. You are very mature, and you have endured a lot at such a young age. It took a lot of strength to get through all you have been through. You just need someone to help guide you."

"Your what zones?" I asked.

"Erroneous Zones. It just means errors. I will write the title down; I hope you will pick it up. I know it will be helpful for you."

"Oh yeah, of course I will! As soon as I leave here."

She read my cards, but to be honest, I don't even remember what the reading revealed. My mind was fixed on this book she mentioned, and that was all I could think about. I paid the five dollars and immediately went to the bookstore and used what little money I had left to buy the book. I couldn't wait to get off work. I had the next two days off, and I had plenty of time to read.

As soon as I got into bed after my long shift of waiting tables, I grabbed the book and ran my hand over the cover, got cozy, and began to read. I couldn't sit it down. Wayne's words of encouragement and stories of his life and how he had overcome so much brought much needed hope and inspiration to me. He had so many answers, advice, and helpful ideas for working through life struggles and what he called "neurotic thinking" that I was experiencing every day of my life.

Wayne grew up in Detroit, just like me, and had a hard life. He ended up in an orphanage and had many struggles throughout his early life. He got his education and overcame so many obstacles and went on to become a counselor, a professor, and a world-renowned motivational speaker. I could relate to his story, and it touched and inspired me in a profound way. His story and the lessons he taught were exactly what I needed to shift out of the hopeless hell I was living in.

I sped through the book in those two days and got up from reading it a different person. I immediately began making better choices and decisions. I started counseling, which was so instrumental in helping me to see my life wasn't over because of the mistakes I had made or the heartaches I had been through. My counselor told me I could be anything I wanted to be if I would just make up my mind to do what it took to get there. No one had ever told me that before.

Between Wayne Dyer's book and this therapist, I felt empowered to rise above where I was and change my thinking. I started believing I could change my life if I wanted to. I could shift from being a victim to becoming victorious. I thought back to all those nights walking the nine miles to work, knowing I wasn't going to stay stuck in a life that made me miserable. I had lost myself through all this hell, and I was ready to find me, maybe for the first time in my life.

I realized during those walks if it was gonna be, it was up to me. I had to make my life what I wanted it to be. Nobody was coming to save me. I shifted my focus from pain and rejection to hope and encouragement. I was determined to get out of the poverty and the survival mode that I had been in for years. I wanted to make a better life for myself. I was desperate for life to change, to feel better, and to live again, and I was willing to do whatever it took to start feeling better.

After the card reading, I quit school and left the Teen Parent Home, grateful for what they offered me but knowing that this was not the right option for me. I attempted to have visitations with Lea, but it was very difficult to work or deal with Charlie. It didn't matter what I did, what I bought her, what I sent her; it was put down, ridiculed, and used against me, and I was just so exhausted, I couldn't find the strength to put us both through the pain every week.

I didn't understand it then but would learn later in life when I was doing some research, what Charlie and his mom were doing by denigrating me, putting me down, and making Lea feel it wasn't okay to love or accept me or my gifts were psychological symptoms of emotional abuse called parental alienation. It occurs when a parent or family member manipulates the child to turn them against the other parent. It is very damaging to a child and their relationship with the other parent.

At the time, I didn't know what to do with what was going on. It was so confusing and hurtful. I could just see how destructive it was and felt we both would be better off if I just went away.

I thought about Lea all the time and hoped that someday in the future, when things were better in my life, I could go back and try again. I shifted my focus and started going to the library after work and studied for my GED. I was determined to get my education. Through reading Wayne's book and using the tools he taught me about standing up for myself and being assertive rather than passive or aggressive, I learned to say no. I learned to ask for what I wanted and saw how doing this got much better results that served me, which helped build my confidence and self-esteem. I had dated a few guys after Charlie who didn't treat me the way I deserved and took advantage of me. After reading *Your Erroneous Zones*, I made up my mind that I would rather be alone than put up with anyone abusing me, running around on me, or treating me with disrespect. I learned I deserved more than that.

Right after the card reading, I ran into Tom. He was my cousin's best friend and someone I had known casually since I was seven years old. He had just graduated from high school and was getting ready to go into the US Marine Corps. We were at a party at my aunt's house, and I was drinking, and my aunt asked him to drive me home. He dated my cousin Stephanie when he was in high school, and to make conversation during the ride, I asked him if he thought they would get back together.

He replied, "Oh, no, I met a girl named Lisa, and we're engaged."

"Oh, that's nice. Are you excited about going into the Marine Corps?"

"Oh yeah, I leave in a couple of weeks."

We chatted about him going into the Marine Corps, and I told him my sister had joined the US Army Reserves. I had thought about going into the service myself, but I didn't know if that was the right path for me. He dropped me off, and I thanked him for the ride.

Three months later, I was staying for a few weeks with my cousin Louise while I was waiting for the apartment I rented to come available after leaving the Teen Parent Home. I was working on myself through counseling and integrating the lessons I had learned from Wayne Dyer's book and beginning to find my inner strength. It was new for me and would take some time to cultivate, but I was learning to stand up for myself, and I was becoming more certain of what I wanted in my life and what I knew I would no longer tolerate.

One evening, while I was staying with her, Tom called. "Hey, Angel! How are you?"

"Really good, thank you."

"Is Stephanie in?"

"No, she is out for the evening. Can I give her a message?"

"Well, no. I'm at a party at your uncle Junior's for your cousin Dallas's sixteenth birthday party. I'm leaving to go back to the Marines tomorrow. I was just checking in to see if she wanted to hang out. What are you doing this evening?"

"Well, I am meeting with my pastor and some people from church for some dessert, but after that I am free."

"Well, hey, why don't you come out and hang out with us?"

"Okay, tomorrow is Louise's fortieth birthday. I think she'd like to come too. Oh, yeah, she just nodded yes to me. We'll be out in a little bit." I had heard he had broken up with his fiancée, Lisa, while he was in boot camp. I wondered how things were going for him and thought it would be nice to catch up.

As soon as I arrived, several guys at the party were trying to talk to me. "Hey, do you know if Tom is still here?" I asked.

"Oh, you don't want that guy. He is leaving tomorrow to go back to California."

I smiled, looked around the room for Tom, and was surprised when I saw him coming to rescue me from the sea of men that surrounded me. He looked nothing like before, just a few months earlier. His body was chiseled and sharp, and he was wearing a tight black Marine Corps T-shirt. His long brown hair was shaved close to his head, and he looked like a completely different person from the guy who drove me home the night after the party just a few months ago. I was stunned and enamored. I thought about how much he had physically changed and reflected on my own internal transformation, and I smiled inside.

My intentions were to hang out as friends. He smiled immediately and took me by the hand and led me away. We spent the whole evening together. We hung out all night and talked for hours. That night was like a breath of fresh air at a time in my life after having gone through so much over the past few years. It felt good to talk to someone who just seemed to get me and was interested in what I had to say. It felt so natural, and we connected on a deep level in a way that I never expected.

We reminisced about the first time we met, when I was seven years old and I was visiting my aunt Jackie during a family trip. He was hanging out with my cousin Dean, his best friend, in the yard when I came out of the house with a jaw full of bubble gum. They were a couple of years older than me and were egging me on to go over and put bubble gum on the door handle of Dean's neighbor's brand-new truck. I loved all the attention from these older kids. It wasn't long before they talked me into it, and I went over and smeared the bubble gum all over the handle and door. It caused quite a commotion when the owner of the truck saw what I was doing, and they ran out, ready to beat my ass. The excitement I felt to please the other kids only moments before turned immediately to fear. A few minutes later, my mom, Aunt Jackie and a whole houseful of relatives ran out in my defense, and a whole scene ensued. "I knew then, Angel, you were someone I wanted to keep my eye on." Tom chuckled.

We laughed about old times and talked about his military experience, which was fascinating to me. "What made you decide to go into the Marines?" I asked.

He laughed. "Well, I was going down the wrong road. I had been partying, smoking pot, and drinking nearly every day and rarely going to school. Throwing raging parties at my house while my mom was at work. My three older brothers, who were all married, would step in when things weren't going well at home, after my dad died when I was seven. My mom called them, worried about me, and they came over one day and told me I needed to get my shit together. I was in the twelfth grade, a few months before graduation, and I was flunking out. A few days later, I came home from school and found a for sale sign in the yard. I asked my mom what was going on.

"She said, 'We're moving, and you're not invited.'

"A few days later at school, two Marine sergeants, fully decked out in their dress blues, came in to do a presentation to recruit students into the Marine Corps. I knew I was at a place in my life where I had to make some hard decisions. My older brother, Bill, went into the Marines during Vietnam, and I felt a connection to the Corps, and I knew I was in a desperate situation. I told them my situation with school, and they talked to the principal and told him I had to graduate in order to get in. The principal made a deal with me that if I didn't miss any more school and completed my assignments, he would make sure I graduated. I joined the Marines that day."

"Wow, that is an incredible story."

I connected with Tom immediately, knowing he had been through a lot in his life too and took care of his mom, helped with the household and his younger sister, like I did for my mom and younger brother, Jake. And I could relate to my mom moving and not being invited. We stayed out until 4 a.m., until the last possible moment when he had to leave so he could catch his plane back to California in just a few hours.

He asked for my phone number and address. "I don't have my apartment yet, but I can give you my mom's address, and you can write to me there." I doubted he would ever call or write, but I appreciated the thought. I felt a bit guilty returning to Louise's and wondered what Stephanie would say. She and Tom had been broken up for years, and she had just started seeing someone new. I felt embarrassed because Tom and I had made out passionately, and he put hickeys on my neck, and I had to face her, but the connection we made was so powerful that the guilt I felt soon faded.

Within a week, I got a letter from Tom. He said he couldn't stop thinking about me and wanted to see me again. He said he couldn't wait six months until he got leave again and wanted to know if I was available the next weekend. He had a long weekend break, and even though he wasn't supposed to go more than a hundred miles from Camp Pendleton in California, he wanted to fly home to see me again. I had just moved into my new apartment, and I told him I would love to see him. We had an incredible weekend. We fell in love hard and fast. It was as if all the stars and planets in the universe aligned in our favor, and within six weeks of his visit, we started talking about getting married. I knew this was moving fast, but deep within my soul, I knew he was the right one for me instantly.

I told him if he married me, there were a few things he needed to know. "First, I don't want any more children. I know you are young, and this may be a dealbreaker, but I have been through so much with Lea and Charlie. I don't think I could ever go through anything like that again. Also, I will never put up with a man mistreating me, abusing me, or running around on me."

"Well, I haven't ever wanted children either, and I would never hurt you. I love you too much."

We were obsessed with each other. He called me every chance he got, and I wrote to him nearly every day, and he wrote back religiously. I couldn't wait to see him again. Six weeks later, I sold all the furniture in my apartment I had just bought and used the money to fly out to San Diego to see him in April. He came home on leave in July, and in December 1986, just before he was to leave to go overseas with the navy for six months, and after only seeing each other face to face a few times, we got married.

After getting married, my relationship with my mom got better. Ben was still an asshole, and not long after I returned from California, my mom ended the relationship. Through working on my own healing and studying the work of Wayne Dyer, I began to learn the value of forgiveness. In Dyer's book, *You'll See It When You Believe It*, he wrote a whole chapter on forgiveness, teaching that forgiveness is an act of self-love. He taught holding on to unforgiveness only causes pain to the person holding it, while the other person is out living their life. He emphasizes that forgiveness doesn't condone the harmful behavior but frees oneself from the resentment. That made a lot of sense to me. I knew in my heart that my mom loved me and always did the best she knew to do at the time. I also recognized that she too was wounded and made many decisions out of pain and survival. I knew she didn't mean to hurt me intentionally, and I loved her. I was able to forgive her, and we were able to build a better relationship and became closer throughout my adult years.

While Tom was overseas, I worked hard and saved as much as possible for our new life together. Tom was stationed at Camp Pendleton in

California near San Diego for his four-year enlistment, with two over-seas tours with the US Navy every two years. After his first overseas de-ployment, I planned to move to California when he returned. Moving away and being married was a fresh start and a new beginning for both of us. I had grown so much after leaving Charlie. Through counseling and reading self-help books, I gained confidence and was ready to cre-ate a better life for myself. When I got to California, I took my GED. Immediately afterward, I started classes at a technical school for dental assisting and graduated at the top of my class. While attending school, I worked at a cleaning company and learned everything I could about how to build a cleaning business. Tom and I loved each other so much and built a wonderful relationship while we were in California. We both changed a lot, being away from our families and the only life we had known back home. Being away gave us the chance to find and discover ourselves without the outside pressure and influence of anyone else.

After Tom finished his four-year contract in the Marine Corps, we re-turned to Michigan. I had big dreams and lofty goals of creating a finan-cially secure life. I was a constant learner and hungry for knowledge that would help catapult me into the life of my wildest dreams. I read all the time and listened to audio cassettes in my car on my way to and from work. I read Norman Vincent Peale's *The Power of Positive Thinking*, Napoleon Hill's *Think and Grow Rich*, James Allen's *As a Man Thinketh*, David Schwarts's *The Magic of Thinking Big*, Tony Robbins's *Awakening the Giant Within*, and Shakti Gawain's *Creative Visualization*. I listened to Earl Nightingale's *Lead the Field* and Brian Tracy's *The Psychology of Achievement* and many other high achievers on cassette tape.

I sat down at twenty years old and wrote out a list of goals that I wanted to achieve in my life. I allowed my imagination to run wild and didn't hold back on any possibility. I learned from these masters that "anything I could believe and conceive, I could achieve." I believed if I was financially independent, I would be happy and all my dreams would come true. I had this knowing, and intuition that was with me always. It helped me survive the dark nights walking through the tough streets of Detroit when I was a young girl. I knew in my heart and soul I could do anything I set my mind to if I was willing and determined to do whatever it took to achieve it. I also knew if someone else had achieved a goal, I could achieve it too. I just needed to do what they had done.

While I was working as a dental assistant, I started my own cleaning business at age twenty. I began by cleaning houses, but before long, I expanded into cleaning office buildings and banks. Soon I converted my business into a commercial cleaning service. This allowed me to work my regular job during the day and clean at night. Tom and I were great partners, and we worked well together as a team. He helped me build the cleaning business, and we worked together at night cleaning after we got off from our day jobs. Sometimes we were so exhausted we slept in our car to get enough energy to finish cleaning all the buildings before we had to return to work the next morning.

The first house we lived in was in Wayne, Michigan, a suburb of Detroit. It was a rental and belonged to one of my brother in-law's best friends, Alex. It was a run-down house that was dated and needed some TLC. We asked Alex if we could use some of our rent money to paint the house and put in some new carpeting and fix it up a bit. He agreed. Tom and I did the work to get it painted and refurbished, and it turned out beautiful. It was our first experience remodeling a house, and it was very rewarding. It was stunning how we could take something so battered and worn down and completely transform it with a little bit of hard work and money. When Alex saw our work, he couldn't believe the transformation. He was stunned and impressed at how ambitious we were. He offered to sell us the house, and we bought our first home when we were in our early twenties.

The transformation of this house intrigued me, and I started researching and learned about real estate investing. I found a book by Russ Whitney called *Building Wealth. From Rags to Riches in Real Estate* and learned how to flip houses. Tom and I found a house in our neighborhood that was in foreclosure. We bought it with a friend and renovated it. Within a few months of hard work, we made $24,000 that we split among us. I had long thought about this as a viable business from the time I was a young kid and saw our neighbor across the street renting out their house. I also thought about it again when I was fourteen years old, living with Charlie in an upper flat. I told him of my vision of buying a property like the one we lived in and renting the upper flat and living in the lower one. I thought it was an excellent business idea, but Charlie shut me down and told me I was stupid and a dreamer. But here I was, less than ten years later, making my dreams come true. Not only did I own my first house at age twenty, but within the next year, I had also bought, renovated, and sold my first house and made more money in a few weeks than most people I knew at that time made in a whole year. I was excited and very motivated.

While I was working as a dental assistant and cleaning commercial businesses at night, I decided to go to college. I knew in order to accomplish such lofty goals, I needed to get a better education. As a dental assistant, I saw that the dental hygienist in our office made three times as much as me and had a lot more autonomy than I did. So, I set my sights on attaining that goal. Since I only had a GED, I went to the local community college for a year, then applied to the University of Michigan for their dental hygiene program. I wasn't sure if I would get in, but I thought, *it doesn't hurt to apply. If I don't get in, they have a program at the community college where I am taking classes, and I can go there.* I had a 4.0 GPA when I applied to the University of Michigan, and I wrote a letter with my application, explaining why I didn't go to high school and all that I had accomplished since getting my GED. They only accepted twenty-eight to thirty students per year out of many applicants. I knew U of M was a prestigious school, so my chances of getting in with my background were probably slim, but I learned through studying high achievers that you only fail if you don't try. So, I polished up my letter and sent it in with my application.

Within a few weeks, I got a personal call from the director of the dental hygiene program at the University of Michigan, letting me know that I was accepted into the program as an alternate. She told me my application had come in at the end of their selection process and they had already accepted all the students for their 1993 incoming class, but they were so impressed with my application and my accomplishment, they were accepting me as a backup, and if someone decided not to attend, I would be accepted for the fall class. She said she would let me know by the beginning of August. She also told me if it didn't work out for this year, I was accepted for the following fall year of 1994. I was ecstatic. I couldn't believe it. *Wow! What were the chances of me, a high school dropout, pregnant at age thirteen, a teen mother at age fourteen, and the only person in my family to go to college, being accepted to such a prestigious school?* Unspeakable joy filled me as tears flowed down my cheeks. Within two weeks, the director called me back to let me know, that someone had decided not to attend the incoming class, and

I was officially accepted to the University of Michigan's dental hygiene program, and classes would be starting in a few weeks. Another dream coming true.

From reading Russ Whitney's book, I learned about "mailbox money." Mailbox money is money that comes in the mail without you having to work for it. Russ amassed his wealth through real estate investing and rental properties. He went from working in a slaughterhouse at age twenty to being a multimillionaire at age twenty-seven. I decided that is exactly what I wanted to do.

There was a lady at our church who traveled whenever she wanted to; she drove a beautiful new Cadillac and seemed to have plenty of money. She told me she had a mobile home park in Arizona and it was a very lucrative investment. I liked her lifestyle and decided I would begin looking into investing in a mobile home park when I saved enough money. While I was at the University of Michigan, I left the dental assistant job but continued the cleaning business, which continued to grow. Tom worked as a purchasing manager at an office supply distribution center, and I went to school during the day and we continued to clean at night. By the time I graduated from dental hygiene school, we had made enough money to sell our first house and have our dream home built near the University of Michigan in a brand-new subdivision in Saline.

We began pursuing our dream of buying a mobile home park. We looked in the Detroit area, but the pricing was too expensive. My two brothers, Jake and David, lived in the Christiansburg, Virginia area, where Tom and I had gotten married eleven years earlier, and we started looking at real estate in that area and found it to be much more affordable. I could see the area was an up-and-coming college town.

So, within a year of graduating from the University of Michigan, and right after turning twenty-eight years old, I took the money we had saved over the years from the cleaning business and the real estate deals, and we bought a twenty-six-unit mobile home park on eleven acres near Christiansburg in Shawsville, Virginia. Nearly two years later, in 1998, we decided to move to Virginia and the warmer weather, to be closer to our investments.

CHAPTER 21

In 1989, nearly a decade earlier, when I returned to Michigan from California, I contacted Charlie's mom, Dottie. I learned that Lea was only living with her grandparents now, and they had left Detroit and moved to Hazard, Kentucky, not far from Harlan. Back to the coal fields from where my family and Charlie's family came. I asked them if I could come for a visit and pick her up for the weekend. They agreed to let me come but told me I could only visit her at their house. It had been nearly three years since I saw her, so I understood, and I agreed. I couldn't wait to see her. I brought her some gifts, and we spent most of the day in her bedroom, playing Barbies, dolls, coloring, laughing, and having a great time. She told me about school, and riding her bike, and playing in the creek. I told her how much I loved and missed her, and I hoped we could visit again soon.

Not long after this, her dad married his new girlfriend, Molly, and Lea came back to the Detroit area to live with them. I hired an attorney and reestablished visitation. We had such a great time together on our visits, but every time she returned home, they would interrogate her and then call and accuse me of not feeding her or some other crazy accusation that wasn't true. Several times during my visits with Lea, Charlie would call me five minutes before I was leaving my house to bring her back causing me to be late getting her home. Then, when I arrived, he jumped all over me for bringing her back late. I told him I was late because he called and kept me on the phone. There was no reasoning with him at all. During the conversation, he threatened to blow my house up with a Molotov cocktail or destroy my life in some way. Eventually it was taking a toll on both me and Lea and my marriage.

One night, not long after our visit, at seven years old, Lea called.

"Hi, honey, how are you?"

"I am calling because I don't want to see you anymore."

"Oh, my goodness! Why, Lea? Is something wrong? Are you sure? We have such a good time when we are together."

"Yes, I am sure. I want Molly to be my mommy."

"Oh, really? Did something happen?"

"No, I just don't have a good time when I am with you, and I don't want to see you anymore. I have to go now."

"Okay, honey. I love you."

"Bye."

She hung up the phone. I was stunned and began crying. I couldn't understand any of this. It just didn't make any sense, but I didn't know what to do. I just knew in my heart Charlie and Molly had made Lea call and say those things. It broke my heart. They made things so difficult, with so much drama and chaos. I just hated putting her through all the craziness and tearing our emotions apart and keeping us both so upset. Tom was also becoming intolerant of Charlie and was ready to take things into his own hands. I knew that wasn't going to work out well for anyone. I was so exhausted of all the turmoil. I felt like I was the only one trying to make this work. It was exhausting. I knew Charlie was never going to let me see Lea in peace, and it wasn't fair or healthy for either one of us. I finally decided to give up my legal rights and hoped that when Lea was older, we would find each other again.

It was another gut-wrenching decision. And it was like losing her all over again.

A few years later, when I was a sophomore in college and still living in Michigan, I came home to find a message from Molly on my answering machine. "Hi, Angel, we are having trouble with Lea, and we talked with a counselor, and she thought it would be helpful if you got back involved in her life. If you wouldn't mind, could you please give me a call?"

I was shocked.

I told Tom, "That doesn't even sound like Molly. Maybe her and Charlie have grown up and matured."

"I wouldn't count on it," he replied.

I called her. "Hi, Molly, this is Angel. I got your message. Is everything okay?"

"Hey, thanks for calling me back. Well, I am pregnant again, and this time it's a boy. And you know, Charlie has always wanted a boy. Since finding out about this, Lea has started acting out, and we thought it would be helpful if she started seeing you again."

"Really. How would that work?"

"Well, we thought we could start with some supervised visits here at the house, and if everything goes well, maybe eventually, she could come with you and have some visits."

"Okay, I would love to see her."

I was thrilled. I couldn't believe it. We arranged a supervised visit with Lea in her bedroom at her home later that week. We had a great time. She told me about school, her friends, and all she had been up to. I told Lea I was sorry things didn't work out before, and I hoped things could be better this time.

She asked me why I left her when she was only three.

"Lea, I love you so much, and we were really close, but things were very difficult back then. I did the best I could to work with your dad, and it just didn't work out. I was very young, and I didn't have any support, and I felt you would be better off staying with your grandmother at the time. I am really sorry that I hurt you. It wasn't because I didn't love you. I have always loved you."

She came and wrapped her arms around me and hugged me so tight, my heart melted with the warmth of her love.

Lea and I had our visits at her house several times, and we had a wonderful time together. They eventually let her come out to my house, but when I took her home, they started yelling and said I was late. I looked at the clock; it was two minutes past the time I said I was going to have her back. I apologized and tried to explain we had started on our way and realized Lea had forgotten an item and I went back and got it. I didn't think we would be late, but it was only two minutes. Of course, it was a huge scene.

They wouldn't let me see her again.

Then, one night a month later, Charlie and Molly got into a huge fight, and the phone was torn off the wall. They sent Lea to call me from Papa Chuck's, who lived next door.

"Mom, this is Lea. Daddy and Mommy are fighting, and they asked me to call you to come and get me. Can you come quickly, please?"

I immediately left and drove thirty minutes to get her. I went up to the door to pick her up and could see through the door the chaos of scattered objects, rearranged furniture, broken dishes, and Lea standing helplessly looking at me defenseless.

Molly came to the door. "Everything is better. She has school tomorrow. We don't need you to take her now."

"Well, I just drove all the way here. If you want to let her go with me, I would be happy to take her to school tomorrow."

"No, she is not going anywhere! Thanks for coming down, but she is not going."

I looked over at Lea. Her eyes were full of disappointment, and I turned and walked away feeling helpless.

The next week, they called and told me I could see her again, but I needed to start paying them child support of thirty-five dollars a week. I said "That is no problem." I couldn't wait to see her. I pulled up, and she ran and got in the car.

"Hurry, let's leave, Mom, before they change their mind."

I pulled away quickly and turned on the radio. We laughed and played her favorite music loud as we drove to my house. But every week it was hell. Always games. She did everything they asked, but if one thing wasn't perfect, they would get her hopes built up, and at the last minute, they would tell her she couldn't come to visit because of some minor thing, like she forgot to dust the top of the television or missed a spot on the dishes when she washed them. She couldn't win. It was heart-wrenching. One time I came to get her, and they sent her out and told me they wanted more money. I was going to confront them and tell them this was ridiculous. Every week there was a new rule.

"Please, Mom," she begged, "just please give them the money so I can go with you." I smiled at her sweet face and conceded. I felt horrible for her to be there and tried to talk to her counselor, but no one would listen to me. I was the absent mother who had no rights.

On one of the visits before I returned to her home, I gave Lea my home phone number and Tom's toll-free work number and told her to keep it in a safe place in case she ever needed it.

Not long after this, Lea was scheduled to come for a visit, and Molly called. "Angel, my car broke down, and I need money to buy a new used car. If you want to keep seeing Lea, I need you to send me the money for the car."

"Molly, I am sick and tired of this shit every week. You are fucking crazy if you think I am going to buy you a car, to continue to be manipulated and treated this way week after week. This is insane. This is awful what you're putting me and Lea through. Do you even understand how all this craziness and chaos is affecting her? Don't you care how this is hurting Lea?"

"You don't know anything about how Lea is. You left her, and she doesn't want to see you anymore. I was trying to work with you, but I should have listened to Charlie. He was right about you. You are nothing but trouble."

"Molly, I have done everything you and Charlie have asked of me, but every week you change the rules. Now I have to buy you a car? What the hell? This is crazy. Please come to your senses and see how wrong this is."

"I am not going to let you turn all this back around on me, Angel. Lea doesn't like coming to see you and complains every time she comes back from a visit with you. We're done with you. You can't see Lea anymore."

"Fine, I am done dealing with all this craziness. Lea isn't going to be little forever!" I slammed the phone down. I was devastated.

Over the next two years, Lea would sneak and call us when she could, and I hoped someday we would get to see each other again.

In the spring of 1996, I was about to graduate from four long years of college and seven long years of working two and sometimes three jobs, focusing on building financial security and success in my life so we could have a better future. It was in the final weeks of my senior year of college at the University of Michigan, and I was studying to take board exams for my dental hygiene license. Tom and I had moved into our dream home that we had built in Saline, just a few miles from the university, six months earlier, and life was finally settling down after nearly a decade of hard work.

Then one night, after a long night of studying, the phone rang, and it was Lea.

"Hi, Mom."

"Hi. I haven't heard from you in a long time. How are you, Lea?"

"Well, a couple of weeks ago, Molly got mad and started hitting me and kicking me with her boot in the shins. Usually, she would keep me home until my bruises or scabs would heal, but she was so mad, she sent me to school. I told Tiffany, my best friend, about it, and she told me I had to tell Mrs. Cooper. I was so afraid, because I knew Daddy would be mad, but I was so scared she would really hurt me this time."

"Oh my God, I am sorry! What happened?"

"When I got to the school and told Mrs. Cooper what happened and showed her my legs and the bruises, she called the police right away. She told me she knew for a long time something bad was going on, but she didn't have enough evidence to turn in a report. She told me it broke her heart every time I was excited to go on a field trip and Molly would cancel it and not let me go. She said she tried to find a way to report her, and she did a couple of times but never heard anything. I told her I always lied when the social workers came to talk to me at the house. She told me I must be honest with the police. Mom, I was so scared this time, I knew I had to tell them, even though I knew Daddy would be so mad at me. I was afraid I might not get another chance to get out."

Tears welled up in my eyes. "Oh, honey, I am sorry. Well, where are you now?"

"I am in family foster care with Daddy's brother, Uncle Randy, and his wife, Aunt Alice. I thought about telling them I wanted to come stay with you, but I was afraid Daddy would be mad. But he hasn't been coming to see me, so I don't care if he's mad."

"It's okay, honey. I am so glad you are safe."

"I would like to see you. Aunt Alice said you could come over and visit, if you wanted to."

"Okay, I will call her and set something up. I love you so much, and I am sorry you have been through all this."

"I love you too, Mom. I hope I get to see you soon."

"You will, I promise. As soon as possible."

I hung up the phone and bawled.

Later, in another conversation, I found out the full truth of what was really happening to Lea. Lea told me when she first came back from Kentucky to live with her dad, Molly was good to her, and she loved her. But after Molly had her first child, Brooke, Lea told me Molly started mistreating her, and it got worse over the years. Lea described times where she was often put into situations that left her with no options. For hours, both Molly and her dad would hold her captive, asking her questions they would never agree were correct. Lea said Molly often promised her she'd be allowed to attend school events right up until the event was about to happen, and then Molly would create chaos and tell Lea she couldn't go. She got angry at Lea over small little things, then punished her.

On one occasion, Lea told me she did something Molly didn't approve of, and she grounded her to her bed and squirted mustard all over her, knowing how much Lea hated mustard, and wouldn't let her out to clean up. Later, after her two brothers were born, Molly put Lea in a psychiatric hospital and accused her of trying to harm the kids, but they released her after a week because they couldn't find any evidence. Lea said she did everything she could do to make her parents happy. Unfortunately, she was in a world where she could never win.

She finally realized at thirteen that leaving was her only option for escape.

I hired an attorney and began working on getting Lea placed in our home. It took a little time, but by summer, when school ended, I was granted guardianship, and she finally came to live with us in Saline.

That summer was a honeymoon period, and things went well. I wanted to give Lea everything she never had. I took her to the mall and let her buy new clothes, took her out to eat at nice restaurants. We went shopping and got new bedding for her room, and I spoiled her with material things. Life was busy for me and Tom. I had just graduated from dental hygiene school and had just started a new job. Tom was still working full time as a purchasing manager at an office-supply distributor, and we were both still cleaning five buildings a night, which took six hours for us both to clean. So, there was little time to spend with Lea, but like most working families, we did the best we could. We took her with us, and she helped us clean some nights.

Other nights, she'd stay with her aunt Alice and uncle Randy, but eventually as she met some friends in the neighborhood, she chose to stay home and hang out with them until we finished our cleaning. On weekends, we took her bowling or out to dinner and tried to do something together as a family. Things seemed to be going well, and we were all adjusting to our new life together.

By fall, Tom decided to quit his job and take over the cleaning business. This way he could work full time with the business, and I could work my dental hygiene job and be home with Lea in the evenings.

As the new school year began, Lea seemed excited about this new beginning. When she lived with Charlie and Molly, she was isolated and wasn't allowed out of the house and was very sheltered. She wasn't allowed to make any decisions for herself, she wasn't allowed to go visit friends, and she was ruled with a tight fist.

Living with Tom and me was a whole new world, and she was nervous. I encouraged her and bought her things to help her fit in. I wanted to give her the best chance at success possible. We were excited she had met a few friends over the summer. When school started, before long, she had met several more new friends. Finally, after all of these years of heartache, things were turning around. At least, I thought so.

As the fall semester continued, things came up, and I saw Lea was struggling. I knew she was a teenager trying to find her own way, while at the same time being plunged into a new family and lifestyle that was completely foreign to her. She had lost her entire family when she was put in foster care because her dad wasn't willing to come see her or let her see her siblings. I thought back to when my parents divorced, and I lost my whole family when I didn't get to see my dad and siblings. I remembered and felt the sadness of those times, and it broke my heart for her. I begged him to stay in her life and have visitation with her, but I think it caused trouble with Molly.

He told me, "I raised her the first part of her life, and I'm backing away to let you raise her for the rest of her life."

He gave up his parental rights and walked away.

Coming to Saline was an adjustment for Lea. It was a difficult time of transition, and we didn't get the support we needed to clearly understand her needs. Other than the visits over the years, which were few and far between, we really didn't have time to get to know each other well. And often during those visits, we were in crisis mode, trying to keep things calm, so we didn't have much time to work on our relationship.

When Lea came to live with us at such a transitional time for all of us, it was tough. I had left her when she was three years old, and now she was thirteen. She was not the same sweet child I dropped off back then, or the sweet seven- or nine-year-old I visited with. She was angry and struggling. I learned what I had suspected: She had been subjected to the demonization of me by her dad and her paternal grandparents from the time I left her at age three. She told me she was spanked or ridiculed if she had behaviors like me. She told me she was shamed for being left-handed like me, and they spanked her hand to try to get her to be right-handed. What she described sounded as though they made her feel bad if she showed love or interest in anything that had to do with me, even the gifts I sent her.

She learned through their actions and words that to love me meant punishment. These ingrained subconscious obstacles were difficult to overcome. And for the first year, I wasn't even aware of the effect it had on her because she hid it very well, trying to fit in. The first time I noticed it, I had taken her to my mom's church for an event. We were sitting in the pew, and I looked at her and smiled, and she looked down and saw we were both sitting with our legs and arms in the exact same position. She shuffled her entire body around and contorted and repositioned herself so she wouldn't be like me. After that, I began to notice more often her disapproval of herself if she reacted or behaved like me, and her disdain toward me grew more evident with time.

As time went on, I pushed Lea out of her comfort zone and introduced her to things that she had never experienced before. She had never been on vacation in her life, other than to see family. During the first fall we were together, we took a mother-daughter trip to Florida to Disney World and Universal Studios during Halloween week, her favorite time of year. In the summer, I made her volunteer as a candy striper at the local hospital to give her some work experience, so she could think about careers as she was moving toward high school. She hated it and let me know she would never be a nurse. I laughed with her and told her I understood, but I was glad she had the experience. I sent her with her close friend to summer camp for three weeks. She called immediately and wanted to come home. The camp counselor adamantly told me not to come get her. She said this happens with kids every year, but once she gets acclimated, she'll enjoy it. One week later, I received a letter in the mail telling me how much she loved it and was so glad she stayed. I was so happy for her.

Even with the good times, the first year was difficult for all of us. Tom and I had been a team, working together for seven years building our business, getting through college, and creating our dreams. This was a huge shift that changed a lot in our lives. We started struggling in our relationship and were silently going through our own marital difficulties. We almost separated the first year after Lea came to live with us and eventually, we did separate for a while a few years later. Tom loved Lea but struggled with the turmoil of having a teenage child we didn't raise in our home.

This situation was especially challenging because her values and standards were very different from ours, and it felt like no one in the house was happy. Tom is a beautiful, loving, kind, funny, amazing man who loves to watch sports, drink beer, and relax. He is a no-nonsense, laid-back, patient person but with little tolerance for drama or bullshit. He doesn't talk a lot, but his actions speak volumes, and when he does speak, people listen. Lea respected him, but they rarely interacted. He was gone a lot because he cleaned the buildings at night and slept most of the day. I imagine this was his way to escape.

I knew our living situation wasn't going to be all roses and butterflies, but I had no idea the challenges that lay ahead. Tom and I made a ton of mistakes with Lea. We controlled things and poked our nose in things we shouldn't have, kept her from being friends with kids we felt were trying to take her down the wrong path in life, and made rules that a kid in her situation didn't need. I was hard on her with her schoolwork, and it took a detrimental toll on our relationship, and she resented me. I was just trying to guide her in a positive direction without recognizing her needs or what resonated with her. I knew my path was successful, and I wanted her to follow it.

I had a lot of shadows around living in poverty and lack. I wanted to escape poverty and the hell it brought me at all costs and believed that she would want a better, more successful life too. I imagine looking back, she never felt accepted or as if she fit in with me and Tom. Our lifestyle and means were far beyond anything she had ever imagined, and it was uncomfortable for her. I believe she also felt things and money were more important to us than her.

Over time she became passive-aggressive, until she became more aggressive. I knew something was wrong. I tried to talk to her, but she wouldn't talk much. I took her to counseling every week, but things got worse. I tried to talk to the counselor and asked for help, but I didn't really get any advice or support. I tried to do the best I knew how, but I didn't know what I was up against and how to help.

I had no idea what it meant to be a mother. Especially to a teenager I didn't raise and one who was raised with completely different values from mine and who was also raised to believe I was a terrible person. I wanted her to join the cheerleading team and do gymnastics and be involved in something at school. I wanted her to hang out with the popular crowd and aim for good grades and become an achiever because I knew that would give her the best life possible. I knew she was smart, and I saw so much potential in her and was frustrated she didn't care about the things I thought were important for her. Social service was involved, but the counselors mostly sided with us and told Lea she needed to do her schoolwork and follow our rules.

I was living in a fantasy world, but I didn't know it. I thought if she had everything she ever wanted, she would thrive. In my mind, subconsciously, I thought I could be the fairy godmother and come in and wave a magic wand and fix everything for her and make everything okay.

CHAPTER 22

In the fall of 1997, Lea started high school at Saline High. She had a best friend named Ashlynn who she spent a lot of time with. She also had many friends at school and enjoyed hanging out with them at the mall, going to movies and having sleepovers on the weekend. I thought things were going well and Lea was finally adjusting to her new life with us.

In October I encouraged her to get a part-time job, and she agreed. She applied to Meijer, a local grocery store, and got the job. On her first day of work, I encouraged her to wear a pair of black pants so she would look professional, and she insisted she was going to wear her torn jeans. We argued over the pants, and she insisted on wearing her jeans. I took her to work and told her I would pick her up at 5 p.m. when she was scheduled to get off. Tom and I went shopping and had lunch, then went back to pick her up at 5 p.m. When I arrived, I waited outside for twenty minutes, but she never came out. I went into the store and asked for her and they said she had left. I was confused and wasn't sure what was going on. I went home and found a voicemail from her saying she was at Ashlynn's house. When I got to Ashlynn's to pick her up, Ashlynn's dad told me she didn't want to come home. He seemed to have an attitude toward me, and it felt judgmental.

The door opened, and Ashlynn's mom came out and joined the conversation and said, "Lea is really upset, and perhaps it would help if she just spent the night."

"Okay, do you know why she is upset?"

"Well, maybe she can tell you."

"Can I see Lea please?"

"Yes, of course. She is in Ashlynn's room. Let me show you the way."

I went inside and knocked on Ashlynn's door, and Lea opened the door and said, "What do you want?"

"I heard you were upset and came to see what you are upset about. I really don't appreciate your attitude."

She rolled her eyes and stood looking at me with her arms crossed.

"I don't appreciate you treating me like this. What is going on here?"

She became extremely angry and said, "I am sick of you, and I don't like you, and I don't want to live with you anymore."

I was stunned. I had no idea where this was coming from. I had been so good to her and had tried so hard to make things work. I was angry and triggered and felt like nothing I did was enough.

"Fine! If you don't want to live with me, I will see what I can do," I said as I walked away feeling devastated, confused, and bewildered as to where this all was coming from.

I began crying. I returned to where Ashlynn's parents were. They could see how upset I was and asked me to wait a minute. Ashlynn's Mom went back in and got Lea, and after a few minutes, they came back.

Lea turned to me and lifted her face and said, "I can't forgive you for never being there for me growing up."

My heart sank. "I am so sorry, Lea. I can't go back and change things. All I can do is do the best I can now. I have done everything I know how to do to make things work."

"Well, it's not working," she said and stood staring at me with anger in her eyes.

I looked at Ashlynn's parents with tears in my eyes. "Do you mind if she stays here until we can figure out some things?"

"Of course. That is no problem at all."

I turned and walked out to my car, climbed inside, and wailed out in tears.

I sobbed over the rejection and pain I felt from Lea and for her, recognizing she must have felt the same pain and rejection as a little girl because I left her. I couldn't have felt more heart-wrenching pain if someone had stabbed me right in the heart.

When I got home and told Tom what had happened, he came and held me and let me sob in his arms. I cried and told him, "She doesn't like me, and I can't fix it. I can't change the past, and I am so sorry I had to leave her when she was so little."

He comforted me and told me, "You really have tried to make things work with her for so many years. I have never seen anyone, Angel, try so hard. Try not to beat yourself up. This hasn't been easy, and she hasn't made it any easier. No matter what you do for her, she treats you terribly, and it is hard for me to watch. I have had to withdraw and let you do your thing. It has been awful. No matter what you do, she treats you like shit and is verbally abusive. I don't know what else you could have done for her. She just refuses to allow you to get close to her. I know this is hard, but I am here for you, and I do love her too, very much, but sometimes love is just not enough, Angel. Sometimes it's just not enough."

"It's just so unfair. It hurts so much. I wanted so badly for this to work. I wanted to make it all better. I wanted her to be happy being here with me, but she is so angry and blames me for everything that has gone wrong in her life. She won't even give me a chance. And I can see. It is my fault that she went through so much. I feel so terrible about what she went through because I wasn't there." I curled up close to Tom and cried out in pain.

"I know, honey, I am so sorry it hasn't worked out."

After a few weeks of staying with her friend Ashlynn, her dad called and said they were exhausted from the shenanigans that Lea and Ashlynn were creating, and I needed to come pick up my kid. I laughed to myself and thought, *yeah, now you know what I have been going through.* I went and picked Lea up, but she didn't want to live with us; she treated me terribly. And even though he wasn't here, I felt like I was being abused by Charlie all over again. So, we decided to call her social worker and have her placed back in foster care.

I failed and lost her again.

She was placed with a single lady in a town called Ypsilanti, about twenty minutes from where we lived. I asked Tom to be home when they came to pick her up, because I couldn't see her leave again. I tried to contact her many times after she left, but she refused to take my calls and told her social worker she didn't want to see me. I sat down and wrote her a long letter.

Dear Lea,

I know you don't want to talk to me and have refused contact with me. I am not even sure you will read this letter, but I am hoping that you will. First, I want you to know I love you so much and I am so sorry for how things have turned out. I never dreamed things would end up like this when you came to live with us. I wanted so badly for things to go well. I thought with time and love that things would just work out. I tried to provide and give you everything I thought you wanted and needed. I was naïve, blind and unaware of what was going on or what to expect. I was just so excited to have you back in my life. It was all I have ever wanted from the time I left you when you were so little. I just wanted so much for us to be close, like we were when you were little, and to share in each other's life.

I didn't know the first thing about being a mother. I really didn't know what my role was supposed to be when you came back after being gone for 10 years. I just love you so much and wanted the best for you. I believed that somehow along the way we would just figure it all out.

When you came to live with us it was a hectic time with so much transition going on for all of us. I know we made a ton of mistakes, and I wish I could have seen things more clearly or would have had some better training so I could have been more prepared.

Instead, I controlled too much and made rules that weren't helpful and made a lot of mistakes. I just thought I was doing what was best for you. What a good responsible parent would do by setting limits and having expectations, but I know now, it wasn't what you needed. To be honest I had no idea what you needed. I just tried to love you and do the best I knew how.

I also heard you when you said you couldn't forgive me for leaving you when you were little. Oh my God, I am so sorry I had to make that decision. There were a lot of things going on back then. I was very young when I had you and I was catapulted from being a child into adulthood and left home at 14 years old and moved in with your dad. I really tried very hard to make things work with him, but they just didn't. It was just a toxic relationship, and we couldn't make it work. I was faced with making a very difficult decision when I was very young and on my own without much support from anyone, not even my parents.

At the time I thought leaving you with your dad and grandma was the best decision for you. It broke my heart to leave you. There was never a day I didn't think about you. I missed you so much and wanted so badly to be in your life, but it was impossible to work with your dad or your grandma, no matter how hard I tried. I take full responsibility for my decision to leave you and I am sorry I hurt you and I am sorry I wasn't there to protect you. I understand if you cannot forgive me. I wanted to at least write this letter and explain these things to you so you know I have always loved you and I always will no matter what. I will always be here for you should you ever decide to reach out. You are so beautiful and so special to me. Words could never express the depths of my love for you. I really do hope I hear from you.

I love you,
Mom

I mailed the letter with love and prayed it would help her understand, and perhaps she would contact me. I didn't hear back from her. As time went by, Tom and I decided to move to Virginia to be closer to our investments and to start a new life. Then I got a call from Lea.

"Hello."

"Hi, Mom!"

"Lea? Oh my God, it is so good to hear your voice."

"I got your letter, and I have been wanting to call you for a long time, but Daddy told me if I had anything to do with you, he wouldn't see me anymore. But after reading your letter, I had to call you."

"Oh, honey, I am so sorry to hear that." Anger welled up inside of me at Charlie and wondered how long he had been interfering in our relationship and if it had been going on the entire time she lived with me. I brushed that thought away and focused on Lea. She caught me up on how school was going and told me she had met several new friends and had a job working at Wendy's. She told me she liked her foster mom and was doing well with her. It was good to hear her laugh and share with me in such a comfortable way. It gave me hope that things could get better. "I would really love to see you, Lea. I miss you so much."

"I will talk to my social worker and see what they say. It was really good talking to you today, Mom."

"You too, Lea! I will look forward to hearing from you again soon. I love you!"

"I love you too, Mom."

I hung up the phone and cried tears of joy. I couldn't wait to see Lea, and I immediately felt conflicted about the decision to move to Virginia.

I talked to Tom and told him about the call and how I was feeling, and we agreed that he would go ahead and move to Virginia, and I would stay back for at least six months, to work on things with Lea and see how things went. The next week after hearing from her, I contacted her caseworker, and he informed me that Charlie and Molly were creating issues.

He said, "We had a family meeting after Lea contacted you and she told them she called you. Immediately things became heated, and me and Lea's foster mom told them they were not allowed to bully Lea and make her feel bad about having a relationship with you."

"Thank you so much. I really appreciate you standing up for her."

"Yes, of course. It is wrong for a parent to keep a child from being with or loving the other parent, and we aren't going to stand for it."

"Thank you. You have no idea how much this means to me. I have never had anyone stand up to them for me."

Hearing this felt so validating. I knew what they were doing was wrong, but I had no way to explain it to anyone. There was just no language or words.

Later, Lea called me and told me about the meeting. "Daddy and I had a big argument this week, and he told me if I continued to see you, he was going to cut me out of his life. Fuck him, he's an asshole. If he can't be mature and not be so selfish, forget him. Him and Molly have been trying to call me all week, but I haven't taken their calls."

I was surprised by her foul language but was happy to hear her stand up for herself to them. It was huge for her to have the courage to speak her truth to them, and I was so proud of her.

"Oh, honey, I am so sorry. I hope they change their mind."

"I don't think so, Mom. They are not reasonable at all, and I am fed up with them."

"I am sorry, Lea."

"It's okay, Mom. I can just see things so much clearer now."

"I am sorry that they are not more reasonable, Lea."

"Yeah, me too."

I could see that Charlie had poisoned her against me for years, and it was difficult for her to see past the lies he had told her about me. He had so much power over her. I realized being in this neutral environment and not living with either of us gave Lea an opportunity to see things from her own perspective and peek past the veil of his deception. Before hanging up, we made plans to begin seeing each other again and scheduled our first visit for the next week.

When I arrived to see her, she was smoking a cigarette, and I was surprised but didn't say anything. We sat and talked, and she told me how things were going for her. Immediately it was apparent she was a different kid from the one who lived with me. She had matured and shifted a lot over the four months since she left my house and was much more streetwise.

The foster home where she lived was in a rough, rundown neighborhood that was known for regular incidents of crime, but she seemed to have adjusted well in the neighborhood. She told me as soon as she arrived, her foster mom gave her a bus pass and told her she had to get a job. She found one at Wendy's at the University of Michigan, twenty minutes away, and took the bus after school and worked in the evenings.

"Yeah, Mom, it has been a big change. I only get to do my laundry every two weeks at the laundromat. I am often on my own because my foster mom is gone a lot, but I have been hanging out in the neighborhood, and my foster mom is related to nearly everyone around here, and they look out for me. They keep an eye on me and protect me." She laughed.

She admitted she had started smoking when she lived with me in Saline and had started smoking pot with the neighborhood kids in the area. She also told me she hated school and was thinking about dropping out. My heart filled with fear, but I didn't say anything. I just listened. She had been through so much, and I was just happy that she was being open and sharing her life with me. It was the deepest conversation we had ever had, and I was soaking in every second, feeling the joy of connecting with her.

Over the next six months, Tom moved to Virginia, and I stayed back in Michigan to work on my relationship with Lea. It was such a beautiful time of bonding with her. Being in foster care gave us the space to get to know each other without the burden of having to be in a parent-child role where I was in control of making rules and telling her what to do. We had space to just share and be with one another. It was a beautiful time.

When Tom was in town, he came to visit her, and they began to build a warm and loving relationship as well.

After Christmas, we talked with Lea and told her I was going to move to Virginia, and we wanted her to come with us. We told her we loved her and would do everything we could to work with the social workers to make this happen. She said she didn't want to move to Virginia right now because she didn't want to leave her friends, but she would think about it. I told her I would come back every month and visit with her and work with her social worker for her to come down to visit us as often as they would allow her to come.

I moved with Tom to Virginia and continued to return to Michigan to visit with Lea at least once a month. Eventually, she was permitted to come and visit us in Virginia and even spent several weeks during the summer with us. We grew closer over time, and just after Christmas in 1999, she decided she was ready to move to Virginia. I was so happy and couldn't wait for her to come home again.

It took many months to work with the system and to get permission for her to return to us, but finally by the spring of 2000, nearly two-and-a-half years after going into foster care and near the end of her junior year of high school, she was placed back into our home. Things seemed to fall into place. She met friends. Had a boyfriend. Was working an after-school job at the County as an administrative assistant, and she was doing amazing. During her senior year of high school, we cosigned for her a brand-new car. She graduated from high school in the spring of 2001 and began taking classes at the community college, and things seemed to be falling into place for her. Our relationship had bloomed, and we were close, like I had always wanted. Things were going well, but there were still cracks beneath the surface.

CHAPTER 23

When I moved to Virginia in 1999, I got my real estate license and worked as a Realtor, invested in real estate, worked as a dental hygienist, and worked to establish our cleaning service in the area, as well as expanding it into a carpet-cleaning business. In the fall of that year, my relationship with Tom was strained. He became depressed and withdrawn, and one day he came to me and told me he wanted to separate, return to Michigan, and wanted a divorce. I was stunned. I asked if he would seek counseling, and he agreed, but after six weeks of therapy, and right before Christmas, he decided to leave. We were separated for four months, and it gave him some time to find himself again and for me to appreciate him in a way I never had before. We talked about what we each needed and how we could make things work. We reconciled just before Lea came to live with us again.

By the time Lea finished her first year of college, I was completely burned out after thriving and overachieving for more than twelve years. I had attained many of the dreams and goals I had set out to accomplish more than a decade before, but I found myself exhausted.

I had everything, but still I was unhappy. We took Lea on a Caribbean cruise to celebrate her success in finishing her first year of college and to unwind and relax for the first time in a long while. During the trip, I realized I needed to make some changes in my life. I took some time to be alone to think about what I really wanted in life. I knew I wanted to give back to others who were struggling and help encourage and support them to overcome the obstacles in their life.

I thought back to reading Wayne Dyer's book *Your Erroneous Zones* when I was sixteen years old. I had always had a desire to be a psychotherapist, but I wasn't ready back then to spend that much time in school. During the cruise, I thought about going to graduate school. It made me excited again about something I was passionate about. I knew this was the right path for me. When I got back from the trip, I resigned my position as a Realtor, reduced my hours as a dental hygienist, and immediately applied to Radford University, a local college in our area, for their master's degree program in counseling and human development. Within a few weeks, I was accepted to the program and started in the fall of 2002. My plan was to eventually open my own counseling and wellness center once I graduated and got my license.

Lea was in college and doing well. She had been dating a guy from high school, but they had started growing in different directions once she started college. The more she moved in a positive direction the more insecure he became, and the relationship became more difficult. They had been together for a year and a half; he had his own place, and she stayed over with him sometimes. Together they had three cats that stayed with him, and when they broke up, we agreed to let her bring her cats home. After a couple of months, we really struggled with having the cats and offered her a mobile home in our park to move into if she wanted to keep the cats.

She moved into the mobile home and seemed excited about her new place. We helped her paint and completely renovate her new home, bought new furniture to help her get started, and she seemed to love it. She had a good job as an administrative assistant at the real estate office where I had worked, she was in college, and seemed to be thriving. In late summer just before starting graduate school, Tom and I took a trip to Michigan and discovered that his sister Cathy's two thirteen-year-old girls, Brianna and Bailey, were struggling and had gotten into some trouble and needed help. I had been close to the twins throughout their lives and often kept them for sleepovers, took them to church, to the movies, and spent time with them when we lived in Michigan. They had been through a lot in their lives and had lived with several family members while their mother struggled to get her life together. Cathy, who was also a teen mom when she had the twins, was again going through some rough times and was in the middle of a divorce from her second husband. She wasn't doing well.

The girls wanted to come back to Virginia and stay with us. I thought about my thirteen-year-old younger self and the struggles I went through and how I wished someone would have been there for me. I wanted to help the girls have a better chance at life and turn things around the way Lea had. We were so proud of Lea and all her accomplishments and felt that having a stable home would give the twins a better chance at life, and Lea could be a good influence on them.

We really didn't think this decision through.

Immediately we packed them up and brought them back to Virginia. Here I was getting ready to start grad school, and we were working hard to build the carpet cleaning side of our cleaning business, along with everything else on our plate, but we figured somehow it would all work out.

A few weeks later, I enrolled them in school, and the problems started. Within the first two weeks, we got a call from the principal to come to the school immediately. They were having an issue with Bailey. When we pulled up in front of the school, there were four Christiansburg police cars there, and we found out Bailey had brought pot to school. The cops filed charges; she was suspended for two weeks and was ultimately put on probation. From that point on, nearly every week, I was called to the school for some problem or issue one of the girls was involved in. I was aggravated and frustrated with them and overwhelmed with juggling everything including grad school, but I loved having the girls with us and wanted so bad to help them and believed that things in time would work out, but it was a roller coaster ride.

Within a few months of the twins' arrival, Lea began to struggle and her attitude toward me began to change. She became moody and distant. She started hanging out with friends from high school who weren't going to college, weren't working, and didn't have any aspirations of doing anything in their lives. She started partying, staying up late at night, her house was a mess, and she started looking sickly. She had lost a lot of weight, she had dark circles under her eyes, she wasn't taking care of herself, she quit her job and stopped going to college. Her life seemed to be unraveling. She got involved with a guy named Matt, who was extremely reckless.

Within a few weeks of dating Matt, she wrecked her car. Then, two weeks later, I got a hysterical call from her crying at 3 a.m. "Mom, I am out with Matt. He was driving too fast and wrecked and flipped his car."

"Oh my God, Lea, are you okay?"

"I think so, but I don't know what to do."

"Is everyone okay?"

"Yes, but I am scared."

" I am sure it was very scary. Are the police there?"

"No, not yet."

"You need to call the police, right now, Lea."

"Okay, Mom, okay I will. I will call you later."

"Where are you? I will come and get you."

"No, we have someone coming to get us. I am fine. I am just scared."

"Lea, I am scared for you. I am happy to come get you if you tell me where you are."

"No, I gotta go. The police are here."

"Call me later and let me know that you are okay."

"Okay, I love you."

"I love you too."

Later, I learned that Matt was intoxicated and had prior charges. He asked Lea to tell the police she was driving so he wouldn't go to jail, and she took responsibility for the wreck, and it was put on her record.

The next day I tried to call her, but she didn't answer my call. I went over to her house to talk to her. I knocked on the door. "Lea, what is going on here?"

"What do you mean?"

"I mean, I am worried to death about you. Things are changing so rapidly in your life. It seems that things are out of control. You have all these people hanging out here. People who have been in jail and on drugs. You have quit your job and college; you are behind in your payments, and this is the second accident you have been in the past two weeks. Are you okay?"

"I am fine!"

"Well, it doesn't look like things are fine. I have gotten calls from your neighbors, my tenants, who have reported that there is a lot of traffic coming in and out of here all hours of the night and day. I can't support what is going on here. This is not good."

"Oh my God, I don't want to talk about this right now. You are so judgmental." She closed the door in my face.

I knocked again. "Lea, please open the door, and let's talk about this." She wouldn't answer the door, and I walked away, frustrated, angry, and scared.

Later she called me. "Mom, I am really sorry for how I acted earlier. I was sleeping when you came, and after everything that happened last night, you made me mad."

"Lea, I am scared that I am going to get a call telling me you have been killed in a car accident. I am worried about you. Do you hear me?"

"I know."

"I need you to get yourself together. What do I need to do to help you?"

"I don't know, Mom."

"Lea, if you will pull yourself together and get rid of all those people in the house and get a job, I will help you. I will pay for the deductible to get your car fixed so you can get back to work. So you can get back on track."

"Okay, Mom, I will do it."

"Oh good, Lea. That is a relief to hear. I love you."

"I love you too, Mom."

The next day, I called the collision shop and arranged for her car to be fixed. The insurance company paid for a car rental and gave her a brand-new car similar to the one she owned. I felt hopeful this would help her get back to work and move in a new direction.

A week later, I got a call from Lea. She was hysterically crying and said she'd wrecked her rental car. I couldn't believe it. She admitted she was drinking and driving and was afraid. So, she told the police the car had been stolen from the driveway and the keys were in it.

"Oh my God, Lea, you have got to be kidding me. Are you okay?"

"Yes, physically I am. I am just so scared."

"Lea, you have to call the police back and tell them the truth."

"I can't, Mom. I will go to jail for filing a false police report."

"Lea, you need to tell them the truth. You need to call the police back. You are going to end up in jail. What are you doing? I thought you got rid of these people and we were turning a corner. We agreed I would help you, and you promised that you would start pulling yourself together."

"I don't want to talk about it. I shouldn't have called you."

She hung up the phone. I tried to call back, but she didn't answer. *What am I doing wrong? No matter what I do to help her, she keeps doing shit to mess up her life. Oh my God, please help her wake up before something really bad happens!*

As the weeks went by, Lea's life continued to spiral, and nothing changed. She continued hanging out partying, not working, and didn't seem to care about any of her responsibilities. I tried to talk to her and get her to wake up, but she wouldn't listen. I could see trying to talk to her wasn't going to work. *She isn't going to make any changes without a big wake-up call. I don't know what to do. What in the hell has happened here? Why is she throwing her life away? I have paid to get the car fixed to try to help her, and she promised to do better, and nothing has changed. It has only gotten worse. Cosigning for her car was a huge mistake. I would have given anything if someone had helped me, when I had nothing, but she doesn't seem to appreciate anything and doesn't seem to care. I thought she was more responsible than this. She makes me so mad.*

As I drove away, I realized, *I have to do something before she kills herself. Unfortunately, she is going to have to go down a hard road before she wakes up. I hate it, but I don't know what else to do. I am going to have to make her move and give back the car. Perhaps this will get her attention, and she will wake up and stop trying to destroy herself.*

I sent her an eviction notice and told her she needed to return the car. After several weeks of arguing, she finally gave back the car and moved in with a friend.

At the same time, things with the twins continued to be sheer chaos. After seven months of working daily to help them get ahead, going to their school nearly every week over some new incident or problem, I was exhausted. A week after the rental car accident, I got a call from the school letting me know the twins had gotten in a fight and were both suspended from school, and I needed to pick them up. I sat down and cried. I had worked so hard to help them to get a fresh start, and it was nothing but crazy all the time. Lea was falling apart, and I couldn't handle this anymore. I felt like I was working harder than everyone and nothing was working. I felt like a failure.

I called Tom and told him about the twins. He said, "That's it, they need to go back home to their mom. We can't do this anymore."

"I feel terrible, but this is more than I can deal with all at the same time. It's too much. I agree they really need to go back home, Tom." I called Cathy and told her we were bringing the girls back home. I talked to both girls and told them how much we loved them and how much we had hoped this would work out, but we couldn't continue to deal with all this chaos. It was taking a toll on everyone. They were sad to leave, and it was hard to see them go, but they also seemed happy to be returning home to Detroit, to the big-city life they were used to.

CHAPTER 24

The first few years we lived in Virginia were very challenging times of transition, and Tom and I worked hard to build the financial success we dreamed about. To purchase the mobile home park, we used savings that we had accumulated over the years of working in the cleaning business. We also used strategies we learned from studying Russ Whitney, including creative financing, using a home equity line of credit, and our credit cards as leverage to get started. It took almost everything we had to make it work, but it was a great investment, and we knew in time it would pay off. We initially moved into our trailer park to save money, then used these same financial strategies to purchase a townhouse nearby in Christiansburg.

As I worked hard to build the real estate investments, my real estate career, the cleaning business, and navigate our personal lives, including working as a dental hygienist, there were times during our journey when expenses came up that were unexpected, and it put us in a financial jam. We had a lot of income coming in, but we also had an enormous mountain of debt and a lot of money that went out. However, we were driven to do whatever it took to strive ahead toward our goals. Tom and I worked around the clock managing and strategizing how to keep afloat and juggling everything. I knew eventually the hard work would pay off, but it would take time.

The pressure was often tough, and it tapped into my financial insecurities and created stress and anxiety on top of all the emotional turmoil I was going through, especially with Lea. When I cosigned for Lea's car, she was doing amazing. I never dreamed we would be in the situation where I would have to take the car back and take on the financial obligation because she wouldn't work. It made me angry for getting into this financial situation to help her out, and she didn't seem to care about the sacrifice I had made to help her. Her attitude seemed to be that I was rich, and my money or finances didn't matter. It really frustrated and triggered me and was a source of contention between us. I had been so poor and was working so hard to build a better life. I struggled with anxiety and depression over all the stress and pressure I was under and often turned to alcohol, something that I started using as a teenager to help me cope. It was often the only thing that made me feel better.

Late one afternoon, a month after Lea moved in with her friend, she showed up at my house and knocked on the door. "Mom, can we talk?"

"Sure, come on in. You look exhausted. Are you okay"

"Well, no not really. I spent all day walking up here from Shawsville. It is almost nine miles, and it gave me a lot of time to think."

"Wow, really!"

"I know I have made a mess of things, and I understand if you don't want to help me, but I am wondering if you would consider letting me come back home. I promise I will get a job and I want to go back to school. Last year, when I was in college, I dated a guy named Jason, and we have been talking again, and it has made me realize I need to make some better decisions."

"Really?"

"Yeah, Mom. I know I need to do better. I am sorry for the mess I've made. I promise if you give me a chance, I will do better."

"Well, Lea, I don't know. You have put us through a lot over the past year, and it has been quite stressful and destructive."

"I know I have made a lot of mistakes, but I promise I will get my life together."

"Let me think about it and talk to Tom. You know if you come home there will be rules. You have broken my trust, and you will need to earn it back."

"I know, Mom."

After Lea moved out, I struggled with a myriad of emotions. I wanted so badly for her to have a great life. I beat myself up over offering for her to move out in the first place over the cats. *Why didn't I just insist on the cats being rehomed or figure out a way to deal with them? I can see now she just wasn't ready or prepared to move out.* I couldn't understand at first, because I couldn't wait to get a car, leave home, and be on my own and in control of my own life. I yearned for freedom and wished someone would have helped me to get a place and offered to help me finance a car. I would have appreciated the opportunity so much and made sure I did everything to honor the agreement, but she seemed angry and seemed to blame me for trying to help her. It frustrated a part of me that she couldn't pull herself together, but then another part of me felt sad for her.

I recognized that perhaps having the twins come to live with us so soon after she moved out must have hurt her. She watched while I took care of the girls, loving them, caring for them, and dealing with the chaos and struggles they continued to get themselves in, with patience and love. She watched me, taking time and energy to try to teach, guide, and direct them. I imagine looking back on it, she must have felt jealous and hurt because I was being a mother to them, when I wasn't there to be a mother to her.

When Lea walked all that way to ask to come back home, I felt compassion for her. It reminded me of the miles I had to walk to work when I was so young and needed my mom, or someone to help me when I needed it most, but no one was there. I also felt that this desperate act of walking so far was an indication that she realized she had made mistakes too and was ready to change and turn things around. I wanted to fix the mistakes I had made. I felt perhaps she just needed some guidance and more structure. I hoped having her come home would give her the opportunity to get back on track, and I wanted things to be better between us. What I didn't remember or recognize then was that once you have been out on your own, it's very hard to come back and live at home and be a child again with rules.

A few days later, I met with Lea. "Tom and I have agreed to let you come back home if you will agree to get a job, stay away from the people who were dragging you down, and move in a more positive direction. Also, I am willing to let you have the car back, but only to go to work and back. You have been reckless with this car, you haven't taken care of it, and I need you to show me I can trust you. If you want to refinance the car and get it out of my name, you can do what you want with the car, but as long as it's in my name and I am financially responsible for it, there will be rules about the car. I also cannot put up with a bunch of stress and turmoil. I am in graduate school, running two businesses, and I can't take a bunch of chaos in my life. If you can't follow the rules, you will have to move back out, and I will take back the car and we will sell it. Do you understand?"

"I totally understand, Mom. I really appreciate you and Tom letting me move back home. I promise I will do better."

I hugged her. "I am happy you are coming home and moving in a new direction. I have been so worried about you."

"I know. I am happy too. I love you, Mom."

"I love you too, Lea."

Lea got a job, and she and Jason grew closer. We really liked him. He had a car, was going to college, and he seemed to really care about her. She started dressing nicer and taking better care of herself. She looked amazing. Several months later, as the summer started winding down, Lea's attitude toward me started changing again. She was distant, grumpy, and snapped at me at the smallest things. I overlooked it and brushed it off. If I asked her about how things were going, she would bite back at me with snide remarks.

"Lea, what is going on with you?"

"Nothing."

"Well, it doesn't seem like nothing."

"You pick at me about everything. If I ask you a simple question, you are rude or roll your eyes at me, and even if I say good morning, you just about bite my head off. I don't understand what is going on."

"Well, to be honest, I don't like you. Nobody likes you, not even Jason or his family. You are too uppity and are so judgmental, and you treat me terribly. Nobody understands how you could treat me the way you do. You are mean, and I can't stand being around you."

My mind started spinning. I was stunned by the words that were coming out of her mouth. "What do you mean? I do everything I can to help you. I don't understand what you are saying to me right now. What have I done wrong to you?"

"Nothing and everything. I just can't stand you. I don't like being around you. You are on my back all the time, asking me questions and in my business."

"Lea, I'm just trying to help you. I just want you to do well, and all I have asked is for you to do your part, and you won't. It's frustrating. I just want you to do what you agreed to do, and I want you to be happy. That's all."

"Well, I am not happy, and it's because of you. You make me miserable."

"I am tired of being treated like this in my own home. I am just exhausted from this whole thing. I am doing everything I can to keep everything together, and I am tired of fighting you. It seems like you haven't ever liked me, and you treat me like shit all the time."

"That is because I haven't ever liked you."

"Oh my God! I don't know what else to do to make you happy. I guess I am just wasting my time here, and you don't give a shit about me. Maybe you just need to move out then and get away from me."

"Oh my God, I can't believe you. Of course. You are going to throw me out again."

"Lea, I am sick to death of all of this. Somehow, it's always my fault."

"Yes, that's because it is your fault, Mom. I am angry at you for leaving me when I was a little girl, and there is nothing you can do to make that up. Nothing! I can't get past it."

"Well, maybe we need counseling to work through this, Lea. I want things to be better between us."

"No, I am not doing counseling. I just don't want to be around *you*!"

"Okay fine then. Then leave and get away from me. Maybe then you will be happy."

"Fine! I will call my dad and tell him he was right about you all along. Maybe he will help me."

I could feel my face flush. "Fine, maybe he will, and maybe it would be better if you went back there to live. I don't know the answer to this anymore, Lea."

I left to get away from her. I couldn't stand the pain any longer. I just wanted to scream. I got in my car and sobbed. I called Tom and told him about the fight.

"What have I done so awful to deserve this? I am so tired of fighting. It just doesn't help. I am so exhausted. I just want to run away."

"I know, Angel. I don't know what to say. You have tried so hard with her. It is hard when you try to take in someone you didn't raise. She doesn't have the same values as you, and she just doesn't seem to want to get herself together. Maybe it would be better if she moved out and got her own place."

"Maybe that would help, Tom. Maybe she has to figure it out herself without my help. Maybe that is better, but it makes me so sad. I wanted things to work. I wanted us to have a relationship and be close, but she just won't let me get close to her. I understand she is hurt. I get it, and I feel horrible about the mistakes I have made in the past. Maybe I was wrong all along, wanting her to come back into my life. Maybe it wasn't the right thing. Maybe she should have stayed in Michigan with her foster mom or went back to live with Charlie. I just don't know. I can't change the past, Tom, no matter how hard I try."

"I know. It is sad. Maybe if she has some space away it will be better. I am sorry you are hurting."

"Thank you for listening and for always supporting me. I don't know what I would do without you. I love you."

"I appreciate you too. Don't be so hard on yourself. You have really tried hard, Angel. More than anyone I know. I love you."

Lea contacted Charlie, and he sent her the money to get her own place. She found a one-bedroom apartment in Fairlawn, a town about twenty minutes from our house. A few days before she moved out, I came to her when she seemed calm. "Lea, I am really sorry things did not work out. I am devastated over all of this. I don't know what the answers are. I love you so much. I just don't know what else we can do to make this work. Maybe some space will help. Maybe in time, we can have a better relationship."

"I don't think so. I don't plan to ever speak to you again."

My voice trembled. "I am really sorry you feel that way. I really do love you, sweetheart, more than you could ever know."

"I know, and I love you too. That is why I am so broken-hearted. I just don't understand, Mom. I just don't understand."

"Me either, Lea."

CHAPTER 25

Lea didn't talk to me for several weeks. Then one afternoon, she got a ride from a friend and came by. I was very surprised and happy to see her. "Mom, I just need someone to talk to. Jason came by earlier and told me he joined the army and didn't even talk to me about it first. He leaves for boot camp in two weeks."

"Oh my gosh, I am so sorry he didn't talk to you before making such a big decision."

"Yeah, I am so mad. I am going to miss him so much. What am I going to do?"

"I know how hard it is to be so far away from someone you love. I went through the same thing with Tom when he was in the service."

"But Mom, he did ask me to marry him when he finishes boot camp in December, and I said yes. He told me I could come with him wherever he ends up stationed once he finishes boot camp."

"Okay, wow, is that what you want?"

"Yes, I think so. I am just so upset with him right now. I just can't believe he would do this without asking me."

"I know that must be really hard."

"How am I going to be away from him for so long?"

"You will get through it. Just write him every day and stay in touch, and the time will go by fast." I hugged her.

"Do you think I could wear your wedding dress, Mom?"

"Of course, I would love for you to wear my dress. Come on, let's go look at it." We went to my room, and I pulled out the dress from my cedar chest, and she tried it on. "Oh my God, you look amazing, Lea."

She stood in front of the mirror, turning from side to side, admiring how she looked in the dress. "Yes, it does look nice."

I hugged her. "Everything is going to be okay."

"Thank you, Mom."

"You are welcome, sweetie."

Oh my God. This kid is all over the place. Her anger is crazy; she can be so mean to me, then she can be so sweet and nice. I never know what I am going to get from her. Maybe getting married would be a good thing. Maybe just getting away from here will be good for her and give her some time to find herself. I know it was good for me being away with Tom when he was in the service. It helped us both grow up a lot. It would be good for me too. I am so tired of this turmoil. She makes life so difficult, and it is hard to be around her sometimes.

When Lea moved out, I took the car back because she wasn't making the payments. She was treating the car with disrespect, and I felt like she was intentionally trying to destroy it to hurt me. This car felt like a symbol of our relationship and the emotional weight and turmoil we each carried.

When Jason left, he told her she could use his car while he was gone, but after he left, his family took the car and didn't let her use it. One evening the doorbell rang, and it was Lea. She was sweaty, hot, tired, and thirsty.

"Lea, come in."

"I just walked from Fairlawn. I walked all day long, and it took me nine hours to get here. I have no cigarettes, no money, no food, and no job. I can't get a job without a car. I promise, Mom, if you will help me and let me have my car back, I will do better."

"I don't know, Lea; I have to think about it." I got her something to eat, bought her some cigarettes, and took her home. Over the next couple of days, I thought about it. I felt bad for her and figured since she was engaged, maybe giving the car back would help her get on the right track. We sat down and talked again. She said all the right things. It hurt me to see her struggle. I thought, *maybe she recognizes how important this car is and she will take care of it this time and get a job and pull herself together.* I agreed to give the car back if she would just get a job, take care of the car, make the payments, and use it to get herself together.

As the weeks went by, her attitude started changing, and she was moody and distant again. She didn't have a job and didn't seem serious about finding one. Jason's letters came to my address because Lea said the mailboxes at her apartment didn't feel safe. I told her she had a stack of letters from Jason that she needed to come by and pick up. She never came to get them. Then one day, I was driving through town and saw Lea in her car with two guys from the trailer park near our house. Immediately my heart sank and hung heavy in my chest.

A few days later, I was disappointed to learn she was seeing a guy named Brad from the trailer park down the street from our house. He was two years younger than Lea, and in my opinion, he wasn't very mature. He had dropped out of high school, wasn't working, and hanging out with his friends was his main focus in life. I was concerned that this was another difficult road she was choosing. When I asked her if she was seeing Brad, she confirmed it.

"Have you told Jason about Brad?"

"No, I haven't. He didn't care about telling me he was joining the army. He left me here alone without a car. Why should I care about him?"

"Lea, it's not fair to Jason. He is far away from home, he is writing to you all the time, and mail means everything when you are in the military, especially boot camp, and on top of that, he thinks you all are getting married in two months. You have to write him and tell him what is going on."

Weeks went by, and she refused to write to Jason. She had moved on to a whole new world and didn't have any care about wrapping up this loose end. She got evicted and put off going to get her things. When she finally decided to go clean out her apartment at the last minute, she discovered the landlord came in and threw out all her belongings and childhood memories. It was heartbreaking. She called crying over all the things she lost. I listened but didn't say much. I was starting to learn that talking really didn't help.

After getting off the phone with her I talked to Tom. "Maybe she has hit bottom and will start to turn things around. It's so devastating to see her go through this and not want better for herself."

"I know, honey. It's hard to watch."

I was frustrated over the whole situation. Letters from Jason kept coming, and I felt so bad for him. Finally, I told her, "If you aren't going to write Jason, I will."

"I don't care if you write him. I am done with that situation."

I wrote Jason a letter and told him that Lea had changed her mind about getting married and that he shouldn't expect any letters from her, and I was really sorry that it didn't work out. Lea gave back his ring, and his mother came by and retrieved it. Lea and I discussed the car, and she agreed to return it to me because she couldn't afford it and she wasn't doing what she agreed to do.

A few days later, she moved in with Brad and his mom.

Within a few months, they got their own place, and other than the struggle of Brad not working and him wanting to run around with his friends, things in Lea's life seemed to settle down. She stepped up, got a job and took care of him.

At the end of summer 2004, she came to me and told me she wanted to go back to college, but she couldn't if she didn't have a car and asked if she could have her car back. I couldn't believe it. Here we were again with the car issues, and it reminded me how important having a car truly is. I was happy to see Lea moving in a good direction and wanted to see her thrive, so I agreed to give the car back to her.

By the fall, she found out she was pregnant. The place she was living in was falling apart; the floors were literally falling in, and the landlord wouldn't fix anything. She'd been working, had gone back to college, and was enjoying it more this time. I was really proud of her. Even without much help from Brad, she was making things work. She asked if I would help her find a better place to move. I found a trailer that was a rent-to-own in a park five minutes from my house. It was in great shape and was located on a nice end lot on a dead-end street. It was a great opportunity for her to have something that was her own.

The park owner agreed to sell the trailer to her if my name was on the agreement. I struggled to get involved in a financial situation with her again, but I could see Lea was really trying and agreed to help her, especially with the baby coming. I wanted her to have a stable home. Soon we began talking about her and Brad getting married, and I agreed to pay for the wedding, even though I was still not sure about Brad. I thought if they got married, maybe it would help him grow up and move in a more positive direction and give Lea security. Since Lea was doing so well with working and school, I decided for Christmas, just before her wedding, to pay off the car I had cosigned for her in high school and give it to her as a gift with a clear title. I hoped giving her the car would end this struggle. And I hoped I would never have to think about this car situation again.

In January 2005, just after Lea turned twenty-two years old and was three months pregnant, she and Brad got married. Six months later, she had her baby girl, Sydney Marie, and we were all thrilled to have this sweet little baby in our lives.

When Sydney was born, I reflected on all the struggles Lea went through during her teen years and how even though she went through so much, she didn't get pregnant as a teenager and was able to break this generational cycle that had gone on for hundreds of years in my family.

CHAPTER 26

In the spring of 2006, both our carpet cleaning and our rental property businesses were doing well. We sold our house in Michigan, paid off what we could, and consolidated loans. Finally, things were going really well financially. I was finishing grad school and had a job opportunity working with at-risk adolescents at an inpatient treatment facility as a therapist where I was doing my internship, and I was thrilled. Tom and I needed help with our rental and carpet cleaning business. Lea had helped us with the administrative side of our business on and off during her pregnancy, and we asked her to come on full time as our office manager, and she agreed. It was a winning situation because she could bring Sydney with her to work and have the flexibility to go to college, and it relieved me of these duties to focus on finishing up grad school.

I was proud of Lea. Getting married and having the baby matured her a lot, and she was doing well taking care of her bills. She was a great mother, and things in her life were going better except for her relationship with Brad, which was stressful and chaotic. He was immature and still wanted to hang out with his friends and party, and he wouldn't keep a job. I hated to see her struggle. I tried to give Brad opportunities for work, but he was unreliable, wouldn't work consistently, and he struggled with addiction. Lea protected him and was willing to work and put up with his instability, disloyalty, and she allowed him to do what he wanted, as long as he'd stay. I didn't recognize it then, but she was continuing the generational cycle of codependency by overcompensating, helping, enabling, and rescuing in her relationship with Brad.

It made me sad that she didn't have more self-esteem and confidence in herself, and I blamed myself. I knew she deserved better than this, but she didn't want to talk about it and got angry if I said anything.

Tom and I loved being grandparents, and we kept Sydney at least one day almost every weekend and spent time with her as often as we could. She had her own room and tons of toys, at our house in town and at our lake house. We often took her on vacation with us and spoiled her at every turn. Because Brad wouldn't help support Lea and Sydney, we helped. We paid for Sydney to go to dance classes, to summer camps, swimming and gymnastics lessons; we bought her school supplies, back-to-school clothes, and made sure she had what she needed in her life. It was hard to watch Lea struggle and put up with being treated with disrespect from Brad, but we tried to stay out of it. During these early years of Sydney's life, Lea and I found common ground with wanting the best for Sydney. We had our differences, and we struggled sometimes and butted heads, but we managed.

Grad school was a wonderful and very fulfilling experience for me. It was so rewarding in many ways and helped fill the longing I had to help others. While studying at the university, I was given the opportunity to teach as a grad teaching assistant and give back to the undergrad students. It also later gave me the opportunity to become an adjunct professor in the Counselor Education Department at Radford University and teach once I graduated. During the four years I was in grad school, the sadness and depression I had suffered during the difficult years with Charlie and Lea dissipated, but the anxiety lingered, and I continued to use alcohol to help when I was stressed. This would continue for many years.

Once I finished grad school and began working, I wasn't around a lot. Lea did a great job managing our businesses and graduated from college with her associate's degree in human services in 2009. We were very proud of her. I finished up my residency and was building my dream of opening my own counseling business. I wanted to create an amazing place for people to work in a healthy, loving environment and a caring, loving place for clients to come for support.

In the summer of 2010, I opened the doors to Life in Balance Counseling and Wellness Center in Christiansburg. It was located in a beautiful brand-new office in the center of town in a medical complex. I hired several psychotherapists, two massage therapists, a Reiki master, and a yoga instructor. I was so excited about accomplishing this lifelong dream. Shortly after opening the business, I asked Lea to come on as my office manager, as well as stay on and manage the other businesses, and she agreed. I was excited to have her come work with me, and I appreciated her help. Through managing the office and working with the therapist, she seemed to gain confidence and thrived, but it was stressful, and things between us became testy at times. I had a lot on me, running the business and seeing a caseload of clients, as well as supervising others and overseeing our other businesses and real estate investments. Lea's marriage continued to be in conflict, and she was moody and seemed stressed.

I could see the office manager position was taking a toll on both of us, and it wasn't working well. I learned through a lady I met who was involved in spiritual practices that she offered a certification program in Reiki. I offered to pay for Lea to get her certification, and she agreed. The situation as my office manager continued to deteriorate because we were both under a lot of stress and there was a lot of turmoil working to build the business. It touched some of my own insecurities, and Lea and I often struggled with each other. As time went on, our moods and frustrations took a toll on both of us, and we struggled to communicate. Lea became more disrespectful to me, bossing me around, and she acted like I worked for her, which really got under my skin. When I asked her to make a phone call for me or do a small task to help me, she would reply, "Do it yourself." I thought, *Why am I putting up with being treated this way? This is insane!* Soon, my patience with her grew short and I fired her.

When things cooled down, I told her I thought it was better for her to move in a different direction, and I was happy to let her build her Reiki practice at my office. I told her the stress for both of us as my office manager was too much, and she agreed. She shifted into building her Reiki practice at my office.

In 2016, the stress of the business and the constant striving, overworking, overachieving, and chaos of the relationship with Lea and my own life had taken a toll and left me feeling burnt out. I knew I needed a break. I also wanted to take a break from alcohol and just take some time to be alone and find a better way to cope with the stresses in my life. When we still lived in Saline, I started practicing yoga and meditation.

Years earlier, I had visited an Ashram in central Virginia called Yogaville for a weekend retreat and learned that they offered a longer stay as a volunteer. I talked to Tom and told him I wanted to go stay at Yogaville for a month as a volunteer and go into stillness and work on healing myself. He knew I was stressed and had been through a lot over the past several years, including helping and dealing with caring for my mother, who was sick after being diagnosed with cancer in 2006. So, I went, and it was good for me to get away and gave me some time to refocus and to work on putting more self-care into my life. I enjoyed my time away and had big plans to relax and implement what I had learned when I returned.

Being away in a secluded place gave me a break and allowed me to detach from everything, including the chaos in Lea's life and the stress of work that had become so overwhelming in my life, and it felt very good. It was so nice not to think about Lea or even hear about what was going on in her life. I even fantasized that I could live here forever and never go back, but I really missed Tom and couldn't wait to see him. It was my plan to incorporate getting up early, meditating, doing yoga, self-care, and continuing to eat well, take better care of myself, set better boundaries, and find healthier ways to deal with my stress and anxiety when I returned home.

However, a week after getting back, I found myself focusing on Lea and her life again. I saw a little house on the outskirts of Radford that was for sale. It was distressed and needed some loving care. I thought, *This would be a great house for Lea, a forever home*, and I decided to buy the property and refurbish it. Tom thought it was a terrible idea and told me not to do it, but I insisted that things with Lea and I had grown and changed over the years and, despite our differences, I thought it was a great opportunity for her and Brad.

A few years earlier, they had moved out of the trailer and got a rental house just a few blocks away from the house I bought. Brad was working steadily for the first time in their marriage, and Lea was still managing our cleaning businesses and rental properties and doing well with her Reiki practice. I heard they were going to have to move out of the rental house and thought this house would be a great fit for them. My idea was they could rent the house from me and work on their credit, and eventually they could buy the house. You would have thought by now I would have learned my lesson about mixing finances and family, but it wasn't even on my radar. Instead, here I was getting ready to dive into this mess again because all I could see was it seemed like a winning situation, and I wanted so bad to help Lea have a better life.

So, without a thought, Tom and I got busy right away getting the house ready for them. We put new linoleum in the bathroom and kitchen; painted the inside of the house; installed a new sink, toilet, and all new wallboard in the bathroom; and had a new ceiling installed in the living room and kitchen. I tried to get Lea to help, but she was bossy, moody, had a bad attitude, and treated me like shit, but I overlooked it and dismissed it as her being stressed. Brad came and helped on several things to try to get the house ready before her lease ended at the end of the month. Even though I had just promised myself I would relax more, here I was trying to show Lea how much I loved her by getting her this house. There were nights that Tom and I got off of work and worked all night, even sleeping in our car in the driveway, trying to get the work done on time for Lea.

A few days before she was supposed to move in, she came over to the house and started bossing me around, barking out orders and ridiculing my work.

"Lea, Tom and I have been over here working our asses off getting this house ready for you, and I don't appreciate you coming in here bitching at me. I have been refurbishing homes for nearly eighteen years. I know what I am doing, and I don't deserve you treating me this way, and I am not going to put up with it. If this is the way you are going to treat me, then you can find a different place to move into, and I will rent this house to someone else."

I wish then that I would have seen the writing on the wall and could have recognized I was getting ready to go right back down the same destructive pathway I had gone many times in the past, but I wanted to help her so badly to move in a better direction, it was almost as if I just couldn't help but help her. It was almost as if something in me was compelled to rescue her, take care of her, and make her life better. It was like an addiction. I wanted so badly for her life to be stable, happy, and prosperous, and I thought if I gave her a hand up, it would make her life better.

Deep down, I needed her to be happy in order for me to be happy. A symptom of my codependency that was buried and out of my aware- ness. I blamed myself for her struggles and for her life being hard. Deep down I believed if only I hadn't left her when she was so little in what became a terrible abusive situation, she wouldn't be so self-destructive, she would make better choices, and she would have married someone who would help her, rather than pull her down. It would take me a long time to really realize that I felt responsible for the struggles in Lea's life and was compelled to save her in an attempt to rid myself of the horrible guilt I felt for leaving her.

The next day she called crying and apologized and begged me to let her move into the house. "Please, Mom. I am so sorry. I am just so stressed over everything. I didn't mean to treat you so mean. I love you, Mom, and this house means everything to me. We have nowhere else to go. Please let us move in."

"Lea, I am not going to put up with you treating me like shit. I don't deserve it. I have worked hard getting this house ready for you before your lease is up, and you have treated me just awful."

"I know, Mom. I don't know what comes over me. I am so sorry. I didn't mean to be so mean. Please let us move into the house. We don't have anywhere else to go."

For a moment, a part of me told me not to give in. I heard Tom's voice in my head say *this is not a good idea.* I even felt relieved to be done with this struggle with Lea. But then this enormous feeling of sadness for her came over me. I hated to see her struggle and be hurt. Her life was already so hard, and I really believed that this house was going to be the very thing that would change her life for the better, and that feeling was so strong. I relented.

I took a deep breath. "Okay, Lea. Let's make this a positive opportunity. I want you to have a nice home and have stability for you and Sydney."

"I know, Mom, and we really appreciate it. It means a lot. I believe this home is a healing home and is going to heal our relationship. I really do, Mom."

"I sure hope so, Lea. I really hope so."

Within a few months of moving in, the rent was late, or she couldn't pay it at all and got behind. Brad quit working, and this put her in a bad financial situation again. He started running around again, hanging out with his friends and getting high. Her life was replete with constant chaos and instability.

For years I was in turmoil and conflict with Lea, begging her to get her life together and constantly bailing her out and overhelping. It was exhausting. I kept giving and trying because of Sydney and the guilt I felt so deeply. I wanted Sydney to have a stable home and not have to move every six months, the way I did after my parents divorced, so I put up with a lot and overlooked things I shouldn't have. I begged Lea to work on getting her credit score up and gave her chance after chance after chance to buy the house, but she made excuses and wouldn't try. It made me so angry and frustrated with her, and it caused us both to pull away from each other. It left me with a low-grade constant aggravation, and I couldn't stand to be around her or talk to her out of feelings of anger and resentment.

I asked her, "Lea why are you so angry, and why do you treat me so mean?"

"I am a bitch, Mom, and I treat everyone that way."

I stood and looked at her with sadness and confusion in my eyes. *Doesn't she want to get better? Doesn't she want a better life for herself and for Sydney? One that is easier, where she doesn't have to struggle so hard all the time? Why does she insist on living in poverty and chaos? Why does she put up with a man who drags her down, runs around on her, won't work or help support her and Sydney, and keeps her upset all the time? She reminds me of my mother and all she put us through hanging on to Percy. Poor Sydney. It makes me so mad.*

I couldn't see it then, but looking back on it, I wonder if even on a subconscious level, Lea felt triggered by or jealous of my relationship with Sydney. Did it bother her that I was there for Sydney and spent so much time, energy, and effort with her throughout her life? Taking her to swimming lessons, taking her on vacations, spending time with her doing crafts, paying for camps, and buying for her. I love Sydney and was grateful to have her in my life. She was like the kid that Tom and I never had.

We were ready for a child when she came into our lives, and we had time, energy, and resources to dedicate to her. I appreciated Lea for letting Tom and me spend so much time with Sydney. She was very generous, sharing her with us, and I believe it helped give Lea a break and time for herself, but I wonder deep down, did this remind her again that I wasn't there for her when she was a child and needed a mom so much? Did it make her feel like I had time for Sydney but didn't take the time for her? Did my overhelping, always buying, and giving to Sydney make Lea feel like I stole her thunder and swooped in as the hero to Sydney and saved the day because I provided things for her that Lea and Brad couldn't afford? Especially at Christmas when I overdid things and left little room for them to shine? Lea never said anything, but she was often passive-aggressive toward me, especially as Sydney became a teenager.

I also felt triggered by Lea and her situation. I couldn't see it clearly then, but I believe on a subconscious level it reminded me of all of my failures and stirred up all the guilt and shame I felt for the mistakes I had made.

A wedge began to form at some point over the years between us. I began to pull away from her because of her negative moods, attitudes, and treatment that hurt and triggered me and made me feel so terrible I didn't want to be around it.

CHAPTER 27

By January 2019, I had financially accomplished nearly all the dreams and goals I had set out to achieve when I was a twenty-year-old girl who had a vision, wrote out a list of goals in a notebook, created a vision board, and got busy putting that vision to work. Together Tom and I traveled all over the world. We had become financially independent in our late thirties. We had built a successful rental property business and a successful carpet cleaning business. I built my dream practice as a therapist and was helping others. We had a beautiful house overlooking the lake in the country, and a townhouse in town. Our marriage was great and stronger than ever, and we were best friends. I had gone back to school while practicing as a therapist and completed a bachelor's degree in the field of metaphysical sciences, which was another passion for me. Then I went on to get a master's degree as a metaphysician and was preparing to work on my dissertation for my PhD in transpersonal counseling. We had great friends and a rewarding life.

But I wasn't okay.

Things with Lea were still strained, and nothing much had changed. I had been using alcohol for years to cope with anxiety, depression, sadness, and stresses in my life, and I felt terrible. I was overweight. I had a pain on my left side under my rib. I had been to several doctors and specialists, trying to figure out what was wrong with me, but they couldn't find anything.

One afternoon, a client of mine came to see me after having just returned from a yoga trip in Costa Rica. She was tan, bubbling over with insight and enlightenment, and feeling amazing after the ten-day trip that she had taken. She spent the entire session talking about all the gifts this self-care trip had given her. I had just turned fifty in November, and although I had spent most of the year before traveling with Tom and our friends, celebrating my fiftieth year on this planet, I was feeling discontented. While listening to my client, my soul began to stir. I felt a calling to take a trip to Costa Rica. I wasn't sure what was calling me, but it was strong and persistent. I knew it wasn't just a yoga retreat. When I told Tom about this yearning, he asked me if I wanted to take our vacation to an all-inclusive resort there in the spring. I told him, "No, it's not a vacation that is calling me. I have no idea what it is, but it seems more spiritual."

The months went by, and the yearning grew stronger. Still, I had no idea what was calling me there, but I trusted my intuition and knew whatever it was, it would find me. I also knew deep down this journey was calling me to come alone.

One evening, seven months later, while watching a documentary on *Gaia.com* called *The Truth about Reality*, it found me.

I had no idea why I picked this particular documentary to watch. It was a story about a movie producer and his friends taking a trip to the

Amazon to heal by taking an Ayahuasca journey. They all were navigating difficult struggles and were looking for answers only a deep soul journey could provide. I had only heard of Ayahuasca once before, ten years earlier. It was a vague encounter with another therapist seeking peer supervision to staff a case concerning a client who had gone down to Ecuador and had taken Ayahuasca and was struggling to integrate her experience once she returned. I couldn't help the therapist because this was out of my scope of practice. I had never heard of this medicine, and I didn't know of anyone else who could help her either.

At the time I thought to myself, *Who in the world would do something like that? Go down to the jungle in the middle of nowhere and take a strange medicine that you don't know what might happen afterwards with no guidance or help?* It sounded crazy to me.

Much like my strong attraction to Wayne Dyer's book as a teenager, immediately this documentary grabbed and pulled me in. I hung on to every word and scene. I listened to Zappy, the producer, tell the story of his extremely wealthy friend Gerry, who sold his company for nearly 100 million dollars, was abusing drugs, drinking a lot of alcohol, his family was in shambles, and he was on the edge of destruction and was silently killing himself. He had gone down to Costa Rica and had a plant medicine experience that completely turned his life around. He quit doing drugs, being reckless, reunited with his family, and his whole life changed. Later he partnered up with Michael Beckwith, a world-renowned New Thought minister and founder of Agape Spiritual Center in California. They opened an Ayahuasca retreat center called Rythmia on the beautiful western coast of Costa Rica in Guanacaste.

"That's it!" I said to myself. "That is where I need to go." Interestingly, a few months earlier, in the spring, I was on a trip with Tom and our best friends, Dave and Jennifer, in Williamsburg, and I heard that Michael Beckwith was going to be at the grand opening of a New Thought Church just an hour away in Virginia Beach. I had been a big fan of Michael's for many years. I was finishing up the last year of my master's degree in metaphysical sciences and thought it would be educational to see and meet him. Unfortunately, our plans changed unexpectedly, and I didn't get to go.

In the documentary I watched, Deepak Chopra, someone I admired and had followed for over twenty years, helped guide Zappy and the others prior to and after their return from the Amazon and their Ayahuasca experience. I had read many books by Deepak and had great respect for him. *This is serendipitous.* There were so many things coming together all at once. I couldn't stop thinking about Rythmia the entire night. The next day I got up and called them. I learned that Michael Beckwith was going to be there in August and in January. I wasn't quite ready to go so quickly in August. To be honest, I was a little nervous and needed to learn more about all of this, but I thought that by January I'd be prepared. I booked the January trip when Michael was going to be a guest speaker at the resort, got the plane tickets, and felt the yearning within me leap with delight.

This was my calling, and I knew it was a divine appointment.

Over the next six months, I read up on Ayahuasca and watched documentaries on psychedelics to learn as much as I could. I began meditating and preparing myself for the journey. I was so desperate to feel better and to heal. I was so worried about my health and even wondered if I had cancer. I was scared. I tried to keep that thought out of my mind and never shared my fears with anyone, not even Tom. Emotionally I was a mess. I had everything in my life I ever wanted, and instead of being happy, I was depressed, anxious, and had an underlying feeling of unfulfillment. My heart ached with sadness, and I just couldn't figure out what was wrong.

I had spent years searching for answers. I had been in therapy nearly constantly since I was sixteen years old, and although it helped me so much over the years, it didn't reach the depths of my pain and discontent. I read books all the time on self-care and overcoming struggles; I meditated and prayed. I exercised and did yoga. I went on personal self-care retreats, visited spas, went to conventions for self-care, and used strategies I learned in my own studies as a therapist to help me heal emotionally, and it helped superficially, but this deep sorrow I lived with, I couldn't shake.

I felt like the pain inside of me was killing me, but I didn't know how to fix it. Drinking helped, but it was taking its toll on me. My relationship with Lea continued to deteriorate after she moved into the rental house. We grew distant and didn't talk very often for years. I saw her each week when I picked up Sydney, but few words were ever exchanged in passing.

After returning from Yogaville and finishing the renovation on Lea's house, my mother's cancer became worse, and I shifted my focus to spending time with Mom and taking care of her. We spent a lot of time together, and she talked about the guilt and regret she felt as a mother. She tried her best to make up for her shortcomings through the years with each one of us kids. I think the years of carrying the guilt took a toll on her health. My sister Jenny and I enjoyed spending time with her and took her on mother-daughter trips. I traveled nearly every month from Virginia to Michigan to help Jenny take care of Mom as her health continued to decline until she died in May of 2017.

In September 2019, Brad left Lea for another woman, and she was devastated, but she didn't reach out to me or tell me he had left. I found out from Sydney during one of our weekend visits. When I saw Lea after hearing about it, I hugged her and told her I was sorry to hear about Brad leaving. She hugged me so tight, and I held her and let her cry in my arms, but after that conversation, she didn't talk to me about it again and remained distant. No matter how much I wanted it, we just couldn't seem to connect. We just seemed to always hurt each other. I know we didn't mean to, but the wounds that were buried deep within each of us, that we couldn't even see but were screaming for our attention, were too painful for us to touch. So, we continued to bury them, hoping we would feel better, but only continued to grow further apart.

CHAPTER 28

My hands were shaking, and my palms were sweaty. My stomach felt queasy. I had traveled three thousand miles and had climbed over a million emotions to get here. The preparation for this journey to Rythmia, in January 2020, to participate in the Ayahuasca ceremony was intense. But I had taken all the steps, followed all the instructions, and prepared my body, mind, and spirit for a journey with this powerful psychedelic medicine that could take the participant on a journey with the spirit of the plant Ayahuasca, which was known by some as Grandmother Ayahuasca, Grandmother Aya, and to others as Mama Ayahuasca or Mama Aya.

Prior to coming to Rythmia, I did some research about Ayahuasca, and once we arrived, the staff spent a lot of time preparing us for the journey prior to our first ceremony. I learned the set and setting was very important and that the medicine should only be done with a shaman in sacred ceremony. I had heard that one ceremony with this medicine can be more helpful than ten years of therapy. I learned Ayahuasca had been successful in the relief of depression, anxiety, alcohol and drug addiction, and various emotional and medical problems. We were told not to have any expectations of the journey because you don't always get what you want, but you always get what you need.

I learned that during an Ayahuasca journey, you can have visions, get auditory messages, see ancestors and loved ones who had passed on. Some people have reported being with God or other spiritual figures, leaving the planet and being out in space, or having encounters with alien beings, fairies, animals, and other beings. Some had experiences going back in time, visiting past lives, or seeing into the future. I learned people often gain profound insights, knowledge, and understandings in miraculous, unbelievable ways. I heard people describe the experience as if a portal opened to deeper levels of consciousness or spiritual dimensions. I learned the journey can be very intense and difficult at times, and this hallucinogenic medicine is very powerful and psychoactive. It isn't a journey that should be taken lightly, nor is it a journey for everyone.

I also learned through my research that this sacred medicine could provide a spiritual awakening and a personal transformation. And I was ready.

Here I was, finally in the jungle of Costa Rica, where I knew my spirit had been called, at Rythmia, getting ready to do something I could have never imagined in my life embarking upon. I had no idea where it was going to take me, I had no idea what was going to happen for me because I learned every experience is different and it works differently for every person, but I knew with every fiber in my soul this was what I had been searching for most of my life. I knew intuitively the answers I was seeking lie in the cup from the vine of this most powerful medicine from the jungles of the Amazon.

I stood in one of two lines, waiting my turn to drink the sacred medicine with nearly a hundred other participants, including physicians, nurses, psychotherapists, lawyers, business owners, executives, dancers, actors, spiritual leaders, and people from all walks of life. The cacophony of chants rang out, the smoke of sage billowed through the room, while beautiful music filled the maloca. We had spent the entire day before and all day this day preparing for this moment; what to expect, and to let go of any expectations; mind your own business. To be aware and understand, no matter how hard it gets, whatever is coming is going; let go and allow; set your intention; and to be sure to speak it into the cup.

It was my turn ... no turning back now. *I am ready!*

As I stepped face to face in front of the shaman, he looked into my eyes and asked, "Have you ever drank Ayahuasca before?"

"No ... this is my first time," I replied.

He was handed a shot glass by a volunteer, then reached for the medicine from one of two glass pitchers behind him and poured the medicine in the shot glass. He prayed over the medicine and blew air from his lungs into the shot glass. He handed me the medicine, and I took a deep breath, put the glass to my mouth, and spoke into the liquid below. "Mama Ayahuasca, I pray for you to show me who I have become."

This was one of three intentions Gerry, the founder of Rythmia and our teacher and instructor on this journey, had instructed us all week to use. And with that, I placed the glass to my lips and swallowed the dark, thick, murky liquid inside. The taste was strong and bitter. It tasted like molasses and black licorice with wooded tree bark–like particles and dirt swirled together. Quickly I swallowed it and knew there was no turning back now.

The room was filled wall to wall with at least a hundred twin-size mattresses, neatly lined up throughout the maloca. At the bottom of each mattress, carefully arranged, was a roll of toilet paper and a bucket to use for purging. I had taken extra precautions by wearing a Depends undergarment, because often when I puke, I pee all over myself. I learned purging was a way to rid the body of what was no longer serving it, and it wasn't uncommon to defecate all over yourself, so I wanted to try to save myself as much embarrassment as possible. I chose a mattress near the door wall of windows, so I could see the night sky. Beside me, near the mattress, I placed my journal, my backpack filled with extra pants, another Depends again just in case, my reading glasses, and my blanket. I stacked two thick, soft pillows behind my back and head, then lay on the mattress and prayed to Mama Ayahuasca, "Please come to me and open up every crack, crevice, and corner of my being and show me what I need to see in order to heal from the pain and agony I had been tormented with and carrying with me for nearly all the fifty years of my life."

We were told the medicine takes about thirty to forty-five minutes to begin and that sometimes Mama doesn't come. Sometimes because the participant didn't follow the *dieta* (the special diet), and other times for no known reason. I had spent much time, money, and effort to get here, and I so dearly wanted Mama to come and visit with me.

I lay back on the pillows and tried to relax and get comfortable and let go of my worries and my apprehensions. I placed the black eye mask I brought with me over my eyes to shut out the world and go inward ... deep into the depths of my soul. I allowed myself to drift into a deep meditation and focused on my breath. Time disappeared and no longer existed … and I invited Mama Aya to come and visit with me, then lay back and rested waiting for her arrival.

As I settled in on my mattress, I said a silent prayer. "I am ready, I am open, and I surrender! Show me who I have become!" I knew the next four days of ceremonies were ahead and prayed for healing. The rustling and preparation of the other participants getting settled into their beds could be heard as I pulled the covers over my body. The smell and smoke of sage filled the room. The lights were dim, and candles were lit around the altar and throughout the maloca.

A team of volunteers, who appeared like angels all dressed in white, swarmed around the room, preparing the space while guiding and giving instructions to the participants as needed. This brought a sense of comfort. Chairs for the volunteers lined the walls around the maloca in front of a sea of mattresses, so they could keep a watchful eye on us, should we need their assistance.

Thirty minutes after taking the medicine, echoes of yawns and puking filled the room. Tears began flowing out of my eyes for no apparent reason. As I reached for the roll of toilet paper at the end of my mattress, I began to yawn repeatedly, as I wiped the tears from my eyes. *Another form of purging*, I remembered as I plumped the pillows behind my head and grabbed a wad of toilet paper in my hand and continued to wipe the tears as they fell. I rested back into meditation, shutting out the racket from the others in the room. I fell deeper into meditation, as the sounds of the others rattled around me. Another reminder floated through my thoughts. *Mind your own business, no matter what else is going on around you.* I focused on my intention. "Mama, show me who I've become." The coolness of the room and the beauty of the music brought comfort, and I sank deeper inward.

Then suddenly, without warning, I felt a heavy warmth coming into my chest and throat as Mama Aya arrived to greet me. Anticipation and worry faded as I smiled and welcomed her. After six months of preparing, I felt honored I would finally meet her. I had no idea what I was in for, but I knew in my heart this was a necessary appointment. The smoke of sage continued to pour from a small pot held by a shaman as he made his way around the maloca. The music rang out as visions of geometric shapes and designs danced vividly in my mind.

Moans, groans, yawns, and puking echoed through the room as my mind faded into the visions that transformed rapidly inside my mind from various colors of checkerboard shapes to concentric circles, to sharp shards of thick black forms and zigzagged lines dancing to the rhythm of the music. Rapidly changing from geometric shapes to visions of toys scattered about with no logical rhyme or reason. A jack-in-the-box toy popped up out of nowhere, while swirls of colors and shapes of various patterns floated through space. So many toys and dolls laying in disarray. I started to get annoyed and aggravated by the constant barrage of toys.

Confusion filled my mind. *Why all these crazy toys? What is this about?* Just as that thought left, *just ask her* popped into my mind. Without words we spoke.

"Mama, why all these toys?"

"Your childhood was cut short, and you didn't have time to be a kid. I thought you'd enjoy some fun. You need to play more."

The message landed hard. Grief and sadness slapped me as I felt the loss of my childhood. I could hear her, but I couldn't see her. I knew Mama Aya was with me. Her presence was strong and powerful. She had authority over me and my journey.

Just like a drill instructor, she had my full attention. My wounds were profound and buried so deep that memory alone did not recall them. Although we had just met, my trust in her was complete. I surrendered as sensations flooded my body. She moved around inside of me like she was taking inventory of every part and checking every system, like a car mechanic when diagnosing a problem. My abdomen contorted as she swam around inside. I could feel her working on my lower chakras. First the root, then the sacral, and finally the solar plexus. My body winced in pain as she pushed on the area under my left rib that I had been so worried about for the past year. My hips shuffled back and forth, as my legs and spine were manipulated as if I was being adjusted by a chiropractor. Tears continued to stream down my face, soaking the eye mask over my eyes.

My intention played in the back of my mind like music in the background as she continued to work through my body. *Who have I become? What will she show me?* I speculated for only a second, then suddenly I was ushered off like Ebenezer Scrooge as she took me back to important memories and visions of various life experiences.

First stop, the ghettos of Detroit, facing the young man who had hurt me more than any other human being on this planet. I saw a little twelve-year-old girl who was thrusted into the world of adulthood at nine, thrown from pillar to post, abused and lost in the world, searching for love and someone who could rescue her.

Right on cue, Charlie arrived.

His shoulder-length blond hair hung in waves, and his blue eyes were piercing. He was fifteen, cocky, and cute. He looked like one of the heartthrob poster boys that hung on the bedroom wall of every teenage girl in the seventies and eighties. When he looked my way, his eyes softened as they penetrated me. My heart melted as oxytocin erupted inside, sending a consuming feeling I had never felt through every cell in my body. I felt like the most important person in the world as his eyes fell upon me. We came together as two broken people forged into a destiny fraught with pain and destruction. My heart beckoned back to that feeling of falling in love for the first time and all of those emotions that I felt for him. Then sadness rushed in from the pain of the hurt, rejection, judgment, violence, and abuse I endured.

I began to cry as these memories flooded in. *Why couldn't he love me? I loved him so much and tried so hard. Why did he hurt me constantly? Why was he so mean? Why did he make it his mission to denigrate me to our child and pour lasting poison in her mind against me? Why did he choose me if all I was going to be was his punching bag? Why?* I cried as I pondered these questions and relived the four years of agony and felt the broken-heartedness all over again of my sixteen-year-old self.

I heard Mama Aya whisper, "He feared your love and was jealous of you because he didn't think he was worthy of you, and he couldn't love you because he didn't love himself. He was hurt as a little boy, and he took his anger and pain out on you." As that message hung on the strings of my heart and the sadness settled in, quickly I flashed through time in the blink of an eye.

The next stop, the greatest heartache of my life. I arrived at Lea's bedside. She was grown, battered and broken down from a lifetime of shattered hopes. Her small, thinly weathered body lay curled up on her bed. Her beautiful ash-blonde curly hair was pulled up into a ponytail on her head, and tears flowed from her sad blue eyes. Sobs from her pain and sorrow were palpable. The pain of her suffering filled me with guilt and shame, as it took me back to a time when she was nearly three years old, and I left her with her grandmother.

I sobbed for her and the hell she endured in my absence. Her wounds were dark and deep. I felt them as though they were my own, and they consumed me. Her feeling of being lost, alone, rejected, abandoned, and misunderstood poured over me like ragged rocks tumbling from an avalanche. As those feelings faded, a rush of anger, hurt, and pain from being abandoned and rejected flooded me, and I doubled over in heartbreak.

As if that pain was not enough, another wave of regret, sadness, and shame for leaving her nearly consumed me. I could see my broken six-teen-year-old self mentally depleted, all odds against her, financially unstable, feeling so broken, suicidal, and hopeless, making a decision that would dig a wound so deep it would cost a lifetime of pain and suffering. The misery was unbearable, and I sobbed. I wished so many times that I could take back the decision to leave her when she was so little and needed me most. I wished I could go back and change things.

Right in front of me, I could see the damage my mistakes had caused her, and it was so painful. I recognized the years of reckless decisions she made were out of desperation for love and acceptance. Her anger and rejection toward me reminded me of Charlie, and I felt it all over again. I saw her entire life and the choices she made and how they pulled her down into poverty, turmoil, chaos, and hell. I looked at her and saw what I feared would have come of me if I had stayed with Charlie. I shuddered and felt as if I would collapse and had to turn away.

While still soaking in this piercing pain, instantly I saw my mother and felt her rejection when I needed her most, when I was fourteen years old, with a six-month-old little baby, when she told me she was moving to the suburbs with Ben, but I wasn't invited. The pain of that moment spilled over me like hot coals, and I sobbed.

Mama Aya showed me that my mother was abandoned herself at age three, when her father died, and again at fifteen, when her mother died. I could see clearly how the mother wound of abandonment, rejection, and needing love and finding it in all the wrong places was in our DNA and ran deep generationally, leaving a painful trail along the way.

Just as I was catching my breath and finding a moment of relief, I heard Mama Aya say, "You have another one you abandoned."

I felt like a dagger was going through my heart, and I began to tremble as I realized I wasn't going to hide anything from her.

My next destination, the second-worst decision and regret of my life. I grabbed my face and winced in anguish, trying to shield my eyes. I felt like I had hit a brick wall, and my knees felt like they were going to buckle beneath me. Sweat pooled up around my neck, and my breathing became labored. I could feel my body pulling back, hoping to disappear.

Just as I was pulling away and trying to shield myself from the pain, my son appeared before me. I couldn't believe my eyes. He was beautiful and perfect. He greeted me with love and sadness. I wondered what his name was, and instantly he said to me, "Zander," and I knew that was right. He was two or three years old. So innocent and small. I could feel so much love and pain as his eyes gazed into mine.

"Why didn't you have me, Mommy? You didn't even give me a chance."

Waves of pain rattled through my body like a machine gun ripping through my flesh, tearing my heart to pieces. I gasped and wailed in anguish. I could feel the pain and suffering coming from my two children simultaneously for the loss of the mother they longed for but never got.

What a terrible, awful mother I am. I felt like the worst piece of shit on the planet. The pain was more than I thought I could bear. I felt the weight of my heart crushing in on top of me, and I didn't think I would survive the pain. The medicine inside of my gut swirled around like rotten sewage. Water filled my mouth, and I knew I had to puke. I raised up so quickly, it felt as though I levitated to the end of the mattress and grabbed my bucket and began to puke from the depths of my soul, screaming out a wail that could peel the paint off the walls. In an instant, four volunteers and a shaman were standing all around me fanning me and spewing water all over me from a bottle of sacred potion they carried with them. I continued to puke profusely, and I didn't think it would ever end.

The shaman sang and chanted over me until the violent episode of purging subsided. I remembered the instructions from the training and looked into the bucket and asked, "What is this?"

Instantly I heard, "This is the pain and sorrow from a lifetime of guilt, shame, and blame that you have been carrying under your left rib for your children. It has been calling for your attention."

I let out a huge sigh of gratitude, then curled up into a fetal position on my mattress and continued to cry. A beautiful volunteer, with long black hair sat with me, handing me tissues to wipe my tears. She nurtured me, like a loving mother comforting her wounded child. I didn't feel like I deserved her kindness, but I was grateful she was so loving and kind to me. I had never felt so much emotional pain in all my life. I welcomed her gentle touch and warm spirit. Individually, Zander then Lea came to me, and I wailed as I thought about the misfortune of them having me as their mother. I lay in my misery.

Zander came over to me, and I peered into his little face and wept. I thought back to the time in the fall of 1999 when I got pregnant with him, soon after we arrived in Virginia. Tom and I were in a bad place in our relationship, and he had just told me he wanted to separate and was leaving to return to Michigan. We talked about the pregnancy, and we both knew that this was not the time for us to have a child. I thought long and hard about it, but after everything I had been through with Lea, I just didn't have the strength to have a child, especially if Tom and I weren't staying together. We agreed that it was best to terminate the pregnancy.

The anguish I felt as I stared at this beautiful little boy consumed me with grief, shame, and guilt. I looked at him and said, "I am so, so, so sorry!" I couldn't even ask him to forgive me, I was so ashamed.

Yet without hesitation he looked at me. "I forgive you, Mommy!"

"Oh my God!" My gut curdling, I shouted out in pain and regret. "How could I have done this to you? I didn't even give you a chance. I am so sorry," I moaned.

The reality of this grave decision pierced me, and I wailed in horror and regret. He came over and curled up next to me to comfort me as I cried. He transformed into a little baby and began to breastfeed and allowed me to nurture him. I held him so close and loved him with every ounce of my being and felt gratitude and unbelievable joy.

I lingered there with him for a little while.

Then I went to Lea and tried to nurture her.

She stood with her arms folded tightly in front of her, with her brow furrowed and her eyes piercing me. I could feel her anger and broken heart, and I crumbled in sorrow. I tried to reach for her, but she turned away from me and wouldn't let me come near her. I could feel her feelings as if they were my own. She didn't trust me and couldn't allow me to hurt her again. I could feel that she felt everything in my life was more important to me than her. She never felt loved and accepted by me for who she truly was. I could feel how much I had hurt her. I was engulfed in sorrow, regret, and pain from the hell I had caused her. I loved her so much, but I didn't know how to love her.

This wound ran deep and was too painful to face. I squirmed and contorted, trying to escape it, but the more I tried to run, the worse it felt. I lay in my misery, grieving for her and bore the pain of the difficult decisions I had made.

I wouldn't find any relief or comfort from Lea. There was no chance she was going to let me get close to her. This wound was far too deep and would take much more time and effort to heal.

There was a call for another cup of medicine.

We were told if we heard the call, then we should drink, not think. So, I called for support to get help to go back up and get another cup, then returned to my mattress. It wasn't long and I was back in the medicine.

My grandmother Dezzy came to me. She was my mother's mom and was part Cherokee Indian, which I felt deeply in my DNA and knew this tribal blood ran thick within me. I even consider that this heritage drew my soul to this sacred medicine journey.

I had never met her; she had died before I was born, but I recognized her. She took me by the hand and led me out to the top of a large hill and said, "You are the one we have been waiting for. You have come to heal the generational curse." She took her hand and waved it and showed me seven generations behind me and seven generations in front of me. I could see her, my mother, and the many women from generations past who let men dominate and destroy them. I could see they were weak and broken down from the abuse. I could also see Lea and Sydney and the generations ahead of them. She said, "Angel, you are very strong and have come to carry these wounds, so we may all heal. When you heal, we all can heal."

I knew instantly this was what had called me here, and I knew this was my purpose. I came to heal so we all could have the opportunity to heal.

As soon as she said this, she was gone. Then Jesus came to me. He asked me to follow him to the cave where he spent forty days and forty nights and was tempted by the devil. I could feel the struggle he had with Satan as he offered him the whole world. He then took me out on the edge of the world, and I could see everything. He showed me all the material things of the world, and he showed me how they seduce us.

I told Jesus I struggled with all the material things I had accumulated and had put before my kids, out of my need to feel secure and helpless as a young girl. I told him I had everything materially I ever wanted, but I wasn't happy, and I felt an emptiness inside.

He looked at me and said, "The devil is our ego, and there is an ongoing struggle within us between the material and the spiritual. You can have both if you understand which one is the master and which one is the servant. Don't let the material own you." He then looked at me with compassion and said, "You are a healer and a warrior. You came into this world to help others find their way to healing. Don't get caught up in the material things of this world."

Next during this Ayahuasca journey, I arrived at the VA Hospital in Salem, Virginia, next to the bedside of Daddy as he was dying. After Hazel came into my dad's life, I lost him. When he was sick and dying of cancer, I tried to visit, but she made my every trip hell. I didn't go visit him when he was near death because I was angry with him over how he let Hazel treat me, and he died without me seeing him again. Mama Aya took me to his bedside so I could reconcile with him.

We talked about the pain I had carried over the rejection I felt by him over Hazel. I told him I didn't come to see him before he died because I was angry but I regretted it. We connected, and I felt our love deeply, and we forgave each other for any past pain and hurt that was caused. I held his hand as he was dying and was there with him as he took his last breath. I felt comfort in knowing he wasn't alone when he died, and it made my heart feel loved and complete. The message "Hurt people, hurt people" came to me and I knew this is what had happened not only between me and my dad, but also between me and Lea.

At this point, I needed fresh air. I decided to go outside and lie down on a bench. The sky was clear, and I could see a million stars flickering through the darkness. The beauty of the night sky was spectacular.

Downloads started coming in from Mama Aya, and my intention came to the surface. "Who have I become?

"I am love.

"I am strong.

"I am independent.

"I am a creator and visionary.

"I am a healer.

"I am a helper.

"I am a mother who is deeply wounded.

"I am hiding and reclusive because of my pain.

"I became like my parents. They rejected me, I rejected my children, and I rejected myself.

"I medicate my pain with alcohol.

"I am a warrior."

I leaned into her messages, and I could accept it. So much information and pain, yet it all felt so necessary.

Over the next three days of ceremonies at Rythmia with Mama Ayahuasca, she sent me back to see Lea again.

Lea was lying in her bed, so broken-hearted because her husband, Brad, had left her for another woman, just like Charlie had done to me. She tried so hard to love him. She tried so hard to fix and rescue him, but he disappointed her at every turn. I could feel her pain; for hours I lay and felt the rejection, disappointment, blame, shame, guilt, disgust, regret, loss, grief, and all her emotions as if they were my own. I cried over Brad leaving her and wallowed in her sadness. All the pain I felt when Charlie left me rushed back in, and I cried for Lea and for my younger self. It was sheer torment.

Jesus came to me and said, "I am the light. Come and walk with me." I wanted to go, but I couldn't leave Lea and chose to stay in her suffering rather than go into the light. I felt like I needed to fix this for her. I blamed myself and felt like it was all my fault. I could not stand to see her suffering so much, so I tried to take it from her.

Jesus looked at me in my suffering and said, "When you fix you, she can heal."

When I returned home, I struggled transitioning back into my life. For weeks I was unsettled and couldn't rest. I needed help but didn't know where to turn. There was no integration aftercare program at Rythmia, and I needed help. I felt the need for a tribe, but I didn't know where to look. I didn't know anyone who had done Ayahuasca and didn't know where to turn. I could now relate with that client who needed help so long ago who had gone to Ecuador to do Ayahuasca, which at the time I thought was crazy.

The life I left before going to Costa Rica was not the same when I returned, because I was not the same. I was still trying to process every-thing that was downloaded, and I still struggled with Lea. I had reached out to her twice while I was in Costa Rica, and it didn't go well. I came to her with humility, but she was rejecting and wouldn't or couldn't hear me, and we clashed. I could see right away how strong her ego and anger were and her need to tell me what she knew, rather than listen. I left both conversations feeling exhausted and defeated.

While I was in Costa Rica, I realized that as long as Lea and I were in a financial situation, we could never heal our relationship. Shortly after I returned, I told her she needed to buy the house she was renting from me. I told her over the next year she needed to talk to the bank and figure out what she needed to do to get a mortgage, so we could get out of this financial relationship with one another, so we both could heal. I also felt she would feel better buying the house and ending this complex financial situation with me that wasn't going well. I also told her if she couldn't buy the house, she needed to move somewhere else. I felt that a year was plenty of time for her to work through this. She agreed she would work on her credit score and talk to the bank.

Over the next month, the call to return to Mama Aya was strong. I knew I had to go back; there was still some unfinished business. I started looking into retreats. I invited Tom to go with me, and we found a place in Peru called Arkana. I booked our trip for May 2020. When I returned from Costa Rica at the end of January 2020, I heard a lot of chatter about a virus in China that sounded scary, but just like the bird flu and the others, I didn't pay much attention. Then, right after I booked my Peru trip, the world shut down due to the COVID pandemic. I thought it would only be for a few weeks and by May, surely things would be back to normal and fall back into place. Of course, that didn't happen, and I had to postpone my trip. I was disappointed and sad. But I knew as soon as it was possible, I had to return to see her.

By January of 2021, after the election, the world seemed to have gone crazy, and it felt like our world would never return to normal again. It was as if the January before in 2020, I got on a plane to Costa Rica to do my first Ayahuasca journey, and the world, inside and out, forever changed. I was at a very low point, and I was searching for answers. I knew I needed to return to see Mama Aya. I got online and found a place in Orlando, Florida, and decided I needed to go right away.

In November, right after the election, I had reconnected with my very close friend Briget, who I hadn't seen in seven years. During our conversation, I told her that I had gone to see Mama Aya and was looking to return for a ceremony. She told me if I found something in the United States, she would go. When I told her about the place in Florida offering weekend ceremonies, she agreed to take the trip with me. We scheduled our trip for early February 2021. I couldn't wait to see Mama again.

My trip to Rythmia was luxurious; the trip to the place in Florida was more primitive, but after having been locked down for a year, I was so happy we were able to even travel to do medicine again. I had learned so much during my last journey, but I knew my healing was not complete. I needed to continue to find the answers I needed to heal. We signed up for a women's-only ceremony, with only twenty-five participants, which was small and intimate, unlike the one hundred participants at Rythmia. During this trip, I got the opportunity to visit Mama Aya during three ceremonies over two days.

The third and final ceremony was the most challenging. We stood in line to get our medicine, and I could feel a little bit of nervousness welling up inside of me. I noticed it and dismissed it. There were some new faces in the group who weren't here the night before and other faces missing that were. One new girl who was a new arrival seemed rambunctious and lively. I noticed her but tried to concentrate inward. I sat down on my mat after receiving my medicine and prayed into the cup. "Show me what I need to heal."

I had such a beautiful journey during the day ceremony, I was hoping Mama Aya would bring more of the beauty, light, and love that I enjoyed just a few hours earlier. The time came to drink our dose, I took a deep breath, held my nose to keep from tasting the nastiness inside, and down it went. Shivers ran through me at the taste, and I took a sip of water to rinse out the remnants. *I will never get used to the awful bitter taste*, I thought. Then on my mat I went.

Mama Aya came again as the music played. And instantly it started off with a deep feeling of sadness. I could tell she was coming this time to get my attention. It was awful. She brought up Lea again. I argued with her, "I thought we went through this already. Not this again." I learned quickly; you can't fight Mama Aya. She always wins.

While in this medicine journey with Mama Aya, she began to show me Lea's life, and all I could see was how awful it was. She showed me how Lea couldn't get her life together. She wouldn't work a regular job that made enough to sustain herself, and I felt frustrated with her. People were screaming and struggling all around me. The rambunctious lady was screaming and was naked by the fire, and I thought for sure she was going to jump into it. I kept getting distracted and worrying about everyone else. I forgot what I had learned at Rythmia, to mind my own business. I was easily distracted and pulled into everything around me.

The guilt, shame, pain, and disgust I felt over Lea's decisions, over my decisions, and how she just could not grow up and be an adult, kept rolling over and over in my mind. I was angry at her and at myself. I blamed myself for her pain, and I blamed her for not getting the help she needed. I felt if she could get her life together, I could stop hurting.

I reflected on how much I helped her, and no matter how much I did, gave, bought, or tried to fix things, it didn't help at all. In fact, it made things worse. Our relationship was strained and had been for years. Especially since the moment I bought the house for her to rent. I was optimistic that it would launch Lea into a stable and comfortable life.

But the house strained our relationship and enabled her and Brad from getting their lives together.

Now Brad had left her, and she was so defeated. I felt I had to help her because of Sydney. I didn't want Sydney to suffer because her parents couldn't get their lives together. I wanted Sydney to have a stable place to live, but I was tired of being in this financial relationship with Lea, and I was tired of being aggravated by this all the time. I went over and over and over and over in my head why this wasn't working. I wondered, *Why can't they see this opportunity and do something to better their lives?* It was exhausting, and I felt frustrated and disappointed in her—and extremely aggravated and agitated that I was dealing with this again.

I couldn't handle it. I called for the volunteers to come help me. Norelle, a beautiful volunteer, came, and I asked if she could make it stop. She encouraged me to stay with it and work through what Mama was teaching me, but it was way too painful, and I couldn't handle it. They offered to give me Hape', a sacred tobacco medicine that helps to ease the negative feedback loops, but I refused it. I was firm that I just wanted it to end. I wanted to get as far away from the endless torture of the negative bombardment of emotions as I could as quickly as possible. It was too awful to bear. She brought me a lemon and some salt and had me suck on it, and soon, I started coming out of the medicine. I took some time to gather my thoughts and went and sat by the fire.

I was still struggling, but it wasn't as intense. I blamed myself for helping so much and for so long, creating learned helplessness and keeping Lea from helping herself. I recognized I had enabled her and kept her from moving forward. I wondered, *Why can't she just get her shit together?* I felt so much anger toward her. I felt like she punished me all the time.

What I would later see more clearly was being in a codependent relationship and being an empath, I wanted so badly to fix her because I felt her pain like it was my own. When she hurt, I hurt. And I wanted to stop hurting. I eventually was able to see more clearly that helping in codependency is often the sunny side of control. I wanted to help or control the situation so Lea and Sydney would feel better, so I could finally feel better about the shame, guilt, and self-judgment I was carrying around. But at this point, I still couldn't see it.

Prior to coming on this trip, I contacted Lea and reminded her she needed to get a loan and buy the house, or she would have to move out in four months, on the first of May, when her lease ended. She seemed shocked. She argued that she had paid her rent on time all year for the first time. I reminded her I had told her the year before that I wanted out of this financial relationship with her. I wanted her to buy the house, but she refused to take the necessary steps to do it. With the interest rates so low, her payment would have only been around $350 per month. Way less than her rent, but she had resistance. I am not sure if she didn't have the confidence to buy the house, didn't value homeownership, felt scared to take on this responsibility, felt more comfortable living in chaos and poverty, wanted to punish me, didn't feel like she deserved the house, or if she felt I owed the house to her. I just didn't understand or comprehend it. I was just so tired of it all. It made me feel awful, and I knew as long as we were in this financial relationship, we could never heal our relationship. It made me feel really frustrated, taken advantage of, and angry.

But I wanted out of this crazy, dysfunctional, codependent situation with her.

I sat by the fire and felt the heat of anger boiling inside of me.

One of the volunteers named Vanessa, who was a divine angel, came and sat with me and let me process my feelings. She told me I was very judgmental toward Lea. I asked how could I not be? I felt annoyed that she said that to me. How could I not feel judgmental? I felt justified in being judgmental toward her. I didn't have much compassion at all for Lea. I was way too angry. I tried to make my case to Vanessa for all the things I had done to help Lea, and all I got back was pain and disappointment. She challenged and worked with me for over an hour, allowing me to process, and I still couldn't shift. The anger I felt was very deep. It would be another two years of working through my healing before I could really see how I was projecting the judgment I had toward myself onto Lea.

I tried to lie down and sleep, but Mama Aya wouldn't let me. I was so aggravated and frustrated that I was dealing with Lea all night. I regretted doing this third ceremony, after having such a wonderful ceremony during the day.

When I couldn't sleep, I got back up and sat with some other volunteers and bitched some more about Lea. I explained how much I had helped her and how I just kept on helping her, like it was an addiction. And no matter how much I helped, things only got worse. One of the volunteers told me I needed to stop helping. She told me her mother threw her out when she was twenty-four, and she had to sleep in her car, but it was the best thing that ever happened to her.

I knew from my own experience as a teen. No one was there to help me. I had to learn young how to survive on my own. That experience taught me to be self-reliant and independent. It drove me to never be in that situation again. I worked hard to overcome poverty because of being on my own so young. I was driven to never be poor or dependent on anyone else. I would have appreciated someone helping me and giving me a hand up.

The night was long, and I didn't sleep at all.

When I returned home from this ceremony, I began doing some integration groups that were offered by the Ayahuasca center in Florida, and met my coach, Penny. We worked together for months, and she helped me very much. One day she told me about a Shadow Ceremony that was offered at the same center, and she thought it would help me work through the shadows, those places within that we hide, deny, and repress, I was still struggling with, especially with Lea. In October 2021, I went back to Florida for the Shadow Ceremony and met Steven Twohig and the Shadow Tribe. It was an amazing experience of healing without psychedelic medicine.

During this healing journey, I uncovered the depths of my broken heart. I found a part of myself, a little girl, who got lost and stuck back in those early years, who was so hurt and broken-hearted, who was waiting for someone to see her.

I learned during my healing journey inward during the ceremony that it was my mother's lack of protection and support for me after her divorce from my dad that crushed me. My mom got lost in herself and survival, and I was a casualty of her wounds.

I touched a deep part of my shadow, a part of me that I had repressed, hidden, and denied and wasn't consciously aware of. I learned so much about myself through the Shadow Tribe and Steven Twohig. It introduced me to a tribe of people who I connected with in a deep way, and their love and support through my journey was medicine for my healing. Steven's knowledge and genius were instrumental in helping me reach back and help heal the wounded child within and helped me recognize so many healing truths about projection and how every trigger within begins and ends with the one who carries it. Therefore, if I am triggered, it's about me; if you are triggered, it is about you. I learned the outside world is just a reflection of our inner world.

This tribe became my family, and I was able to find true unconditional love and acceptance unlike anything I had experienced in a family before. They saw me for who I truly am, and I trusted them.

Many years earlier, in 2016, when I was struggling and went to Yogaville looking for answers and healing, I met the beautiful Swami Arivananda. I asked her to pray and give me a spiritual name. She was very humbled by my request, and a few days later, she got back to me and gave me the name Premanjali. I tried for years to let the name settle in, but it didn't quite fit. After returning from my Ayahuasca journey in Florida, I prayed about it. One night I woke up, and God came to me and said, "Your new name is Anjalia." It is pronounced On ja lea.

"Ah ha! That's it! Thank you, God!" Immediately I knew it was right. I knew I was transitioning from the person I had been.

During my early years of life, I was called Angel. She was a tough young girl who was a fighter and a survivor. After I met Tom and began college, I became Angela. She was a driven, ambitious overachiever and a dynamic creator who built an empire from her strength and determination, and now I was transitioning again into my true higher, wiser spiritual self, and Anjalia was the perfect fit.

I knew all the parts of me were going to still be within me, but I was ready to move in a new direction. It was scary to think about changing my name, but it was time, and I found a tribe who genuinely loved me. I asked them if I could take on my new name with them before I introduced it to the world, and they were very supportive. It gave me a safe space to transition into who I was becoming.

In May 2022, I returned to Florida for another journey with Mama Aya. I had spent a lot of time working on myself and integrating the messages, lessons, insights, and downloads from the work I had gained from the previous journeys with her. I still felt there was more work and knowledge I needed to heal. I could feel Mama Aya calling me back to her, and she was much gentler with me this time. I took a moment to acknowledge how I was here doing all this inner healing around the mother wound with a plant medicine called Mama Ayahuasca. And what a healing mother she is. Tears welled and I took a little time to revere her with my gratitude.

She came to me this time like a loving mother with comfort and compassion and showed me how much I had grown since my first encounter with her, nearly two and a half years earlier.

She showed me how much I am loved and how much good I have done in my life, especially in my granddaughter Sydney's life. I told her I carried a lot of guilt for not being a better mother to Lea and blamed myself over the struggles Sydney endured because her mom is so wounded because of the mistakes I had made. Jesus was with Mama Aya, and they both said to me, "You must stop trying to help Lea and Sydney, unless they ask you for your help. Don't help them! You are disempowering them by continuing to try to fix things for them. You are the problem in this situation." *Oh my God, I am the problem, yet I keep feeding it. Why? Why can't I stop doing this?* "You must get out of their way. You need to leave them alone." I allowed it to sink in, but it was difficult.

Then I heard Mama Aya again. "You rob others of their gift of giving because you don't know how to receive."

"I know, Mama Aya; it is just so hard for me to receive." I remembered when I was young and poor in Detroit, if I was given anything, I was always made to feel like I owed someone something for it.

Just as that realization came through, a beautiful volunteer named Grace came and gave me so much love, and I was able to receive it. It was so beautiful. As soon as Grace left, I could hear my inner child crying for me. Mama Aya said, "Stop letting her hurt. Go to her and nurture her." I spent time hugging my inner child.

Then Mama Aya said, "If you give a gift, give it without expectations or attachment. If you are giving an opportunity that has strings attached, you need to be clear of the expectations. This is where the confusion happens. You must ask, how can I give this gift without you feeling like you owe me? And if you are offering an opportunity, be clear and say, this is an opportunity, and here are the terms."

Jesus then said to me, "There is nothing greater than a mother's love. Show that love to Lea."

"I try, Lord. She doesn't accept it. I don't know what I am doing wrong."

"You can't take Lea's suffering away, no matter how hard you try. This is her journey. Just let her know you are here for her when she is ready. You are light and love. Your vibration in a relationship must match, or it won't work. You can only show up with your light and love, and if someone doesn't accept it, it just means they are not ready or able to accept it yet. Send her love and move on. When she is ready, she will find you. You can't pull anyone up unless they want to vibrate higher."

I took in the information but still felt sad for her. It was hard to accept that I couldn't fix it, and it would take more time for me to really hear and own the messages that I was given.

CHAPTER 29

In the fall of 2023, I took a much-needed trip to one of my favorite places in the world, Sedona, Arizona. It had been a long year of healing, and I had been through so much. I knew I needed some time away to reflect and do some more healing. There was a continuing education program being offered at Mago Retreat Center on Dr. Dick Schwartz's Internal Family Systems Theory for six days, and I thought, *this is the perfect time and place for me.*

The past six months weighed heavily on me. Things were swirling around I thought I had healed, but somehow my need to help took me right back into another difficult situation with Sydney. Old patterns die hard for sure, and this one had been with me since early adulthood, nearly thirty-five years. I had gone down this road many times. Always with good intentions and with a big heart, but nearly always steeped with a lesson for me to learn, most often, the hard way.

The past year had brought about a lot of challenges that had come from some deeper healings I had experienced earlier through my plant medicine and integration work, including the Shadow work I had been doing. In the spring of 2021, when the deadline for Lea to move out was fast approaching, Sydney was visiting and broke down and cried over having to move out of the house. It broke my heart. She had been through so much with her parents' separation. I felt terrible for her. I wrestled all night and couldn't sleep, thinking about how devastated she was. The next morning, I asked Sydney to go to breakfast so we could have an adult conversation. I had never talked to Sydney before about her parents in an open, adult way, but I felt I needed to have this conversation under the circumstances.

"Sydney, I don't want to have to make you move. It breaks my heart we are in this situation. I have tried everything to help your mom, but it isn't helping. It just seems to make mine and your mom's relationship more difficult."

"I know, Grammie. Mom has been struggling since Dad left, and I have had to take care of her a lot. She just cries all the time and can't seem to pull herself together."

"I am so sorry, Sydney; I hate that your mom is struggling. I don't know what to do. I want better for you. I just want to help you get through high school and into college, so you can have a better life. If you would agree to stay focused in school, go to college, and not go down the same road as your parents, I will talk to your mom and try to work something out so the two of you can stay in the house till you graduate high school. But I can't make any promises; all I can do is try."

"Oh, Grammie, that would really mean so much to me."

"Okay. I love you, girl!"

"I love you too, Grammie."

I contacted Lea and told her I would agree to let them stay, but we had to make a new lease with a rent increase to cover the improvements on the house that were made and the tax increases. I agreed to a two-year lease, which would take her through to Sydney's graduation, then they would have to move or buy the house. I emphasized, "The rent must be paid on time, or I will have to evict you, and when the lease is up, you will need to buy the house or move. I want out of this financial relationship. Do you understand?"

"Yes, Mom, I can do that. I really appreciate it."

"No problem, just get yourself together. I want you to feel better and for you to move in a better direction."

"I know, Mom."

We signed the new lease. After the initial first month's rent, she paid rent two more times and never paid again. She found out that due to COVID, you didn't have to pay your rent, and you could have your landlord apply for a government program, and they would pay your rent. I was so angry with her for not following through on our agreement—again. I was mad at myself for giving her another chance, and I was very frustrated having to deal with this government program. I did everything the program asked, then got a letter that they were changing their system, and I had to reapply in this new system. I did what they asked a second time, then got a letter saying they needed more information. For nearly a year, I tried to jump through all their hoops, but it never went through.

Finally in September 2022, when the program ended and there were no funds left, and I never got paid, I sent Lea a letter, letting her know I would be filing for eviction beginning in October, due to unpaid rent for thirteen months. I didn't get a response from her.

I finally got an eviction trial date set for late December, but due to circumstances I was unaware of and some new paperwork they required, we had to reschedule the date for February 2023. This whole process was heartbreaking to me. Lea seemed to be intentionally defiant and incompliant, and it broke my heart to have to evict her and Sydney, just a few months before Syndey's graduation, leaving them nowhere to go.

Not only was Lea not paying rent, but she also let Sydney's boyfriend move in with them. I just couldn't understand why she was making the decisions she was making. It seemed like she was intentionally being disrespectful and trying to hurt me. I felt like she didn't care at all about my feelings. She had what seemed to me to be an attitude that I was rich and I owed this house to her, and was mad that I made things so hard for her. I was so tired of being in this codependent relationship where I tried to help, took on all the responsibilities and consequences, and she got all the benefits and none of the responsibilities or consequences.

Finally in February 2023, we went to court, and she was evicted.

Lea had started dating a guy named John and made plans to move in with him. Sydney didn't like John and didn't want to go live with her mother at his house. So, I asked her if she wanted to come stay with me until she finished high school in May. The plan was that after graduation, she would go to college, and I wanted to help her have the best opportunity and pathway forward as possible.

Sydney moved in with me, and at first, everything was good. But soon things started to shift. It seemed as if Sydney didn't want to be there. It seemed it didn't feel like home to her, and we had rules she wasn't used to following. We had a large house, and the entire basement was finished, with a bedroom, living room, dining room, bathroom, and kitchenette. It was like having her own apartment. All we asked was for her to keep it clean. But she seemed unhappy, withdrawn, and avoided me and Tom most of the time. I figured this had to do with being a teenager, and I could tell she was struggling with some depression and encouraged her to see a counselor, but she chose not to.

I gave her a lot of leeway because she had been through so much, and I knew losing her home and having to be uprooted was devastating. I overlooked a lot of things and just tried to be supportive while she worked on finishing high school.

In July she had made plans to have her online best friend, Kaylee, who lived in South Carolina, come and stay two weeks with us for her eighteenth birthday present. We agreed to drive down and pick her up and take her back. This seemed to perk her up and gave her something to look forward to.

I left her on her own to hang out with her friend and didn't bother them while she was visiting. Then one day I went down to check on them and found the entire basement a complete mess. You couldn't see the floor, the countertop, or the table. There were food wrappers everywhere, half-full beverages on our new couch, the trash was overflowing, and it looked like a garbage dump. I was stunned. "Sydney what in the hell has happened down here?" She cocked her head with attitude and stared at me. I clenched my jaw and said, "After all I have done for you, Sydney, I can't believe this mess. Please get it cleaned up!"

She stared at me then rolled her eyes and reacted flippantly toward me. "I hate when you say, 'After all you have done for me.' It makes me mad, Gram."

"Well, Sydney, it is hard for me to believe the condition of this place. Please get it cleaned up." I had never seen her act this way in her whole life. I was stunned. I didn't want to embarrass her in front of her friend, so I let it go, but later let her know we needed to meet with her.

During the meeting, we told her we could tell something was wrong and asked her if she was struggling with going to college. She told us nothing was wrong and that she had to go to college if she wanted to have the lifestyle she wanted. We told her there were other options, but college would give her the best opportunities and that college could be a lot of fun once she got started and met some people there.

We encouraged her to live on campus, but she let us know she absolutely didn't want to live on campus. We discussed our expectations for her living with us and for keeping her space clean. She agreed to comply, and we left the meeting feeling like we were moving in a positive direction.

The next week, right before college was set to start, we sat down with Sydney and discussed getting her a car. She had no way to get to college every day unless we drove her, and with Tom's and my busy schedule, it didn't seem practical. I had saved for years for Sydney to go to college, and since she had done so well in high school and received a full-ride scholarship to Radford University, the money was available to help with a car.

Six months earlier, we had helped her get a car at a small dealership for $5,600, and within two weeks of getting the car, the engine seized up because it didn't have any oil in it. We were all very disappointed, especially Sydney. When Tom and I discussed helping Sydney get another car, we looked at better used cars in the area. The prices were outrageous for used cars that had less than 100,000 miles on them, and they didn't come with a warranty. We rationalized that we had $8,000 to put down on the car. With help from Sydney's scholarship, she could put in $2,000, and we could get the payment down to under $300, and she could have a brand-new car with a full warranty that would last her for years, and she would have her own car to get back and forth to college. In my mind, I rationalized that getting this car was a different situation with Sydney than the one with Lea.

We researched the most dependable, affordable new car on the market and found Toyota Corollas were ranked the most reliable car in our price range. I remembered what Mama Aya had told me about gifts and opportunities. So, when we discussed getting the car with Sydney, we explained this car was an opportunity, not a gift. We told her if she went to college and kept her GPA up to retain her scholarship, we would pay half of the car payment and insurance, and she could pay half with the money she had left over each semester from her scholarship. We felt like it could be a winning situation for her. We also told her if she decided not to go to college, she would need to get a job and take over the payments, or we would take the car back and sell it. No questions asked. She agreed and seemed excited about getting a new car.

College began a few weeks later, and we were excited for Sydney.

However, within a few weeks of college starting, I could tell something was off. Sydney wasn't getting up for her morning classes. When I asked her about it, she told me they offered online classroom attendance. I didn't want to micromanage, so I didn't pry, but I had concerns.

She started staying out until 2 a.m. and avoiding us more and more. When I asked her about it, she said she hated school, but she was going to make it through it because she had to. I told her again she didn't have to go to college, there were other options, but since she started the semester, it was best for her to finish it, and if she needed to take a break or consider other options after the semester ended, she could. This way she wouldn't burn any bridges. I also encouraged her to think hard about the decisions she was making. "Sydney, you are standing at a crossroads, and there are two paths you can go down. You can work nine to five for someone else in a low-paying job that you are not passionate about, or you can go to college and have a career that opens a lot of doors for you, doing something you love and enjoy. But ultimately the choice is yours."

"I don't want to talk about this, Grammie. Talking about school makes me mad and stresses me out."

"Okay. I am just trying to help you think about your options." I could tell things were not going well. Her living space continued to deteriorate, she stopped keeping herself up, she looked tired and overwhelmed, and anytime I tried to say anything, it didn't go well. She left and didn't say goodbye and wouldn't come home until we were in bed.

One morning in early October, I was having my coffee. I looked out our front window and noticed her car was six feet from the curb, and it was wrecked. I went out and looked at the car, and from bumper to bumper, down both sides of the car, it was damaged from end to end. *Oh my God, what has happened here?* I went down to her room and knocked on the door.

"What?"

"Sydney, what happened last night? Your car is wrecked?"

"I don't know. I don't remember."

"What do you mean, you don't remember? Were you drinking and driving or high? The car is sitting six feet out in the road, and it is wrecked. Did you hit someone?"

"I don't know. I don't want to talk about this right now."

"Sydney, we have to talk about this."

"Okay, when I get up."

"Ugh!" I left worried and went upstairs and told Tom.

"What do you mean she doesn't remember what happened?"

"I don't know, that's what she said."

He gave her a little time and then went down to talk to her. "What happened to the car, Sydney? Grammie said you can't remember what happened? That is very concerning."

"Poppy, I was asleep when Grammie came down here, and I was scared. I wrecked my car last night taking my friend home. She lives down a country dirt road, and it was dark. When I was trying to back out of her driveway, I couldn't see and backed in between two trees. I am so sorry."

"Okay. Well, that makes better sense. You need to be honest with us. We will get the car fixed. I will have Grammie call and have it put into the shop."

"Does it have to go in the shop, Poppy? It drives just fine."

"Yes, Sydney, the car has to be fixed. It is a brand-new car, and you have insurance. The car is getting fixed. You understand."

"Okay."

Later, when things calmed down, we had a long discussion about her lying and about school. We told her we knew she was struggling, and if she didn't want to go to college, we would support her in making some different decisions, and again I told her she needed to finish up this semester.

She responded, "I need to go to college; this is the only option I have."

She told us she was passing and doing well in her classes and needed to finish school. I offered to help her look at classes for next semester that might fit better in her life and that were offered later in the day, rather than having morning classes, since she didn't like getting up so early.

"Yeah, Gram, that's a good idea. That would be very helpful."

"Great, we are always here to help you. I know you are going through a lot, and I know this accident was scary, but it's okay. It happens. We will get the car fixed. We love you."

"I love you all too."

Sydney continued to distance herself from us, and one day she came home, cleaned the entire basement, then came upstairs with her bags packed and said she was going to stay with her dad and his girlfriend for a while and left.

Just before I left for Sedona, we took the car in for the repairs.

During my stay at Mago in Sedona, I did an energy healing with one of the Master Healers there. I wasn't sure what I was signing up for, but I was told it was an amazing service, so I agreed. It was a cool afternoon when I arrived for my session. I waited in the meeting area for the Master to arrive. I spent some time contemplating what I wanted to heal. I had already done so much healing over the past nearly four years with my plant medicine and with Shadow work, but I knew there was still a bit more left to conquer.

What lay heaviest on my heart was the situation with Sydney. I hated to think about having to take the car back. It broke my heart. I had learned while I was at Mago that she had dropped out of college, and I knew we were going to have to talk about it when I got home. I instantly regretted cosigning for the car. I didn't know what to do to resolve this terrible situation I had gotten myself into again with another person I loved dearly.

Yuno, the Master, finally arrived for my session and took me to a quaint room off from the yoga studio. The air in the room was quite chilly, but the warmth from this Master Healer radiated from her with intense force. She guided me to a mat on the floor and asked me what I felt needed healing. I told her I was struggling with an issue with my granddaughter, and I wanted some clarity on how to handle the situation in the most loving, healthy, and healing way possible, so we could both move forward without damaging our relationship.

She asked me to notice where in my body I was holding this energy.

I responded, "In my heart."

She asked me to lie down, and for the next hour, she began pressing and knocking on various parts of my meridian points, pulling out and releasing energy from all over my body. It was intense, and at times I felt like she was beating the crap out of me. It wasn't awful, just uncomfortable. However, by the time we were finished, I felt an amazing relief that I hadn't felt in a very long time. She asked me to sit up and close my eyes, go within and ask again how to resolve this situation. Immediately, Sydney's higher self appeared to me in a vision and said, "Grammie, you have to let me go."

I felt some sadness, but I knew it was the truth. I had to let her go and find her own way. I had to get out of her way.

Wow! I have to let her go.

I instantly felt relief. It was incredible. I still wasn't completely resolved, but this helped a lot. Even though at the time it seemed like
a different situation in my mind, I could see clearly, I was making the
same mistakes and going down the same path with Sydney that I went
down with Lea. It wasn't working, and it wasn't healthy.

When the retreat ended, I planned to spend the rest of the day in
Sedona. A week before, I had found a practitioner in Sedona named
Stacey Zimberg, who did Theta healing. I had never heard of this before,
but she explained that while she is in a Theta brainwave state, she guides
you along with her to find the source of your struggles. She explained
that she finds the bottom beliefs that are blocking you, does healings,
manifestations, cancels contracts, and does soul retrieval.

It sounded amazing and resonated with my soul, which is always my
guiding source, so I booked the session for after my retreat. After leaving
Mago, I drove into Sedona and did a little shopping, then spent some
time among the amazing red rock formations. I wanted to take it all in
and just be present with the energy of the unbelievable beauty of this
stunning place before arriving at Stacey's home for my appointment.

Stacey lives just past Bell Rock, and the drive down AZ-179 South is
a trip I had taken many times. It is a very scenic drive past the Chapel
of the Holy Cross, the trailhead to Cathedral Rock, and of course Bell
Rock. It was a beautiful sunny day, and the warmth was welcoming,

after experiencing mostly gloomy, chilly days much of the week during the retreat. As I drove through the many traffic circles on my way to Stacey's, I thought about all the healing I had experienced over the past year, and even the tremendous work I had experienced at Mago, and wasn't quite sure what I wanted to focus on. I felt pretty complete, but I trusted the universe and knew my soul was guiding me here for a reason.

I arrived a couple of minutes early and was sitting in the car, gathering my things, when Stacey came out to greet me with a big smile. She was a little older than me, probably in her sixties, and had long, flowing, dark-brown hair with hints of gray that were just beginning to show through. Her skin was weathered by the sun, and she had a soft gentleness that made me feel immediately welcome.

"Good afternoon, Angela. I hope you had a nice drive in!"

"Yes, it was quite beautiful, thank you!"

She guided me into her beautiful home and presented me with a glass of water from the canyon. I sat on her couch, and right away we began the session. She said a prayer, asked me to close my eyes, and began asking me questions and directing me back to a time, which could be even before this lifetime, when I felt the most hurt or sadness.

I replied, "I was born with a broken heart."

"Really! "Tell me about your childhood."

I was very open and told her I had often felt rejected and as if I didn't belong in my family. She asked me what was going on that made me feel this way. I told her my parents had split up a year before I was born, and my mother had met someone during the breakup, but then my parents got back together, and not long afterward, my mother found out she was pregnant. When I was born, Mom knew right away I belonged to the man she had met during the breakup and not the man I called and knew as my dad. I also told her my two older siblings were three and five years older than me and were very close, and they often shunned, pushed me away, threw things at me, and called me names. I told her my family gave me the nickname "Devil" because I had so much energy and was always getting into trouble. She gasped in repulsion upon hearing this and immediately cleared that energy and said a prayer to cleanse this energy from me.

Then she asked me to go back into my mother's womb and asked me what it was like in there. I visualized being in my mother's womb, and within a few seconds, I was floating around in the amniotic fluid. "What are you feeling?" she asked.

"I feel a lot of sadness."

She said, "This is not your sadness. This is your mother's sadness, and doesn't belong to you." She began praying and clearing the energy in the womb, filling it with a bright golden light of love and healing. Removing all sadness or any other negativity or energy that didn't serve my highest good. I could instantly feel the change, and the sadness went away.

She went through all the struggles of my childhood and cut cords and cleared energy. I told her I was molested for the first time at age five by a friend of my father's, and it went on until my parents divorced when I was nine. I told her I was molested for years by Doug and Percy, who preyed upon me when I was young girl when I lived in Detroit. She cut the cords and cleared all that energy and said a prayer over me.

She then asked about the divorce, and I told her my parents divorced when I was nine. I explained all the responsibilities I had to take on after the divorce. I told her I met Charlie when I was twelve, and he began to pressure me to get pregnant. I told her I was so unhappy at home and wanted out of the abusive situation, so eventually I gave in and got pregnant at age thirteen to get out of that abusive situation, but ended up going into an even more abusive and hurtful situation with Charlie.

She asked me who had hurt me most in my life.

I instantly replied, "Charlie hurt me more than anyone ever has, and the pain he caused me has been carried with me through my daughter all my life."

As I said these words, tears welled up in my eyes. I could feel all the pain, hurt, and resentment of the hell that I had been through with him and all the pain he planted in Lea when she was such a young child that created distrust and distance between us that I could never bridge. She immediately asked me to go to Charlie and look him in the eyes and tell him everything that I ever wanted to tell him.

I began to sob, and I could see him right in front of me.

I did as she asked and looked him in the eyes, and I began to get loud. I asked him, "How could you hurt me so bad and treat me so terribly?" I cried and wailed from a part of me that was so deep and had been hidden for over forty years. I screamed at him and asked, "What did I ever do to you to deserve the pain that you heaped on me? And worst of all, not only did you hurt me, you hurt Lea and did everything you could to turn her against me!"

"All I ever did was try to love you!" I shouted. The pain, hurt, and anger was deep. I had never felt so much disgust coming out of my body in my life.

Stacey was chanting and praying over me. She asked me, "What is Charlie doing right now?"

I told her he couldn't look me in the eyes. "He's looking away in shame."

She cut the cord with Charlie and then asked me, "Can you forgive him?"

Immediately in defiance and anger, I said, "I don't think so. I thought I had forgiven him years ago, but I know now I have not."

She continued to pray over me. A gentleness fell on my heart, and I knew I had to forgive him to set myself free.

My sobbing began to subside, and I told her with tears still running down my face, "I need to forgive him."

She began to guide me while chanting and saying prayers over me. I closed my eyes and went back in. He was recoiling in a corner and began shrinking. I looked again, and I saw him as a little boy, maybe around four or five years old. His blond hair was shaved close to his head, and his blue eyes were sad and lonely. I could see he was hurting. My heart had compassion, and tears welled up in my eyes as I said to him, "I don't know who hurt you so badly to make you become so mean, destructive, and abusive and hurt me and our daughter Lea but—" I paused as a lump welled up in my throat "—I forgive you. I forgive you, Charlie!"

A feeling of relief filled my entire body as Stacey continued to chant and pray over me while I surrendered more than forty years of pain and agony. She cut and cleared the cords between me and Charlie. Then she focused on me and Lea and any pain that was still lingering from the past. She asked me to go back to my pregnancy and feel Lea in my womb. She asked me to check in and see what I was feeling during my pregnancy. I said "There's a lot of sadness. I endured a lot of turmoil and abuse during that time." She began to pray and chant and cleared all the sadness and negative energy inside the womb. She cleared all the amniotic fluid of any negative vibrations. She restored health and harmony to my pregnancy, and I could feel a vibration of healing showering over me and Lea. She then cleared all cords from ten generations back and ten generations ahead of me. I could feel the energy of healing swirling around my entire body. Then she opened her eyes and said, "I feel this session is complete."

I felt completely drained and spent the next three days sleeping a lot out of exhaustion, but something was different. I could taste real emotional freedom for the first time!

CHAPTER 30

As soon as I returned from Arizona, I learned that Sydney had stopped going to classes in October. I tried to contact her, but she didn't return my calls. I decided to email her a letter.

Sydney,

I have tried to contact you but haven't gotten a response. I am aware of the decisions you have made with dropping out of college and highly suggest you go to the Dean of Students and let them know that you have been struggling and made a mess of this past semester so they may possibly clear up your record. I promise, you do not want this mess on your records. If you need help with this matter, please let me know.

Sydney, Poppy and I love you very much and no matter what we will always love you and we are here for you. And the past six months have been hard to watch. It is very apparent now you were not ready for college, and we made a mistake getting this car. When we got involved with this car it was a perfect situation if you were going to go to college and let your scholarship help pay for the vehicle, but that is no longer the situation. As a matter of fact, things have changed dramatically, and we are no longer in the situation that we were in when this all started and what we agreed to is no longer the case.

Poppy and I are no longer willing to be involved in this car situation with you. You are responsible for where we are right now. How do you want to resolve it? We have a couple of suggestions if you are interested. The car will remain parked with us until this is resolved. Please let us know.

I have spoken to your professors, and they have asked you to reach out to them and let them know that you are struggling. They want to help you, so you don't ruin your academic record. I know right now you don't care, but you may change your mind in the future. It is never good or helpful to burn bridges. I would highly recommend you take care of this as soon as possible.

I love you more than I could ever express. I look forward to hearing from you.

Grammie

She immediately sent back an email response.

Grammie,

I don't really have the time or energy to type a reply right now and I may not for a while but just know I love you and I am finally figuring out how to live for myself. I am so tired of talking about the car and you know I hate the family meetings. I understand I'm responsible and I'm not saying you are bad or wrong, I just don't want you to think I'm ignoring it.

Sydney

I didn't hear back from her except for a "Merry Christmas" and for New Year's a "Happy New Year."

Tom and I talked and decided to give her some time to think through things. The car payments were paid through April, and I figured that would give her some time to decide if she wanted to get a job and a loan and take over the car. I didn't hear from her.

I learned that Lea had gotten a job near my office, working at an equipment rental company as an office manager. I had gotten her a birthday card, some rocks, and a bracelet while I was in Sedona and decided to stop by and bring her the card, along with $50 I put inside.

When I arrived at her office, she came over and hugged me and cried. She was sad over some unfortunate things that were going on with her sister Brooke, who was in some trouble. I held her for a long time and just listened. We had a great conversation. It was the first time after the eviction nearly a year before that she was kind toward me. I felt grateful and a glimmer of hope that perhaps now that she was out of the financial situation with me and was finding her own way in the world, maybe we could heal our relationship.

She filled me in about Sydney. "She's staying with me at John's house. She's just nesting right now and needs some time to work through all she's been through. Things are not going well with me and John. I have talked with Brad's dad, Paul, and he agreed to let me and Sydney move into his one-bedroom apartment. He has a hospital bed in the living room where he sleeps and offered us his bedroom to help us out."

"I am glad Sydney is taking some time for herself. She has been through a lot. Please tell her I love her when you see her."

"I will. She is really, really mad right now, so I wouldn't expect to hear from her for a while."

"Okay. I love you. Happy birthday!"

"I love you too, Mom."

I left her office feeling overwhelmed with love. *Wow! That was a nice visit. Hmmm, very interesting. It's good to see Lea's doing better. It will be interesting to see how this all unfolds. I love them both so much. I am going to keep sending them love and light metaphysically through my prayers and meditation and hope that they can find their way to healing and peace.*

In March, a few months later, I still hadn't heard anything from Sydney about the car, and we needed to make a decision about selling it, if she didn't want it. I emailed Sydney.

Hello Sydney, it has been a while. I wanted to check in and see if you would be available to have lunch or dinner soon? I have some time on Thursday March 14th which is a week and a half from

now. I could do something after 2pm. Let me know if you are
available. If that day doesn't work, let me know when you are free.

I love you,
Gram

I waited a week and didn't get a response. I sent a second email.

Hi Sydney, I hope you are doing well. I sent an email last week,
but I am not sure you got it. I have been waiting to hear from you
because you said it would be awhile... and I figured you needed
some time to think through things. It has been since December,
and I wanted to check in. We wanted to see if you have had some
time to think about what you want to do about the car. We need
to make a decision about it. Would you like to try to get a loan,
and keep the car or should we sell it? If we sell it, we will need
to have you sign off on the title. It is a beautiful car and worth
holding onto if you can afford it and want to make a long term
commitment and investment into it. If you take care of the car and
don't run the miles up, the car could last you 10 years or more. But
that is up to you.

We need to discuss this as we are making the payments on it and
the insurance, and we need to make a decision. No lectures, we just
want to know how we can move forward from here. We love you
very much and we only wish you happiness, health, and love in

your life. That is all we have ever wanted for you. We look forward to hearing from you.

We love you,
Gram & Pops

It took a few days, but she finally responded.

Grammie,

I planned to type a very long and well thought out email, but you seem to have an urgency for me to type this and I won't be able to do that anytime soon. I've been avoiding emailing you because I don't want to come across as rude, but I'm just going to be real. I had already assumed you had sold my car, feel free to go ahead and do so. That was a very nice opportunity and I appreciate it, but the honest truth is I always knew that wasn't my car. I knew I wouldn't be able to do college ever since orientation. Every time I mentioned waiting you said I'd never go, and each time I said something about not going at all you said, "Well if you want to work a 9-5 and slave away for the man 5 days a week for your whole life and that makes you happy that's okay." I don't care what tone of voice you say that in it comes across as judgment. Especially when it's repeated every single time.

The reality is that we don't live in a world where I have to go to college. If I want to start making crafts and figure out shipping, I could have several simple online businesses by tomorrow. I'm not *ready for any of that. I'm still accepting that I lost my house. I'm still getting over the fact I'm not friends with almost anyone I was just this time last year. I'm coping with the fact that I didn't step up and it caused me to have to permanently rehome my dog. I'm still not over the first car I lost. I haven't had 5 seconds in the past two years until these past few months to even realize what all has happened around me. I know life happens and things are hard, I know you can't just shut down every time things get hard. What I'm saying is I had a foundation at our house in Radford and it was shattered. I had found a way to get myself where I needed to be even without a vehicle, I had a job I knew was mine when I was ready. I had a safe space. I am now $10 in gas away from home with no job, no transportation, not even my own room. However, I am being the most authentic to myself I have been since I was 16. I am happier sharing a bedroom with my mother, at Paw Paw's house, than I was in any of the 3 other rooms I've had these past two years. It's not because of where I am, but it's the people I'm surrounding myself with and the boundaries I'm keeping. I'm sorry if this seems like I'm rambling, but I want you to know exactly how I feel.*

I know you want me to talk to you and have dinner, but I'm not in a place where that's something I'm going to be doing. I'm sorry about any financial repercussions I have caused you with the past couple of deals with the car. I think we were meant to break a cycle Gram, and not in the way we thought. The entire cycle was unhealthy, not just the way it has ended. Business and love are two things that must be kept completely separate. If I love you, I am going to make sure you have everything you need as long as you are trying. Business is you meet your end of the deal as long as I meet mine. When money and things (cars, houses, trips) are brought into it there are too many conflicting feelings. I love you endlessly and I thank you for how much you have taught me on my journey so far. I'm sure we have more to learn from each other, but right now I have too many negative feelings to allow that. I hope you are able to take this in in a way that you don't feel judged. You have called me out on my shit and I'm calling you out on yours. That's not mean, it's not hateful, it's real. Thank you for your understanding.

Sincerely,
Sydney

I took a few days to process it all. *Wow, that was very mature. This is coming from a loving place within her heart. She is hurting, and I can hear it. Man, what a mess I have made. All I have ever wanted to do is to help them see how beautiful, amazing, and powerful they are and guide them into a better direction. But I have made a mess and have made a ton of mistakes. OMG!*

I took some time to reflect on my need to fix the car and housing situation for Lea and later Sydney and wondered what that was all about for me.

It came to me. *Oh my God, having a car and a house meant so much to me because Percy wouldn't work and Mom's car got repossessed. It sank us down so far below what I felt was already the bottom. I remembered the devastation in my mom's eyes and listening to her cry for days over losing her car. Without a car, she couldn't get to work and provide for us. We lost our apartment, we had no way to get to the grocery store or laundromat, and no one was there to help us. Because we lived in poverty, no matter how hard Mom tried, life kept knocking her down.*

I thought back to those times when I walked nine miles to get to work and sometimes back home if I couldn't get a ride. I remembered the rejection and disappointment I felt if I asked others to help me with a ride and they wouldn't. The pain I felt not having a car wounded me deeply and made me determined to do whatever it took to get a car and to never be without one. I never wanted Lea or Sydney to feel that much desperation or pain. I had the same feelings about having a house. Because Percy would never work and help Mom, we struggled financially and moved constantly. I never started or finished the same school from fourth grade, when my parents divorced, until I was in the seventh grade. I never felt secure or safe. Later I went on to invest in real estate, and I now own thirty houses. I am sure I did this subconsciously to overcompensate for not having the security of a home after my parents divorced.

I wanted Lea to have a home and a car. Subconsciously, a car and a home were symbols of ultimate security and happiness, and I wanted them to have this so badly so they could be happy. I didn't want her to suffer the way I did. When Lea got involved with Brad, and he wouldn't work, ran around on her, was rarely home, put drugs and his needs before her and Sydney, and Lea put up with it and kept rescuing him, she reminded me of my mother, who I resented for putting up with Percy. And when Sydney, as a young teenager, had to take care of herself and her mother after Brad left, it reminded me of me and what I had been through as a parentified child. I felt compelled to stop the pain and the patterns from repeating themselves. *This is why I have worked so hard to encourage and help Sydney go to college and make a better life for herself and break that pattern. I can see now; this isn't what she wanted at all. This was not about them; this was always about me.*

I sent her back an email.

Sydney,

Girl, Go do you! Have fun, enjoy life, go find whatever it is that makes your heart sing and that you are compassionate about. Live life to its fullest and don't get hung up on the little things or what other people think about you. Who am I to judge? I've learned through all of this struggle, we are all different and we all have different values and aspirations. I have only always wanted the best for you. I apologize for making you feel pressured into doing something you didn't want to do. That was not my intention. I am sorry I didn't hear you. You are beautiful, talented, magical, and only you know what your truth is. I see and hear you. And I love you very much!

Thanks for getting back with me about the car. We will move forward then, and Poppy can contact you when it sells to sign the title.

I love you and wish you only the best. I am always here when you are ready.

Love,
Grammie

I took a deep breath and hit the send button. I remembered what her higher self had said to me during my healing session in Sedona. *I need to let her go. I can see now I must get out of their way. I have wanted so badly to help them, yet I hindered them by over-helping, over-giving, and reacting out of my own fear and pain, and it has not been helpful. Oh my God. I have created a lot of hell along the way by trying to rescue them. When all along it was me, my inner wounded child that I projected onto them. It was me that needed to be rescued. I judged them because they were heading down a road toward poverty and struggle, and it scared the hell out of me.* I sat and cried and allowed myself to feel my pain, sadness, loss, regret, and grief. It was overwhelming and heartbreaking, but healing.

Two months later, at the end of May, my sister Jenny called and asked me if I heard that Sydney's Paw Paw Paul had died.

"No, I didn't hear that."

"Oh, I am friends with Brad on Facebook, and I saw his dad passed away."

"Oh no, I hate to hear that. Hmmm, Lea and Sydney have been living with him for the past few months. I wonder what happened?"

"Didn't they call you and tell you?"

"No, they didn't. Maybe they will in the next few days." I never heard from them.

I looked on Brad's Facebook page and saw the funeral announcement and told Tom even though we hadn't heard from anyone, we needed to go to the visitation at the funeral home. He agreed. We arrived at the funeral home and stayed until the funeral was about to start, but Brad, Lea, and Sydney had not arrived. Brad was always notoriously late.

I told Tom, "We won't stay for the funeral, but let's wait until 2 p.m. and see if they arrive."

At one fifty-nine, Brad pulled into the parking lot with his brother, Lea, and Sydney. I drove around, and Tom and I got out of our car. You could tell they were surprised to see us and were in a hurry to get inside. We hugged each one of them quickly and told them we were sorry for their loss, then left.

As I slid into the car to leave, I felt like an outsider, and I thought about all the things I had done to push them away. How I tried to control and influence them to do what I thought was best for them but made them unhappy.

All I ever wanted to do for them was to make their lives better.

Hmmm, and yet what I have done is conveyed the message I didn't believe in them. I thought if I helped give them a hand up, it would encourage them to move in a positive direction, and their pain would stop, and so would mine.

A few days later, I called Lea and told her, "I've been thinking of you and just wanted to check in."

"Yeah, it has been a lot. Paul had been sick for a long time with liver failure, and things had gotten bad over the past few months. I could see he was declining, and I called Brad and told him he needed to take Paul to the hospital, that something was seriously wrong. He came and took him to the hospital, and within a few days, he died."

"I am really sorry to hear that."

"Yes, it is sad. He just turned fifty-nine a few days before he died."

"Wow, that is too bad. Well thanks for letting me know what happened. I am thinking about you all and sending my love."

"Thanks, Mom. I love you too!"

A month later, I was thinking about Lea, and I sent her a text, *"Thinking of you today and sending love and light."*

I got a text back immediately. *"I sign my lease for Paul's apartment on Sunday!!"*

"Oh, that is so good to hear!! I am so happy for you! That must feel really good!"

"It's been a long road, Mom, but I am glad to be here."

"Yes, it has. I am happy for you. Great big hugs! I love you!"

"I love you too."

Wow, that is wonderful news. She is finally moving in a good direction. I am proud of her.

The next week, I texted her and asked if I could stop by; I had a housewarming gift for her.

"Oh yeah, come on by."

"I will pull in the driveway, if you just want to come out."

When I arrived, she was waiting for me.

"Hey, congratulations on your new place." I gave her the gift. "I am really proud of you."

"Yeah, me too."

"Well, this is the perfect place for you. It is close to the grocery store and the bus stop, and if you want, this could be a forever home."

"Yeah, I am really happy. It has been a journey over the past few weeks. Brad and his girlfriend were evicted and have been staying here after Paul died. I told them I was going to rent the apartment, and Brad asked if he could stay here until they could find a place to live. I said there was no way he was staying here, and he needed to get his life together for Sydney. I reminded him his dad just died at fifty-nine years old. I let him know everything I felt about him leaving me and Sydney and all the hell and heartache he caused me over the years. And how him leaving us nearly broke me and it has taken me this long to get back on my feet. I explained it wasn't my responsibility to rescue him, and he needed to get his life together. I told him Sydney had been through so much because of the hell she had been through after he left, and I need to focus on her and support her as she finds her way into adulthood. He was mad, but they left, thank God."

"Oh, Lea, I am so proud of you for speaking your truth and standing up for yourself."

"Yeah, it felt really good, Mom. I am excited about the progress I have made. We are going to be okay. We've been taking the bus to work since I don't have a car, but I am saving and looking for one, and hopefully, I will find one soon."

"Well, that is good. I am glad you are finding your way."

"Yes, a lot of good things are happening for me. I have started practicing Reiki again and have found a place to practice that is affordable, and it is going really well."

"Oh, that is wonderful news, Lea. I am so glad to hear that."

"Yes, it has taken some time, but I am getting there, and Sydney is doing well too. She is working with me at the office, and she is planning a trip to see her friend Kaylee in South Carolina for her birthday next week. She has been through a lot, but she is finding her way too. I am really proud of her."

"Well, I am really glad to hear that things are falling into place for both of you. I love you both very much."

"I know, Mom, and we love you too."

A few days later, I was surprised to get a text from Sydney. I had sent her a text when her Paw Paw died, but I never heard from her.

She texted, *"Hey Gram, I just now actually saw the last text you sent me. Thank you! I love you more. I need to set up direct deposit for work and I was wondering if you knew the bank account number for the account you helped me set up when I lived with you."*

I sent her the account number with a heart emoji.

She texted back, *"Awesome! Thank you!"* with a heart emoji.

I responded, *"You're welcome!!"* with a heart emoji.

Wow, that was so nice. My heart is so full. I love Lea and Sydney more than words can express. It was so good to hear from both of them this week and hear them moving in a positive direction.

CHAPTER 31

I didn't hear much from Lea after she got her apartment. And these days, I'm not in much contact with her and Sydney, but I am in a lot more contact with myself. After my trip to Sedona, I sat and reflected on my life and all I had learned over the past four years after taking my journey with plant medicine. It was a difficult process, and it took a lot of courage and strength to face the wounds within. To look at myself in the mirror, face the truth, and take responsibility for how my wounds played out through the journey of my life. To look at how I unintentionally hurt Lea. I was so blinded by my wounds, I ran from them, buried them, projected them, or medicated them with work, school, new projects, alcohol, or anything that kept me from being still. It took being still and facing the wounds within to discover the source of my pain and how it drove my behavior and my decisions.

My wounds were the underlying juice that fueled the vehicle of my life. In many ways, along with my drive and passion, they drove me to be successful, compassionate, and kind to others, loving deeply and giving generously to those in need, and in ways they helped me. And in some ways, they were detrimental, especially with Lea. I also believe there are no accidents. Everything happens for a reason.

I can see clearly that my life has been an incredible journey of the heart. I know as a therapist, one difficult or tragic event in someone's life can change everything. I had multiple ongoing events throughout my life that resulted in what we in the psychological field call complex trauma. I came from loving parents who meant well, and I also struggled through poverty, heartache, abuse, neglect, and pain, and faced obstacles that were mountains to climb to attain success unimaginable for someone who had the challenges I had. I learned from great masters that if I could believe something, change my limited thinking from lack to possibilities, and take the necessary steps, I could achieve anything I put my heart into. I am grateful for these lessons and for the ambition to create a better life and live the American Dream. I worked hard overcoming so much to prove to myself I was enough and I was worthy.

The wounds from my unfolding were fueled by my determination to move beyond poverty and focus on abundance. By the time I was in my mid-thirties, I had built a significant financial foundation, but I didn't believe or trust it. I didn't think it was enough. I was still stuck in scarcity. These engrained generational beliefs were difficult to overcome. They were like poison in my subconscious mind. They clouded my perception, and I lived my entire life through the lens of not enough.

So, I built more.

I couldn't stop. It was like an addiction that was fueled by the fear of returning to a life of heartache, even though it didn't make logical sense. Nothing was ever enough, because I didn't feel like I was enough. As soon as I finished one degree or made a business successful, I started another; as soon as I built one dream home, I started focusing on building the next project. Since the results were success, it was easy to ignore the dysfunctional pattern I had created of always striving but never arriving and running myself into exhaustion. I had everything I ever wanted, but no matter how much I attained, it was never enough to heal the pain inside.

I recognize now the answers I was seeking were within me. I also appreciate what Jesus told me: There is nothing wrong with striving, success, money, education, or material things, unless they become your master and rule your life, and you become their servant.

My mother was very judgmental and highly critical of me, and I became a perfectionist and an overachiever. I can see now that she was a young mom with three other children, who was exhausted by an overactive child who was relentless and determined to do things her way. It completely overwhelmed her. She didn't know how to constructively manage my hyperactivity, so she did what she knew how to do, verbally chastise me. She constantly riddled me with statements like, "Angel you can't do nothing right. You're just always in the way, getting into something and rattling my nerves. Why can't you just sit still? Why do you have to be so bad all the time? You are just the devil. You are so clumsy and careless. Why do you have to talk so much and ask so many questions? Can't you ever just be quiet for a little while? It's enough to drive me crazy. Why do you have to be so picky and hard to please? Why are you so needy all the time? Nothing is ever enough for you, is it?" or "You're always causing trouble. You never give me a minute's peace. Why can't you just settle down? You are going to drive me to an early grave."

I know she didn't mean to hurt me, but as a kid, those messages are like poison, and they infect your mind and become the inner voice of the child. I not only heard these messages from her, but from most of my family. I took on these messages, and they crushed me. I felt damaged. I was extremely hard on myself, and it drove me into a state of depression and burnout, trying to be enough.

Just like my deep gratitude for the new path I found after discovering Wayne Dyer's teaching, I also realize now that without plant medicine, I wouldn't have awakened to the insights, understandings, and enlightenment that was necessary and absolutely what my soul needed to begin the healing process. This path is not for everyone, and it isn't a quick fix. Actually, it is a deep journey within, and I am grateful I found the answers my soul needed so I could be free and at peace. I am also grateful it took away my need to lean on alcohol and freed me from that struggle.

It has taken me a lot of years to really embrace and let go of the self-blame, guilt, and shame I felt as a mother for the difficult decisions I made to leave Lea. It's helpful to believe that she chose me and Charlie to be her parents and that we had a soul contract to complete, because we each had lessons to learn from each other.

I spent a lifetime trying to overcome, overcompensate, rescue, repair, fix, and to undo the damage I caused by having a child at fourteen years old with a man who brought me the greatest pain and heartache I would ever endure, and who taught me some of the greatest lessons in my life. I believe it was all a necessary assignment, and everything plays out the way it needs to for each of us to face our challenges and decide if we are ready to learn the lessons that we divinely chose before we came here or we continue to face the challenges of repeating them until we do.

Through this journey with Charlie, I saw the power and destruction of parental alienation. I never knew it had a formal name until I became a therapist and worked with families going through custody battles. I experienced it firsthand, and it was heartbreaking. The first time I learned about it, I was working with a large family with many children, and one of the parents had ostracized two of the children, and the other parent and isolated them from the others. The ostracized children and the other parent couldn't understand why their siblings/children wouldn't talk to them and treated them so badly. They were very confused and reported how painful it was to be rejected and hated by their parent/spouse and their siblings/children whom they love. It broke my heart to hear their stories. I also listened to the alienated parent, who was so hurt and scared that they were losing the children who stayed behind because they refused to have visits or spend time with them. It was heartbreaking to see the toll it was taking on them. And it took four long years of court battles to finally help this family reunite and be whole again.

Two other therapists and I worked together to understand this very complex and disturbing case that was fraught with abuse and alienation. Through our research and studies, we found C. A. Childress, PsyD, and Dr. Richard Warshak, both of whom wrote several books and recorded videos on this very disturbing complex abuse that surfaces during highly conflictual divorce or custody battles.

The term parental alienation syndrome was first coined by psychiatrist Richard Gardner, MD, in 1985 and later became known in the psychological community as parental alienation and is defined by ncsc.org (National Center State Courts) as:

"… a strategy whereby one parent intentionally displays to the child unjustified negativity aimed at the other parent. The purpose of this strategy is to damage the child's relationship with the other parent and to turn the child's emotions against that other parent" parental_alien-ation_Lewis.pdf (ncsc.org).

Ah ha! That's it! I remember thinking when I learned about this. "That is what Charlie did to Lea for all those years!" I felt validated to know I wasn't crazy. I knew something sinister was going on, but I couldn't label or explain it. This gave me a feeling of vindication.

For the first time, I had a name for what I had gone through with Charlie. Parental Alienation. What an awful thing for a parent to do to their child.

As a therapist, I learned that often it comes from childhood abuse, attachment disorders, or trauma in the parent, and they play out their wounds through the child to punish the other parent. After learning about this disorder, I worked for years to teach other therapists, lawyers, and the courts about this very destructive abuse that is detrimental to the parent-child relationship.

What I know in my case is that it caused a lot of damage to mine and Lea's relationship. I don't know if she ever got past what I imagine was the ingrained, brainwashing, indoctrinated, constant bombardment of vilification, poison, lies, and pressure to reject me that were spun in her mind about me while she was growing up. I am not sure of the emotional and mental toll it took on her for being punished because she loved me or enjoyed spending time with me and had to lie about it or hide her true feelings. I am not sure how it affected her being ridiculed, criticized, and negatively judged because she was left-handed like me or had any qualities like me. I am not sure the toll it took on her being interrogated after returning from visits with me that lasted hours if she didn't give the answers they wanted to hear and they wouldn't relent until she gave in. I imagine it contributed to her feelings of not being loved and accepted, and it reinforced that her feelings didn't matter, and I wasn't safe to love, and in fact it was punishable to love me. I imagine she also learned that love was conditional by their constant indoctrination of the message "If you love your mom, you won't be loved and accepted by us." It breaks my heart what she went through.

I often wondered if the generational patterns of parental alienation continued with Lea as grandparent alienation. Did Lea, out of her own fears, insecurities, and wounds, say things to influence Sydney in a negative way toward me? I noticed starting around her preteens, after Lea moved into our rental house, Sydney began to change. Her attitude toward me was more negative, and things were different in our relationship. It got worse when she came to live with me her senior year in high school. Was I denigrated, put down, and demonized to her? Was she told negative things about me, and was I blamed over them losing the house, even though I did everything to help, encourage, and plead for Lea to do the right thing? I don't know, but I felt it, and intuitively over the years, it felt evident. Unless you see it through the lens of alienation. I may be wrong, and I take responsibility for my judgments and any hurt I may have caused, but I do wonder what happened.

I know that children love both of their parents and have qualities from each of them. When a child is made to feel that their parent doesn't love them, or is ridiculed, punished, or degraded in any way because they love the other parent or are like the other parent, or wants to spend time with the other parent, the person who gets hurt the most is the child. It is emotional abuse and creates cognitive dissonance and deep wounds. They feel like they have to protect the wounded parent who is doing the denigration, or they will lose their love or favor with that parent.

It can instill the belief, *if my parent doesn't love me or something is wrong with my parent, there must be something wrong with me.* And often these wounds and poison last a lifetime and harm the child's self-esteem and potentially a healthy relationship with the other parent. It is a very sad and unhealthy thing to do to a child. I think subconsciously, these deeply held messages kept her guarded, and I don't think she ever allowed herself to get close to me, out of the fear and distrust that were placed in her heart and mind when she was a little girl. I still don't even think she really knows me. I think she only knows the person she thinks I am.

I would never wish this kind of hurt on any parent, grandparent, or child.

And of course, I had a part in the dysfunction too. I wanted to save Lea from suffering the heartache and worries I had gone through and experienced. When she suffered or made poor decisions, it triggered me and made me so angry at her for not getting her life together, because I could see how it was creating chaos and pain in her life and in my life too. As an empath, I felt her pain as if it was my own. Deep inside, unaware of it, I wanted her to stop hurting so I could stop hurting. What I didn't realize at the time and came to learn through plant medicine and shadow work with Steven Twohig, was that I was projecting my pain and wounds onto her.

I also know the first seven years of a child's life are crucial, and what is learned during that time is carried with the child throughout their lives. She grew up in sheer chaos most of the time. Perhaps, when things were too calm or quiet, it created anxiety and discomfort, so subconsciously she created the chaos she was used to and was comfortable with. She also grew up with a generational poverty mindset, and it is hard to overcome our programming. Our beliefs are very powerful. It is uncomfortable to shift and move from a place we have always known into uncertainty and the unknown. It takes a lot of courage or pain to change. Many times, people choose to stay comfortable or stuck, even when it is difficult and harmful.

I also saw my younger self in Lea. During the struggles she had with Brad and wanting so bad for things to work out, I could feel her pain and see myself back as a very young girl waiting for Charlie to come home from work when he was seeing Elaine and hoping he was going to choose me.

I could also see myself through her emotional and financial struggles and trying to find her way. I remember those early years when I was sixteen and on my own, with no one there to help me or even give me any ounce of encouragement. I could also see how hard she tried to work and pull Brad up. I saw her frustration when he wouldn't help her, and I could feel how devastating that was. I wanted to help her so much, but I just didn't know how to do it without it being dysfunctional because I was too wounded.

When I looked at her life in poverty and pain, it resembled the life I imagined I would have had if I had stayed with Charlie. The pain of seeing her stuck in this place triggered every cell in my body, and I wanted to get her out and save her at any cost. I projected, judged, and criticized Lea, because that is how I felt about myself. Not intentionally. I didn't even recognize what I was doing. Once I was able to see this and turn within and find the wounded little girl inside of me and help give her what she needed, it helped me in my healing process. Looking back now, I can see clearly how the wounds from my childhood and teenage trauma drove my behaviors and my life. I saw the world through the darkness of these wounds and unforgiveness of myself, which clouded my perception and kept me from seeing clearly. It took a lot of work to clear the windshield and see into the mirror past my wounds and pain and recognize that it wasn't about Lea or Sydney, it was about me. It was my inner child and inner wounds that were screaming out for my attention. I was the one who needed rescuing, and I was the one who needed to heal.

I've learned that we each must take our own hero's journey. My life and struggles were my hero's journey. Leaving Charlie was one of my calls to action. I had to face my circumstances and fears and decide which path I would take. I could wallow around as a victim and stay stuck, or I could make a different choice that would require me stepping out of my comfort zone. I chose to face the uncomfortable, difficult obstacles that stood before me. Another call to action was realizing the chaos helping and trying to control others, especially Lea, caused in the lives of those I loved.

When I was in grad school, I read a beautiful story that illustrates this dynamic very well, but it didn't really sink in at the time. Then, one morning, while going through the eviction with Lea, I remembered this story and realized this was powerful medicine for me.

The Butterfly Story
(Author Unknown)

One day an old man found a cocoon of a butterfly and scooped it up and took it home and placed it on his windowsill. He watched the butterfly struggle for hours trying to emerge from a small hole in the bottom of the cocoon. Then it seemed to stop making any progress. So, the man, wanting to help the butterfly, took a pair of scissors and cut a larger hole in the cocoon. Soon, the butterfly flopped out with a swollen body and shriveled up wings. The man continued to watch expecting the butterfly's wing to emerge and for it to fly. Neither happened. Instead of reaching its potential, the butterfly spent the rest of its life crawling around on its belly and never could fly. What the man in his kindness and haste didn't recognize was it was necessary for the butterfly to struggle through the small hole forcing the fluid out of the body and into the wings so it would be ready for flight when it emerged. Sometimes struggles are exactly what we need in our life. If we went through our life without any obstacles, it would cripple us. We would not be as strong as we are, and we would never fly.

Sometimes we can't recognize what is right before our own eyes. We can see and give advice to others in a similar situation, but our own wounds are often too close for us to see. What I painstakingly realized through looking within, I prevented Lea from launching into adulthood much earlier and finding her inner strengths by constantly rescuing her from the challenges and struggles that were necessary for her to find her inner hero and overcome the obstacles that were placed before her. I unknowingly did this because I was so stuck in this pattern of being a hopeless helper and a codependent, who was compelled or addicted to help her. And without awareness, I started to do the same thing to Sydney. I knew better, especially as a therapist, but in my own life, it was difficult to see. Thank God, my eyes were opened, and I finally woke up from the delusions of my pain and wounds, so that I could set them free and ultimately free myself.

I made so many mistakes with Lea and later Sydney, just like my mother made so many mistakes with me, but she didn't rescue me. She let me live with the consequences of the choices I made. I was angry with her for not helping when I felt like she should have. The desperation I felt, not having anyone to help support me when I was so young, drove my addictive helping behaviors, because I didn't want anyone to suffer the pain I had gone through. I helped others because I wanted so desperately for someone to help me.

However, a part of me feels grateful to my mom for leaving me out there homeless sometimes, alone, without anything. I can see now it was what I needed, and it is one the greatest gifts she gave me. To leave me alone so I could face my greatest challenges, take my own hero's journey toward finding my own way to victory, and it made me who I am.

Lea and Sydney didn't want or need me to rescue them.

They really just wanted me to love and accept them and get out of their way.

They are both so powerful, beautiful, amazing, and their light is so bright. I know they will find their own way to what works best for them in their lives. I will always pray that someday they will come back into my life, and we can find love and acceptance of each other without judgment. I have felt their judgment over the years as well, and I understand the pain of judgment, and the desire to be free from it. I do hope we can have a relationship that comes from the heart, based on pure unconditional love.

Here's the hard truth: Just because you are the mother or the child or a family member, it doesn't mean that things always work out the way we want.

When I finally let this truth in and I got to a place where I could no longer stand the pain and constantly wallowing around in it, I decided *I'm not going to live on this street anymore. I am not even going to live in this neighborhood! I am done causing myself pain and heartache, and I am moving on.*

I have come to terms that Lea, Sydney, and I may not be able to find common ground, even though I know we all love each other very much. It takes a lot of surrendering to accept that sometimes things don't always work out the way we hoped. I don't know what the future holds. I do accept that it is okay to let go and surrender with love and peace. I also trust, if it is meant to be and healing can occur, that love will find a way.

Even if we can't find common ground or have a relationship, I am so grateful they came into my life and were two of my greatest teachers, who helped me heal the deepest wounds within and have shown me how deep the human spirit can love.

Mama Aya and Jesus were right, when I heal, they too can heal.

What we are all searching for is freedom, love, and acceptance without judgment.

Freedom to be who we genuinely are.

Freedom to explore and live the way we choose.

Freedom to just be free and be in peace.

I believe we will find what we are seeking if we can be still and look within.

I know we all have the capacity to heal and create with love a more beautiful world, life, and relationships that only our hearts can imagine.

EPILOGUE:

A LOVE LETTER TO
THE CHILD WITHIN

I have changed, grown, and healed so much in writing this book and going through this journey. I have learned there are many parts of ourselves that hold our wounds, just like all the chapters holding this story. This is why there are so many layers to our pain. We pick up these wounds along our life's journey at different times and ages and through different events or traumas in our life. If we can't deal with them at the time because it isn't safe or we don't have the capacity to do so, we often bury these wounds and carry them throughout our life as our inner wounded child. It is through tapping in and connecting with the wounds within that we can heal.

One very helpful technique I learned through shadow work with Steven Twohig is turning within. He taught me that when I am triggered, I must acknowledge, notice, feel into, and allow myself to feel the wounds, pain, and disturbances. Then ask the feeling, "If you had a voice, what would you say?" Then listen and acknowledge that voice.

Then go within all the way back to where the pain originated, to the first time the pain was ever felt, notice what is happening and what the inner child needed but didn't get. Then he guided me to find the hero within, that powerful higher self that has been kind and helpful to others and have that part go back and rescue that little wounded one by giving that wounded part what it needed.

This is some deep shadow work and often requires a trained guide to help you navigate this journey. I am grateful for learning this technique through Steven's work and his organization, Mastering Change. I have also learned some similar techniques through my studies with Dr. Dick Schwartz, the well-known marriage and family therapist, through his Internal Family Systems Theory.

I am so grateful for my higher self and for finding her within. She is the higher, wiser inner mother that I have always needed, and she is always with me. Here is a letter she wanted to write to my inner wounded parts that I call my inner child.

Dear Angel (Angela), My Inner Child Within,

I am writing to tell you I have compassion for you and recognize that you have suffered by taking on the wounds of other wounded ones. You are a beautiful, loving child, and you came onto this planet in pure love and light from God.

You are special, beautiful, and a unique, divine child of God. The high energy, sensitive, hyperactive, picky, boundary-pushing, fussy, determined, relentless child that you were is a beautiful part of who you are. And it caused triggers in others who were wounded and couldn't handle the overwhelming and powerful way you showed up in this world. It didn't make you bad or the "devil" the way you were told. These were gifts that weren't able to be received by your family because they ruffled feathers and were overwhelming. These very attributes were gifts that led to so many talents that you have.

It took a lot of strength to take responsibility to face the wounds within, look into the mirror, and see yourself as you truly are. It took a lot of courage to face the pain, heartache, and shadows and do the work necessary to finally free yourself from the prison of guilt, shame, self-judgment, and fear that you carried for over forty years. I am so proud of you.

The challenges you faced were opportunities to find your gifts within that gave you the sheer determination to face the many obstacles to overcome so much. Your empathy and compelling desire to help others not suffer came from your struggles and created the compassionate, caring, generous, loving, kind, amazing, successful person you are today. I am grateful for who you are.

You are so deserving of all you ever needed. You are loved so much unconditionally, flaws and all. I accept you as you are without judgment. I am here for you anytime you are feeling low, hurt, triggered, abandoned, rejected, hated, ridiculed, scared, or spiraling from the wounds within.

I promise to do my best to notice and be aware when you are hurting and come and help you go within and find the source of the pain and to give you what you needed but didn't get at the time.

I know the people who hurt you didn't intend to cause you pain. They were just projecting onto you the pain they felt inside that you, your behaviors, or responses triggered and mirrored in them. And the fierceness of their response reflected the depths of their suffering. It wasn't about you at all; it was about their wound. I am grateful that you have such a loving heart and have learned to forgive them and send them love. All of them.

But perhaps most importantly, I am so grateful you are finally learning to forgive yourself. It wasn't easy going through all you went through as a young mother. You were such a baby yourself. I can see how difficult it was to make the heart-wrenching decisions that you made. You too, like Lea, your mother, and grandmother before you, were also a child that was left behind to fend for yourself on your own, and I know you did the very best you could at the time.

I forgive you for continuing the dysfunctional codependent patterns of hopelessly helping, rescuing, and fixing. I know it was out of guilt, shame, and desperation to stop your own pain and to give to Lea what you yourself didn't get. I know you were doing what you felt was necessary.

I forgive you!

*I forgive you for what I know you have felt was unforgivable …
being a mother who left your child behind.*

*I know it felt like a scarlet letter of shame that you have worn on
your heart and have beaten yourself up so much over the years, for
leaving her when she was so young, and the decisions you made
as a mother. But I know you really did the best you knew how at
the time.*

Honey, I forgive you! I forgive you! I forgive you!

*I forgive you for all the mistakes you made as a mother and as
a grandmother. I know you will continue to make mistakes because
you are human. And I will always be here to nurture, love, and
support you as you work through the lessons that life has to teach.*

*I love you from the deepest part of my soul, and I am always here
for you.*

Always, Anjalia (Your highest, wisest self)
Namaste

ACKNOWLEDGMENTS

I knew when I was sixteen years old that I had to write this book, but it wasn't ready to be written until now. It took a lifetime of learning and most importantly healing, to get here.

Thank you to my beautiful, amazing husband Tom, for your undying devotion, unconditional love and support, and for your unwavering encouragement through all the hurdles, heartaches, and hell that I went through in order to face the mirror I could not see and find my path to healing. I am eternally grateful to you. I couldn't have done this without your support.

To my parents in heaven. I love you both dearly, and I appreciate you for teaching me so much about life. I know you did the best you knew how, and I am grateful.

To my brother David. Thank you for helping me when I was a teenager, all alone, at my lowest point, with nowhere to turn. You gave me an opportunity to shift and turn things around, and I have never forgotten your love and kindness.

To my sister Jenny. Thank you for being my constant companion and sounding board. I appreciate your love, understanding, acceptance, friendship, and for always listening. I know no matter what, I always have you.

To my brother Jake. Thank you for helping me learn to love more deeply and understand more clearly the power of forgiveness and letting go. I love you!

To Wayne Dyer, whose work, genius, and spirit has been my closest guide and companion while writing this book and throughout my life. God sent you to me as a gift.

To my best friend, Jennifer. I cannot even imagine my world without you in it. Thank you for showing me how deeply I am loved, for being there every step of the way to listen, reflect, advise, suggest, and for being the one to read my first draft. Your input and feedback were priceless. I love you! You are special to me beyond words.

To Silent Dave. Your love and light shines so bright, words are not necessary. I am grateful you are on this journey. Thanks for stepping into my sacred circle.

To Stacy, my beautiful spiritual sister. Thank you so much for your love and support through my healing journey and for holding on to your end of the rope, letting me know you are always there. Thank you for being with me along the way. I am so blessed to have you in my life.

To my sister-friend Sheila. I appreciate the long nights, the deep conversations, and for taking me within the depths of my own well. I am grateful for your patience and kindness, and for loving and seeing me in my darkest moments. You helped prepare the way for me to break wide open and see the truth of who I truly am. Thank you for holding such powerful space.

To Barbara, thank you for listening and supporting me for over 20 years. I am grateful for your wisdom and your kind words. You are a gem, and I am blessed to have found you.

To Henry, thank you for your love, support, and guidance. You mean more to me than I could ever express. I love you endlessly.

To Penny and Lori, your love, support, and encouragement on this journey have been constant companions, and I know you are always available to support me when I am in need. I treasure you both!

To Steven, thank you for being my teacher. I am grateful for the container and space you created to allow me to delve deep into my shadow, find and slay the dragon, and come out on the other side being able to see more clearly. And thank you for your advice, companionship, and support on this arduous journey of writing and publishing.

To the Shadow Tribe, Valerie, Michelle, Kelly, John, Yanira, Neilsen, Sheila, Tim, Andrew, Jamie, Virginia, all the guides, practitioners, seekers, and teachers. You are my family, and I love you.

To my developmental editor and coach, Brianna McCabe, thank you for your wisdom, expertise, love, support, and for being the beautiful spiritual guide I needed to put all the words, paragraphs, and chapters in the right place. I am so grateful for your love and support.

To all the experts and advisers who helped me put my book together so beautifully, including copyeditor Joe Pierson, book cover designer Rajendra Kumar Mourya, interior designer Ines Monnet, and marketing strategist Rodney Hatfield. You all did amazing work. I am blessed to have worked with such talented professionals.

To my attorney, Kirk T. Schroder, thank you for helping me release this work into the world with confidence.

To Kim and Lisa, my personal assistants, thank you for taking care of everything so I could step away and write with confidence, knowing you had my back. I am so blessed to have you both in my life!

To all my practitioners at LIB, Alan, Cindy, Andrew, Erin S., Angela, Jenny, Liz, Donna, Sarah, Lisa K., Erin J., Makenna, Deanna, Anda, Arielle, Chloe, Melissa, and Whitney, thank you for your loving support. It means the world to me.

To Mama Ayahuasca, plant medicine, and my spiritual guides. Words cannot express the gratitude I have for your gifts. I wouldn't be where I am without you.

To Jesus, thank you for being by my side each step of the way from the beginning, forever and always. You are the light in my world, and you shine so brightly to show me mine.

To my amazing, creative granddaughter. Thank you for being one of the greatest gifts in my life. You have brought me so much joy and taught me how to turn around and see my own judgment and dysfunctions. What a gift.

To my beautiful, amazing daughter. Thank you for being my greatest teacher, for showing up being exactly who you are, for being my mirror and challenging me to look within and see myself so that I could see you more clearly. Thank you for your patience while I healed. I love you more than anything!

And finally, to all of those who wounded, bullied, kicked me when I was down, preyed upon me, and caused me to suffer. You helped me learn what I didn't want in my life. Thank you for being some of my greatest teachers.

ABOUT THE AUTHOR

Anjalia McGoldrick is a licensed professional counselor, hypnotherapist, metaphysician, entrepreneur, and author dedicated to empowering others through her unique blend of professional expertise and deeply personal experiences. Starting her journey as a teen mother, Anjalia faced significant challenges, navigating life on her own from a young age. Despite these obstacles, she has transformed adversity into a source of strength, cultivating the hope and courage necessary to break cycles of poverty, confront abuse, and realize her dreams.

Her unwavering resilience and drive have made Anjalia not only a respected counselor but also an empathetic advocate who intimately understands the struggles her clients face. Never forgetting the trials of her own past, she channels her compassion and love for humanity into every aspect of her work, inspiring and uplifting those who are determined to overcome their own hardships.

Anjalia was born in Cincinnati, Ohio, raised in Detroit, Michigan, and now lives in the beautiful Blue Ridge Mountains of Christiansburg, Virginia, with her husband, Tom.

Subscribe to Anjalia McGoldrick's email list at:
www.anjaliamcgoldrick.com

To discuss booking Anjalia McGoldrick for
media or speaking events, email at:
anjalia@anjaliamcgoldrick.com

Website: www.anjaliamcgoldrick.com

Facebook: Anjalia McGoldrick, Author

Instagram: @anjalia_mcgoldrick

X: @anjaliaauthor

www.ingramcontent.com/pod-product-compliance
Lightning Source LLC
Chambersburg PA
CBHW021214130626
46554CB00004B/1217